MW00340639

INTO THE DISTANCE

INTO THE DISTANCE

The Lost World of Long-Haul Trucking

George Bennett

Copyright © 2023 George Bennett

The moral right of the author has been asserted.

Apart from any fair dealing for the purposes of research or private study,
or criticism or review, as permitted under the Copyright, Designs and Patents
Act 1988, this publication may only be reproduced, stored or transmitted, in
any form or by any means, with the prior permission in writing of the
publishers, or in the case of reprographic reproduction in accordance with
the terms of licences issued by the Copyright Licensing Agency. Enquiries
concerning reproduction outside those terms should be sent to the publishers.

Matador
Unit E2 Airfield Business Park,
Harrison Road, Market Harborough,
Leicestershire. LE16 7UL
Tel: 0116 2792299
Email: books@troubador.co.uk
Web: www.troubador.co.uk/matador
Twitter: @matadorbooks

ISBN 978 1803137 155

British Library Cataloguing in Publication Data.
A catalogue record for this book is available from the British Library.

Typeset in 12pt Adobe Garamond Pro by Troubador Publishing Ltd, Leicester, UK

Matador is an imprint of Troubador Publishing Ltd

To the memory of Jane, who has a walk-on part in this story, but played a major role in my life.

CONTENTS

INTRODUCTION

During the first half of 2021, something strange started to happen across the UK. Supermarket shelves began to look like gap-toothed children, and there were shortages of anything from fresh vegetables and common groceries to components on which all kinds of manufacturing depend. The delivery of goods – a function taken for granted by everyone from the prime minister to a primary school child – was no longer occurring with its usual reliability. Even commonplace staples were suddenly in short supply, and it took a while for everyone to realise what was happening behind the scenes. The fact that few people were prepared for these shortages is a testament to the unseen efficiency with which goods of all kinds had been delivered for decades. Every part of the economy, from farming and manufacturing to retail, imports and exports – even internet shopping – depends on road transport or, as the York Trailer company's slogan put it in the 1970s: 'If you've got it, a truck brought it'. Now, this unappreciated system was tottering. To the surprise of most people, and apparently without warning, there was a chronic lack of drivers for the number of heavy goods vehicles that the economy needed on the road every day of the year.

There were, of course, short-term reasons for the rapid decline in the number of truck drivers, including the Covid pandemic, the departure of continental drivers in the aftermath of Brexit, and the accompanying lack of preparation by the government for the consequences of its attitude to foreign workers. All of these were paraded as causes of the driver deficit, but they just brought to crisis point a trend dating back at least two or three decades, and anyone paying attention to the road transport industry over that period might have seen it coming.

Truck driving has simply become an increasingly unattractive profession. Wages – always low considering the skill required to drive a heavy truck – have remained stagnant for years, apart from occasional settlements in the very large transport fleets. Traffic has grown steadily heavier, and the road system increasingly clogged, while adherence to delivery times has become ever more demanding. Perhaps more significant, however, is the fact that a job that once came with considerable flexibility and freedom has now become heavily regulated and constantly monitored, and the steadily increasing surveillance has done much to diminish driver satisfaction. When I began working full-time as a professional driver in 1975, the relatively low wages paid to long-distance drivers were mitigated by the significant latitude with which we did our jobs. Close supervision by management was impossible in the days before mobile phones and the global positioning system (GPS), but these brought a radical change to the life and work of long-distance drivers.

The use of satellite tracking and communication has allowed truck companies to monitor their drivers every second of the day. Not only can transport managers now locate every one of their trucks to within a few metres, they can tell which gear the driver is using, what speed the truck is doing, and retrace every detail of the vehicle's route. In the days when I worked as a driver, there were many sources of job satisfaction, but one of the most attractive was the fact that we drivers were largely unsupervised. Once we drove out of the company yard, the only way our managers could speak to us was if we phoned them. And the further afield we travelled, the more we had to make our own decisions, about routes, timing and troubleshooting. Now, instructions can be transmitted through a mobile phone or in-cab computer, and the driver is available to the boss at any time of the day or night. As a result, the freedom and initiative that used to compensate for being away from home for days – and often weeks – at a time has largely disappeared. It is, perhaps, little wonder that long-haul driving has become less attractive as a career. After all, if driving has become as supervised as working in a factory or an office, you might as well do the latter, and sleep in your own bed every night.

Not surprisingly, the first people to step away from the wheel in recent years were older drivers who didn't like the gradual accumulation of changes, but the transport industry has not been able to attract enough young people to take their place. This is not simply a British problem; there is a similar scarcity of drivers in most of Western Europe, and in the United States, where transport companies – many with thousands of trucks – are constantly advertising for new drivers. Annual driver turnover in America is a staggering ninety per cent across most large firms, even though the payment per mile for long-haul drivers has almost doubled in the past ten years. In Britain, where the recent critical driver shortage was met with wage increases as high as forty per cent, drivers are still not staying.

Added to the disincentive of constant monitoring, modern drivers are faced with the requirement to make 'just-in-time' deliveries, where whatever they are carrying has to arrive at a factory or supermarket distribution centre according to a tightly scripted schedule. Drivers can *even* be penalised for being early, something that never happened when I was a full-time driver. The combination of strict delivery times and ever-increasing traffic is a recipe for stress, whether a driver is running for long distances over several days or gets home every night. Even younger drivers now cite this as a reason for choosing another way of life. It may sound trite, but truck driving is simply no longer a satisfying job, let alone fun. But it once was, as this book sets out to demonstrate.

My interest in truck driving as a profession began with my childhood enthusiasm for vehicles in general, and the ambition I formed as a six-year-old child back in the 1950s to be able to drive a big lorry. As soon as I reached the age of twenty-one – the minimum age for a heavy goods vehicle driving licence – I took and passed the driving test that allowed me to drive the largest trucks on the road. I discovered, as I'd imagined as an infant, that it was both exciting and satisfying to be able to drive a full-sized articulated truck, fifty-five feet long and weighing in at thirty-two tons – the maximum size at that time. To do so required skill and flexibility, particularly back in the 1970s, before trucks began to be automated. When I took up driving full-time, there was always something new to learn, whether it was a different type of gearbox, a new kind of load or a hitherto unknown country. There was a constantly changing view from behind the wheel, and an astonishing variety of scenery, from the moorlands of Scotland to the deserts of Arabia; from the orderly urban landscape of Dusseldorf to the chaos of Damascus.

Moreover, the task of a driver is to deliver something to someone who needs it, and that gives every working day an immediate and achievable goal. I found that to load a truck, drive it anything from a hundred to several thousand miles, and deliver the goods, was a repeated source of satisfaction. When I lived in North Wales, I carried cheese to England that was made from milk produced by farmers who were my neighbours, and I brought back animal feed and equipment that those same neighbours needed. I hauled cars on transporters to dealers and their customers, and exported British beef and lamb all over the Continent, bringing back all kinds of fresh fruit from orchards in Italy and southern France, dairy produce from southern Germany and oven-ready poultry from the Netherlands. I travelled from the English Midlands to Dubai, carrying components to build the vast Jebel Ali desalination plant that was the physical foundation of that city's spectacular development. Whatever the distance, and whatever the load, there was always that moment of satisfaction and anticipation when the truck was unloaded, and it and I were ready for something new.

Perhaps best of all was that driving a truck meant I was paid to indulge my love of travelling. As a traveller, I have always been at least as interested in the process of travel as I have in the final destination, and truck driving is all about the mechanics of moving. As a professional driver, I journeyed to a score or more countries, and drove hundreds of thousands of miles. I visited dozens of cities across Europe and the Middle East and, as I drove between them, the views I saw from my cab were predominantly rural, in terrain as varied as the French Alps and the plains of Hungary. It is true that I rarely saw the famous sights of the lands I visited, but I made a quite different connection with those countries, and the people who lived there, than it is possible for a tourist to do. Wherever I loaded or delivered, my reason for being there was clear, and my presence was necessary. I had friendly – and occasionally not so friendly – interactions with farmers and factory workers, customs officers, loaders at fruit-packing stations, abattoirs or wholesale markets across most of Europe. I learned to appreciate and understand a range of different cultures and how to negotiate them. I ordered food in cafes and restaurants with just a few words of several European languages, and I juggled with a clutch of different currencies, sometimes in unreadable scripts.

So much has changed since those days that the world of work this memoir describes has, in many essentials, disappeared. The five transport companies for whom I worked in the 1970s and early '80s – including three quite big ones – have long since closed down. The simple business of 'road haulage', conducted by small and medium-sized firms carrying goods from point to point, has been largely overtaken by 'logistics', involving a wide range of functions performed by sprawling corporations. In nearly every firm I worked for, drivers were on first-name terms with the boss and could take any grievance to him directly. This is no longer the case when the driver is just a small piece in a logistics jigsaw. And while trucks operating up and down the highways of the western world still have a driver at the wheel, that driver's role has greatly changed, and significantly diminished, in ways I have outlined. Driving has become more regulated and more prosaic, less buccaneering and, in my view at least, much less interesting.

After I gave up my life as a full-time driver, I worked for twenty years in various roles as a magazine journalist, editor and publisher, specialising in the road transport and truck manufacturing industries. From behind the wheel, and in hundreds of interviews with truck manufacturers, operators and drivers, I watched as the traditional trucking industry was transformed in ways that were unthinkable when I passed my class one heavy goods driving test in 1972, during the final year of my undergraduate degree. A profession that required skill, initiative and independence has been gradually replaced by a routine job in which the driver's role has been steadily reduced, so that now, in the words of one American driver I interviewed for a magazine article in 2018, it amounts to little more than 'keeping the truck between the lines on the road'. And even that function is being automated.

The irony is that the trucks themselves have improved out of all recognition compared with the wooden-framed, fibreglass cabs and low-powered engines that I wrestled with back in the 1970s. Modern cabs are spacious, convenient and quiet, with enough room to live in comfort for days or weeks at a time, and even short-haul trucks are as well appointed as a luxury car. Under the floor, powerful engines not only make driving easier, but they have an efficiency far greater than their underpowered predecessors of four decades ago. The pleasure of driving a large truck is possibly greater than ever, but in parallel with all this technical progress, drivers themselves have been gradually devalued. When I was a journalist, truck manufacturers often boasted about how much they were making their trucks impervious to driver error, which they did by making their products less and less demanding to drive, and explicitly discounting and devaluing the skills that driving once required, and that drivers were proud to possess.

The process of marginalising the driver has been under way for decades, though perhaps not with the results that truck manufacturers intended. In the twenty-odd years I worked as a 'truck journalist', I wrote articles about successively greater automation of heavy trucks, beginning with semi-automated gearboxes, and continuing to fully automated transmissions, adaptive cruise control and more. Onboard computers have been designed to take care of vehicle distancing and lane control, and the driver's role is being relentlessly reduced. In recent years, there has been much media excitement about 'driverless' cars and even some general interest in fully automated trucks. It is presented as a given that this is progress and, as in so many other industries where automation was easier and has therefore already occurred, not enough thought is given to what happens to the people whose jobs are replaced by automata. In a driverless future, this would include drivers numbered in millions across Europe and North America alone. In any case, even if automating the driving itself proves to be technically possible or legally feasible – and one can only imagine how lawyers will battle over insurance liability – it overlooks how much of a long-haul truck driver's job is done away from the wheel.

Forty-plus years ago, this was considerably more than it is now. In those days, we had to be able to put a load on a truck (sometimes by our own labour) and secure it, usually with ropes and tarpaulins. International drivers had to understand complex customs paperwork and border procedures, and deal with a wide variety of workers and officials. We might have to change a wheel and carry out repairs, sometimes improvising a solution in the absence of spares or specific tools. There were no satellite navigation systems, so we needed to exercise the ancient art of map-reading and work out our own routes. Part of my working toolkit was a box of street maps covering major cities in Germany, France and Italy, which I gradually acquired each time I visited somewhere new. Failing that, we had to be able to ask directions from people with whom we had no common language and understand their answers. And between all these activities, we were responsible for controlling a large and complex articulated vehicle through all kinds of weather, over long distances and through widely variable terrain, to deliver a load to someone who needed it.

Some of this work away from the wheel still exists, but in the ways I have already outlined, the job as a whole has altered quite significantly, and thereby become less attractive. Having to make our own decisions, as long-distance drivers far from home, with tenuous or non-existent means of communication with the company's management, was sometimes challenging or worse, but when everything went well or we overcame some obstacle, it was both exciting and satisfying. It also required a practical intelligence, which is quite different from the picture of intelligence as conventionally measured.

But for all the interest and excitement in solving problems when things went awry, I found the greatest satisfaction came from the act of driving itself, in a vehicle that was completely familiar from hundreds – if not thousands – of hours behind the wheel. As an American truck-driver friend once told me, there are 'truckers' and people who simply drive trucks for a living. I was definitely the former. I loved the process of driving, the vehicles themselves, and the commanding position high in the cab that allowed me to see far more than a car driver can. I enjoyed the steady accumulation of knowledge and skill I gained from every new situation I found myself in. The moment of climbing into the cab, once my truck was loaded and ready for the road, always gave me a feeling of anticipation and even excitement, wherever I was heading. Just letting in the clutch to begin a journey that might take days or weeks was a moment to notice and savour. To be driving through the south of France into an endless summer evening, crossing a lonely desert on an empty road, or negotiating a tricky switchback climb towards the Alps, always with the familiar and comforting growl of a large diesel engine beneath the floor, was a pleasure that never got old.

SAUDI ARABIA, OCTOBER 12TH 1978

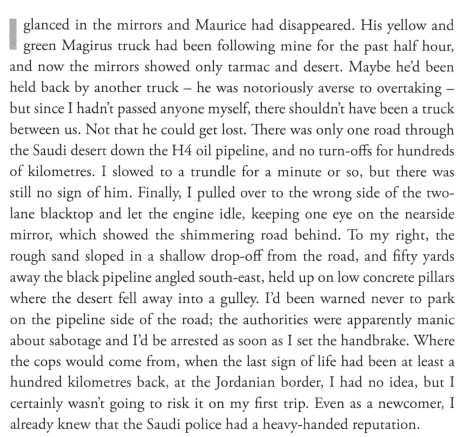

I glanced in the mirrors and Maurice had disappeared. His yellow and green Magirus truck had been following mine for the past half hour, and now the mirrors showed only tarmac and desert. Maybe he'd been held back by another truck – he was notoriously averse to overtaking – but since I hadn't passed anyone myself, there shouldn't have been a truck between us. Not that he could get lost. There was only one road through the Saudi desert down the H4 oil pipeline, and no turn-offs for hundreds of kilometres. I slowed to a trundle for a minute or so, but there was still no sign of him. Finally, I pulled over to the wrong side of the two-lane blacktop and let the engine idle, keeping one eye on the nearside mirror, which showed the shimmering road behind. To my right, the rough sand sloped in a shallow drop-off from the road, and fifty yards away the black pipeline angled south-east, held up on low concrete pillars where the desert fell away into a gulley. I'd been warned never to park on the pipeline side of the road; the authorities were apparently manic about sabotage and I'd be arrested as soon as I set the handbrake. Where the cops would come from, when the last sign of life had been at least a hundred kilometres back, at the Jordanian border, I had no idea, but I certainly wasn't going to risk it on my first trip. Even as a newcomer, I already knew that the Saudi police had a heavy-handed reputation.

I gave the engine a couple of minutes to cool down and switched it off. The sudden silence was broken only by the ticking of contracting metal beneath the cab. I fidgeted in my seat, wondering whether and when to go back for Maurice. After another five minutes, the decision was made for me. A large Jordanian Mercedes truck appeared, tall and rugged on twenty-four-inch desert wheels and tyres, with its wide, imposing bonnet in the standard sun-faded orange of Middle Eastern Mercs. The driver drew up beside me and gesticulated back the way we'd come; I didn't need any Arabic to know that my running mate was in trouble some way back. I waved my thanks and the Jordanian set off again. I fired up the Magirus's V10 engine, checked that the sand beside the road looked solid, and swung the articulated truck round in a wide arc to avoid bogging down. I regained the tarmac facing the way I had come and set off again, cursing Maurice roundly.

The desert road undulated beside a rocky outcrop at that point, obscuring the road I'd come by, and I'd gone a few kilometres before I saw what I'd feared. Maurice was in deep trouble. His truck had ploughed off the road and was up to its front bumper in soft sand. The rear of his trailer was clear of the road, so the momentum of his truck – grossing 32 tons plus – had carried him at least twenty yards off the blacktop. Maurice was standing by the cab of his Magirus, waving at me. I slowed my own Maggie to a stop on the road and climbed down.

"Where've you been?" Maurice demanded, as if it were my fault he'd run into the sand.

"I was waiting for you," I said, "and a Jordanian told me you were in trouble. What happened?"

"Blowout, on the front."

Another one? I could hardly believe it. This was the fourth tyre Maurice had blown since we'd entered Yugoslavia a week earlier. Nobody could be that unlucky. As Lady Bracknell might have said – if she'd known what a tyre was – to lose one tyre might be regarded as a misfortune; to lose two looked like carelessness. And Maurice had lost four. The only reason we still had a spare between us was that we'd met some homeward-bound colleagues the previous evening and between them they'd given us three replacements. I knelt down in the warming sand to examine the problem. The Maggie's front wheels were sunk in deeply and the right front tyre had collapsed, leaving the axle at sand level. Maurice and I looked at each other. We both knew what was coming next; he didn't have a jack. As usual, he'd be using mine.

Maurice was a likeable guy, and we got on well enough, but we were a mismatched pair, and our driving styles were sufficiently different to have caused a slight, unspoken friction since we'd set off from England ten days earlier. And leaving without a jack was a weird mistake for an old hand to make, setting out on a journey of nearly 8000 miles, on a round trip across Eastern Europe and the deserts of Arabia to Dubai. For, all appearances to the contrary, Maurice was the experienced one, and had spent two years driving within Saudi Arabia, doing what was known as 'internals'. This was my first trip to the Middle East and my new boss, Jack Harrison, had partnered me with Maurice so he could show me the ropes. I was learning, but not the way Jack had intended.

The front tyre is the worst one to blow on a big articulated truck. For one reason, it's easy to lose control, as Maurice had done, and for a second, the wheel drops onto the rim, so it has to be lifted higher than the extension on a truck's ten-ton bottle jack before the new wheel and tyre can be accommodated. At the rear, the wheels are twinned, so if one tyre blows, the other gives it some support, and the wheels normally clear the ground with one lift of the jack. In this case, we'd have to hoist the front axle, support it somehow while we repositioned the jack, and then raise it a second time. And we'd be doing it on soft sand. It would have been an interesting problem, but for the time of day. Maurice and I had set off at dawn from our overnight stop, to cover some miles before the thermometer climbed to its midday level of forty degrees Celsius or more, and it was now getting on for eight in the morning. The temperature was already becoming noticeable and we both wanted to get the heavy job done before the heat became unpleasant to work in. I lugged my jack across the sand, took a block of timber from under my trailer and started work. I scrabbled some sand away and shimmied the timber and jack into position under the axle. As a temporary support, while we repositioned the jack for a second lift, we used the spare wheel on its side. It wasn't ideal, but it worked.

It's heavy work to change a 75kg truck wheel, but after half an hour or so we'd managed it. Now all we had to do was get Maurice back on the road. We scooped the sand away from behind his wheels and hitched a chain from the back of his trailer to the rear of mine. I pulled forward far enough to take up the slack, and Maurice let in his clutch and tried to reverse out with the help of my truck up on the blacktop. The trailers swayed into line with each other, and with much over-revving, Maurice's truck scrabbled its way off the loose sand and onto the hard road. We grinned at each other. Whatever the cause of the original problem, we'd laboured together to solve it and it felt satisfying.

"Tea?" suggested Maurice.

Once more heading deeper into Saudi Arabia, and towards Qatar 1500 kilometres away, we drove on for a couple of minutes until we'd found sand hard enough to park on. We swung off the road and pulled up side by side, our two yellow and green Magirus tractor units, and red rental trailers, looking in much better shape than their drivers. Using some of our precious water supply, we washed ourselves and put on the kettle.

Two mugs of tea and a half hour later, we were on our way again. This time, Maurice took the lead and I dropped back a couple of hundred metres behind him. No need to crowd together on a virtually empty road. Occasionally, another truck passed us heading north, and once Maurice swung across the road to skirt a broken-down vehicle. In what I discovered was the standard Middle East practice, the driver had left a warning line of rocks angled across the road behind his truck, but had then apparently abandoned it. The road was mostly flat and straight, with occasional bends around small rocky outcrops. I scanned the truck's instruments as usual and then looked again. The air pressure gauges were dropping. They continued to drop as I watched them, and at any second I would have no air to actuate the brakes. I depressed the clutch and revved the engine, but the air compressor didn't respond; the needles kept falling. In my preoccupation with the air pressure, I'd lost sight of Maurice round another outcrop and couldn't flash my lights at him to pull over. I rolled to a stop and the fail-safe system clamped the brakes on. On a truck with brakes actuated by air pressure – as all trucks have been equipped since the 1960s – the brakes won't come off unless there's enough air pressure in the system, with the very sensible intention that if the truck has insufficient air pressure to stop it, it shouldn't be able to start. Unless I could build the pressure up to at least 80psi, the brakes wouldn't disengage again and the truck wouldn't move.

My first thought – unfortunate as it turned out – was to tilt the cab and investigate the compressor. In a 'cab-over' truck – the universal European design – the engine and all ancillaries are under the cab, which has to be tilted for any kind of maintenance or repair. I bundled my possessions into the passenger-side footwell so they wouldn't crash through the screen when the cab rocked forward, and groped for the cab tilt bar from behind my seat. I jumped down from the truck, brandishing the bar, and inserted it into the small hydraulic pump behind the cab. As I pumped furiously, the cab started lifting and tilting, and only when it lurched sideways as well as forwards did I remember that one of the front cab mountings was broken, a legacy of hard use on the road to Tehran in the hands of the truck's previous driver. I was lucky the whole cab hadn't fallen off, but at least I could get at the compressor. I had just tilted, and partially dismounted, the cab when Maurice turned up. Now the boot was on the other foot. Maurice was, strangely, more panicky than I was. He listened to my description of the breakdown and quickly offered his diagnosis.

"It's the compressor; it's knackered."

If he was right, I was in serious trouble. The compressor provided air pressure to power the air brakes, and without it I'd have no way of stopping, even if I could have moved in the first place. Heaven alone knew where the nearest replacement was, and any sort of town was several hundred kilometres away.

"You won't be able to go anywhere," Maurice stated the obvious. We considered our options, and with almost indecent haste, he came up with a solution. "You'll have to stay here while I tip my trailer, then I'll come back for yours and I'll go and tip that. Then when I come back again, we'll find a way to get your truck onto mine." In the back of both our minds was the resourcefulness of the new colleagues we'd met the previous afternoon as they were heading home. They had managed to load a broken-down truck – and its trailer – onto two other trucks in the middle of the desert, without having a crane at their disposal.

I thought about it. The one virtue of the plan, unspoken but obvious to both of us, was that we'd no longer have to live with each other. In all other respects, it was unsettling. I figured it would take Maurice about a week to get to Dubai, unload his trailer and get back to me. And then I'd have to wait another week while he delivered the contents of my trailer. It was a crazy idea, but he was sure it was the only solution and, after all, he was the experienced Saudi driver.

"I'll leave you some of my water," he said, "and I'll be as quick as I can." Oh yes, and he'd have to take my jack, which, with his record of blowing tyres, he was likely to need.

Less than half an hour after Maurice had come back to find me, he was again on his way to Dubai and I was left alone with my truck, stranded in the middle of Saudi Arabia. Only then, in the silence of the desert, did I begin to think. To begin with, I had broken a key rule of Middle East driving. "If anything goes wrong," an old hand had told me a few days earlier, "don't do anything until you've had a cup of tea." This very British advice actually made perfect sense, because the time it takes to make and drink a cup of tea is the time you need to ponder your problem, whatever it is. If I'd paused to brew up, I might not have tipped the cab off its broken mounting; even if I were able to sort out the air problem, getting the cab back in place was going to be a real headache. I sat with my tea in the shade of the trailer and applied myself to the facts, thankful that I no longer had Maurice chattering at me. The sand stretched to the horizon, with no sign of life apart from a solitary small bird that startled me by swooping into the shade of the truck and perching on a spare tyre. It cheered me for a moment, but it didn't diminish my predicament. But one thing was certain, whatever else happened I wasn't about to sit in the desert for two weeks, waiting for Maurice to sort me out.

FIRST STEPS

It had taken me several years to reach, at the age of twenty-seven, this low point in my trucking career, but my interest in trucks took hold long before I was old enough to drive them. It began, rather improbably, in the experimental spiritual community near London in which I was brought up. The community, led by my own father, the writer and philosopher J.G. Bennett, numbered about fifty residents, with non-resident associates in the hundreds. It was dedicated to finding a way to bring science and spirituality together, and was experimental in the sense that its members tried a wide variety of different spiritual and scientific approaches, as well as working with the ideas and practices of the philosopher and teacher G.I. Gurdjieff. It was also a highly practical place, in which the community restored and maintained a number of large buildings and gardens, and grew much of its own food. When I was eighteen, one of the residents shepherded me through the process of rebuilding a diesel engine in my first vehicle, a Land Rover, which I had, imprudently but cheaply, bought with a connecting rod poking through the side of the cylinder block. Peter was something of a hero to me because he had been an aircraft mechanic in the war, working on enormous Sunderland flying boats, and was later a ship's engineer. He also took part – with the other community members and regular visitors – in the building of a large nine-sided meeting hall, whose design was remarkable enough to attract a visit from the architect Frank Lloyd Wright.

The building project took two years and it was a regular source of entertainment for the community's children. At one stage, the structure required a stream of ready-mixed concrete lorries to deliver concrete to form the walls of the building's underground lobby. I was fascinated by these trucks, with their rumbling diesel engines and concrete mixer barrels that clanged and groaned mysteriously as they poured liquid concrete through a cement-spattered trough at the rear. It seemed to my six-year-old imagination that nothing could be more glamorous than driving such an impressive vehicle. My parents regarded this with some amusement, but long after I had moved on, they remembered. When, fifteen years later, at the age of twenty-one, I passed my class one heavy goods vehicle test, my father asked whether this meant I could now drive a ready-mixed concrete lorry. "Yes," I said, "but now I don't want to." What I wanted, and what I was now qualified to do, was to drive articulated trucks.

Not only did I want to drive them, I wanted to drive them for long distances. I had been brought up from an early age to be a traveller, as my father and grandfather had been. I knew little about my grandfather, who died thirty years before I was born, but I did know that he had knocked about in the Middle East and southern Europe for many years, and had been a correspondent for Reuters. My father – born at the tail end of the nineteenth century – was a gifted linguist, and had served in British army intelligence in Constantinople in the aftermath of World War I. Fluent in Turkish and Greek – as well as Italian, French, German and, later, Indonesian – he had travelled all over the Middle East, lived in Greece for several years and visited every continent. When I was seven, he and my mother took my younger brother, Ben, and me around the world for six months, as they travelled in connection with a new spiritual movement, Subud, which they were helping to introduce in the USA, Australia, Ceylon (now known as Sri Lanka) and India.

Travel on this scale was unusual for a child in the 1950s, but not only did my parents take Ben and me to many countries themselves, they also encouraged us to be independent. When I was eleven, and Ben still nine, we were sent to stay with a family in France by ourselves and not by the straightforward means of a plane. Instead, we boarded the boat-train from London to Dover, got ourselves across the Channel and onto a train to Paris, all unaccompanied. We boys thought this was quite unremarkable, but it seems incredible by modern parenting standards. We took independence a step further when, a week into our three-week stay with a family whose two children disliked us as much as we did them, we decided to run away. We managed to get ourselves by train into the centre of Paris from the southern suburbs, cross the city on the metro to the Gare du Nord, and were just boarding the train for Calais when we were apprehended by our distraught host. We stayed the course after that, but our passports were confiscated.

Just before my eighteenth birthday, in February 1969, I set off on an overland trip to India with my then girlfriend, Jocelyn. The six-month trip was a further lesson in independent travel and how to deal with a variety of cultures, but it also gave me a glimpse of a possible future for myself. We spent many weeks travelling around Turkey and I once saw two road-weary trucks on the quayside in Istanbul, waiting for a ferry across the Bosphorus to the Asian side. They belonged to the pioneering British company, Asian Transport, which later became the famous Middle East trucking specialist, Astran. I immediately saw the potential of trucks as a means of taking me long distances, which was reinforced as we hitchhiked home a few months later and got a lift through Eastern Europe in a truck from Iran.

When we returned from our travels, I began a four-year degree course at Keele University, near the Midlands city of Stoke-on-Trent. My interest in trucks was brought into sharper focus as a result of my university studies or, more accurately, the amount of time I spent hitchhiking between Keele and my home in Kingston upon Thames, south-west of London. One of Keele's unadvertised virtues was its proximity to the M6 motorway service area of the same name, where truck rides were often forthcoming. I learned to recognise different brands of truck, and to know which ones were good to ride in and which were best left alone. I began to appreciate the finer points of an ERF or a Leyland and once, to my astonishment and pleasure, I got a ride in a new Volvo F88, one of the superior Swedish imports whose arrival in the UK heralded the eventual demise of the British truck industry. Land Rovers were no longer my ideal vehicle; heavy trucks had replaced them in my affections.

I passed my class one heavy goods vehicle test in 1972, as soon as I reached the minimum age for the licence, in the early days of my last year at university. During the long summer vacation, I had, as usual, worked long hours for several weeks in the local hospital kitchen in Kingston, and I then spent some of my earnings on a week-long truck-driving course. This was run by the quaintly named Blox Services, in the low-rent part of Wimbledon, in south-west London. The training school advised me to start with a class two licence, which would allow me to drive what was officially described as a 'multi-wheeled rigid vehicle above 3.5 tons'. In those days, vehicles in this category were usually tippers, either twenty-four-ton six-wheelers or thirty-ton eight-wheelers, neither of which appealed to me. What did appeal was Blox's assurance that I would almost certainly pass the class two test after a week of full-time training, while a class one licence might be a bit of a stretch in only five days. With my own money at stake, I went for the sure thing.

I arrived at the training school on a Monday morning, feeling somewhat self-conscious and anxious not to screw up. The course began in the classroom where, with an assorted group of would-be drivers, I listened to a retired policeman run through the principles of truck driving. Some of us were learning to drive class one articulated trucks or 'artics'. Several, like me, were training on six-wheelers and a few – including two firemen needing licences to drive a fire engine – were learning on humble four-wheeled sixteen-tonners. When it came to questions, one of the prospective artic drivers asked what he should do if his truck started to skid.

"Try to get in the first few words of Our Father," said the ex-copper, laconically. We laughed dutifully.

"But seriously?"

"Try to get in the first words of Our Father," the trainer insisted. The laughter died. Were these vehicles really that difficult and unforgiving? Years later, with probably a lot more varied driving experience than my former instructor, I got out of a skid quite simply, but even so, it may have been the prayer that did it.

I spent the rest of the week in a Ford D-Series six-wheeler, partnered with another trainee. We took turns to drive, giving us each a total of four hours at the wheel. While one of us drove, the other trainee observed from the passenger bench, which we shared with our instructor. The D-Series had a modest cab and I suppose it was cramped, but I didn't care as I practised manoeuvring a vehicle many times the size of the cars and Land Rovers I was used to, and learned to reverse using only the door mirrors. I also negotiated the mysteries of double declutching, a vital skill in the days when nearly all trucks had non-synchromesh gearboxes. This required dipping the clutch to shift out of one gear, lifting off the clutch pedal in neutral, and pressing it down again to engage the next gear. When downshifting, we also had to blip the accelerator to bring the engine up to speed to match the lower gear. It took a day or two to learn – amid embarrassing crunching of mismatched gears – but eventually became as automatic as walking.

Our training routes varied from central London, where I found myself struggling past Harrods in heavy traffic, to the Surrey hills on runs that seemed almost long-distance. We ate in transport cafes, and gossiped about vehicles and the severity of the various test centres we might be sent to. By the end of the course, I would have been quite happy to give up my studies and become a permanent part of the fraternity of drivers that I was starting to recognise around me. And at the end of the week, I passed my class two test with ease. Now I wondered whether I shouldn't have risked the full-blown class one training, but there was no more time before my university term began, and I couldn't really afford another week's tuition.

I returned to Keele to prepare for my fourth and final year, but I already felt dissatisfied with my class two licence, because it wouldn't give me access to the long-distance articulated trucks I'd set my mind on. So, in the first two weeks of term, I fitted my academic schedule around a series of one-day artic lessons, at £16 a day, at a driving school in nearby Crewe. This time I was driving an odd-looking Dodge 500 Series tractor unit, with a broad, shallow grille that gave it the wide-mouthed appearance of the future animated clay character, Wallace. It was coupled to a short, thirty-foot unladen trailer that I thought was chosen to be easier on trainees. Later, I found that longer trailers were actually easier to reverse, but the thirty-footer was probably cheaper to buy. The laid-back driving school parked its trucks overnight on a large piece of waste ground and, to give us time to practise manoeuvres before our formal lessons, left the keys in the bumper for us to help ourselves. Along with the more committed of my fellow students, I gave myself at least an hour of reversing practice before our training sessions began.

Reversing with any sort of trailer is counter-intuitive; if you want to go left, you steer right, and steering any sort of intentional course requires constant correction at the wheel. If you over-correct, an articulated truck ends up like a partly folded pocket knife and there is no recourse but to drive forward until you've got the tractor unit and trailer in a straight line again, and start over. I practised every morning until I could perform the zigzag reversing manoeuvre required in the test, but I was hardly a competent reverser, and hopeless going backwards in a straight line. The following summer, in my first full-time job, I found myself delivering twenty tons of kerb stones to the Abingdon bypass south of Oxford, which was then under construction. The only way to the delivery point was to reverse for half a mile down a half-finished section of the new road. My progress was a nightmare as I kept over-correcting the wheel, so that the trailer veered from side to side like a weaving drunkard. Every fifty yards or so I had to stop, drive forward to straighten the trailer, and then reverse again. The fact that I was doing it under the incredulous eye of the site foreman didn't help, neither did the ponderous unassisted steering of the Atkinson tractor unit I was driving at the time. Eventually, I did figure out how to reverse straight back, for as long as I wanted, but it took time and much more practice than I could fit into a few days of training.

Meanwhile, I still had to pass the class one artic test. The training set-up was the same as before: two students and an instructor per vehicle. The Dodge cab was wider than the Ford's had been, but the relationship between the three of us was still quite intimate, thanks to the friendly girth of our instructor. In other respects, the lessons were quite different. In place of the cramped suburbs of south London, we ranged along the roads of Cheshire and west Staffordshire, and into the ageing streets of Stoke-on-Trent. This was the best known of the five towns – also known as 'The Potteries' – of Arnold Bennett's novels, built on the ceramics industry that had made it one of Britain's first industrial centres. By this time, however, it was a fading city, still dotted with disused brick-built 'bottle' kilns and empty factories. The narrow streets were lined with low, red-brick terraced houses and we manoeuvred our way along them, as we learned the intricacies of the ten-speed gearbox.

Like the six-wheeled Ford I'd been driving a few weeks earlier, the Dodge had a non-synchromesh gearbox, but with ten gears instead of the six in the lighter Ford twenty-four-tonner. One requirement of the test was to start in bottom gear (or crawler) and shift smoothly through every ratio from first to top and down again, to ensure that we could find every one of them when we needed it, double declutching all the while. Since an unladen truck never needed to go below third gear, this exercise was somewhat academic, but was aimed at preparing us for the realities of driving a loaded vehicle.

I discovered how to swing the tractor unit wide at corners, to give the trailer room to follow without climbing the kerb, all the while watching it in the nearside mirror to make sure I wasn't mowing down pedestrians. I learned to look as far ahead as I could see, anticipating hills or other changes in the road, and watching for the idiocies of car drivers who didn't appreciate how large our vehicle was. And I began to rely on the door-mounted mirrors, checking them constantly when on the move and trying to believe what they showed me when I was reversing. Each day I spent about four hours at the wheel and another four observing my colleague, and I staggered back to my university flat exhausted by the effort of attention.

On the fifth of my training days, we headed to the test centre, about ten miles south of Stoke in the village of Swynnerton. It was raining hard and I worried about skidding or jack-knifing the unladen truck with the examiner on board to watch. The two-hour test started with forward and reversing manoeuvres and a rather tame emergency stop. This was technically named 'stopping under full control', by which the ministry men meant 'stopping as quickly as you can without jack-knifing the bloody thing' and involved accelerating to 25mph and tramping on the brake pedal as you passed a pair of cones. I completed all three off-road preliminaries and we were off, heading into Stoke and the streets I was beginning to find familiar. The heavy rain and spray made for bad visibility, so I leaned forward to reach the light switch on the fascia by my right knee and turned on the headlights. The examiner didn't comment; indeed, his only conversation was a series of instructions, "left at the lights", "continue straight on", "pull over here and stop". This last command was for the hill start test and I was nervous enough to select fifth gear instead of third. As soon as I began to let in the clutch, I could feel the mistake through my foot, as the combination of an eight-ton truck and too high a gear threatened to stall the engine. I trod firmly back on the clutch and reengaged the handbrake.

"Sorry, wrong gear," I apologised to the impassive examiner, as I selected third gear and started again. Maybe that one error would fail me, but to my relief he made no mark on his recording sheet and I completed the rest of the road test without incident. Back at the test centre, the examiner launched into a series of questions about the Highway Code and driving in general.

Finally, he asked, "Is it a good idea to use your lights when visibility is poor?" What did he mean? That's what I'd done, wasn't it? Surely that was right?

"Yes, it is," I said. "That's why I switched them on when we were on the A34." The examiner looked surprised; perhaps he hadn't noticed, but in any case it stopped his questions and I'd passed. Now, finally, I had my class one heavy goods vehicle licence, or HGV 1, and could drive any heavy goods vehicle on the road.

First, however, was the small matter of finishing my studies. I stepped out of the world of trucks and back into the life of a potential academic, and applied myself to getting a respectable grade in my degree. For the next eight months I never set foot in a truck, but when I did graduate, in June 1973, it was my class one HGV, and not my degree in History and American Studies, that helped me earn a living.

CHAPTER 2
LEARNING THE ROPES

From Keele, I moved into a flat in Leicester with Jocelyn, now my wife, and our two-year-old son, Ben. After four years as an impecunious student, I badly needed a job, so the day after we moved in, I went down to the labour exchange. No dole office is a happy place and I was ushered into a large room filled with people displaying varying degrees of dejection. Slumped back in chairs asleep, or leaning forward nervously and peering around them, the job-seekers had an unsettling air of permanence. The clerk wasn't much more encouraging, until I said, "I've got an HGV 1," at which point she brightened considerably.

"Have you? We've got several driving jobs available." Within minutes, I was leaving with appointments at A.M. Walker of Cosby and at Hercock & Simpson.

Emerging from the gloom of the labour exchange into the bright June day, I set off for Hercock's yard on the edge of the city. Hercock was the one I was interested in; they did international work. I parked outside their office and found the transport manager. He wasn't concerned about my lack of driving experience – there was evidently a shortage of trained drivers – and promised to start me immediately.

"We'll put you on a four-wheeler to begin with," he said, "and then when you're twenty-five, you can switch to an artic." Twenty-five? That was three years away. For the first time, I considered what it would be like to have a permanent job as a driver, but I couldn't yet imagine myself working for three years for anyone, let alone as the driver of a lowly four-wheeler. "It's the insurance," the transport manager explained. "It costs too much to insure drivers under twenty-five for artics." That was his problem, not mine; I hadn't paid for a class one licence just to drive a class three four-wheeler. Besides, smaller trucks meant shorter distances and less interesting work so, taking a chance on finding a better offer, I turned him down and set off to visit A.M. Walker in the village of Cosby, a few miles south of the city.

Walker's yard was a vast sea of hard-packed gravel with a small area of tarmac outside a squat brick office building. In the distance, beyond a row of parked trailers was a line of corrugated iron workshops. I presented myself to a Mr. Parry, the transport manager, who was as enthusiastic as Hercock's man, but without his insurance hang-ups. I explained my lack of experience, but Mr. Parry was unperturbed. He walked me across the yard to the corrugated iron workshops, from which emerged a heavy-set swarthy man who turned out to be the workshop foreman. We shook hands. "Bill will give you a road test," Parry explained, "and if that goes well, you can start on Monday."

Bill led me across the yard to a line of loaded trailers, one of which was fronted by an Atkinson Borderer. This classic British tractor unit had a wide, fibreglass cab and a split windscreen whose sloping bottom edges gave the truck a somewhat lachrymose appearance. I eyed it apprehensively and I was made more nervous by the forty-foot trailer. Not only was it ten feet longer than the trailer I'd trained with all those months ago, but it was also loaded with twenty tons of paving stones, lashed at the rear with criss-crossed ropes. My heart gave a lurch as I realised the obvious – for the first time I'd be driving an artic loaded to its maximum of thirty-two tons, instead of the eight tons of unladen Dodge back in Crewe.

I climbed into the cab, through the narrow, wood-framed door, and sat in the driver's seat. In front of me was a large, almost horizontal steering wheel and a semi-circular dashboard filled with switches and dials. Chief among them were the rev counter and speedometer, with gauges for air pressure – three of them – fuel, battery charging and oil pressure arrayed on either side. It looked thoroughly intimidating compared with the homely Dodge I'd driven as a trainee. On my left, and almost as high as my elbow, a large flat engine cover filled a third of the cab. The heavy gearstick stood up from the floor well, with a large round black knob to the left of the wheel.

Bill explained the gearbox, a simple six-speed David Brown transmission, and helped me adjust the nearside mirror to my liking. He showed me the starter button and I fired up the 180hp Gardner engine, which rumbled into life under the engine cover. I engaged first gear and carefully let in the clutch. The weight of the truck immediately made it feel different from the vehicles I'd learned on, but it also supplied a satisfying momentum. I trundled the Atkinson across the yard and out onto the road. Compared to an unladen truck, everything was in slow motion. I shifted carefully up through the unfamiliar gearbox and took extra time to bring all thirty-two tons to a stop at every junction. If I displayed any nerves, Bill didn't comment on them, and within a couple of miles we were chatting quite affably. We must have been out for half an hour before I found myself swinging the Atkinson back into Walker's yard. Mr. Parry came out to meet us and, although I didn't notice him do it, Bill must have given Mr. Parry the nod before he turned away to his workshop, because I was told to start on Monday.

I would be paid a 'tip and load' bonus. The basic wage was a princely £4 a day, with an extra £2.50 every time I loaded and £2 for 'tipping', or unloading, which was usually quicker and easier. I discovered that it would be an exceptional day in which I could do any more than one load and tip in a single shift, so I was looking at a daily payment of no more than £8.50, and weekly earnings considerably less than the wages I'd earned as a student, working long hours in the kitchens of our local hospital. Mr. Parry told me that for the first two weeks, and more if necessary, I would ride and drive with another driver, who would show me the ropes.

This was no mere figure of speech. My first week was with Terry and I rapidly discovered that being able to drive a truck was only the beginning. The first thing I needed to learn was how to load a flatbed trailer – as most trailers were in those days – and then how to secure the load with ropes and tarpaulins. In doing so, I discovered a whole new vocabulary. Tarpaulins were 'sheets'; the rounded section of steel that ran along each side of the wooden-floored trailer, an inch clear of the floorboards, was called the 'rave' – I never discovered why – and the knot that tightened all the ropes was known universally as a 'dolly'.

Terry and I began our week delivering a trailer that had been loaded the previous Friday. When we arrived at the delivery point, we had to start by unsheeting the load, and the process was anything but random. First, we walked round the trailer freeing the ropes from the series of hooks located under the trailer sides, about fifteen inches apart. The ropes and knots were rigid with tension, but Terry showed me how the dolly knot could be untied simply by pulling on the loop at the top of it and sliding the rest of the knot around it. With the rope loosened, we had only to slip the lower loop off the hook and pull, at which point the whole dolly dissolved into a straight piece of rope. I thought it was brilliant then and, nearly fifty years later, I still do. The next step was to coil the half-dozen ropes that were pooled on the ground. Terry demonstrated how to make a neat coil by holding the rope tightly in one hand and letting it slide through the other as I swung my arms out to full stretch and back together again, each time picking up a new loop that was the same length as the rest. We wound the looped end of the rope around the coil a few times, threaded the end through it and tightened it by banging the whole coil to the ground.

Next came the sheets, which were secured in place by thinner lengths of rope attached to the sheets themselves, which cinched the edges of the sheets against the rave. These were easily undone, leaving each sheet hanging loosely down each side of the trailer. Terry and I then pulled each sheet off the trailer, taking care not to dislodge the load itself, which in this case consisted of cartons stacked on pallets. Now came the crucial part, folding each sheet ready to use for the next time. I kept quiet about my brief previous experience of sheets.

Shortly after getting my class two licence, and before my last year began at Keele University, I had found a week's work with the driver agency Manpower in Stoke-on-Trent, during which I'd been assigned to a company running a single drop-side Dodge four-wheeler. Manpower had neglected to check whether I knew how to rope and sheet – in fact they never even met me, but hired me on the strength of a single phone call – and of course this vital skill hadn't featured in my driving lessons. In that particular job, however, it didn't matter most of the time, since my loads never rose above the drop-sides and the weather was fine. However, towards the end of my week with the Dodge, I'd come in to find it neatly roped and sheeted.

I arrived at my delivery destination in Birmingham and managed to wrestle the ropes off their hooks – not appreciating the genius of the slip-off dolly knot – and unsheet the load. Once I'd tipped, I bundled the sheet behind the headboard, having no idea that there was a proper way to fold it. Naturally, it started flapping as soon as I hit the road, and I had to weigh it down with some short lengths of timber that had been left in the load-bed of the Dodge. I divulged none of this to Terry.

Our sheets were large tarpaulins about twenty by thirty feet, and two were enough for most loads on a forty-foot trailer. Terry directed me to one corner of the first sheet and he took the other end of the same side. Pulling it taut between us, we dragged the sheet onto an open space so that it lay completely flat. Then we folded it about three-fifths of the way across the rest of the width of the sheet and back again. We repeated the process with the other edge until we had the whole thing folded into fifths, in such a way that when we unrolled it on the top of a load, the sheet would unfold evenly on each side. Back in Stoke, I could have spent a week and never worked out the folds for myself. Once each sheet was folded lengthwise, we brought each end in to the middle before rolling the whole sheet up and stamping on it to make it sit snugly back on the trailer once it had been unloaded. After about fifteen minutes, we were ready to take the load off. Most goods we carried were stacked on pallets and our job now was simply to watch a forklift driver lift each pallet off and, usually, squirrel it away in some warehouse. Other loads, I would discover, were 'handballed' – unloaded by hand – by the driver, sometimes with help from someone at the delivery point, and too often without.

We set off to collect our next load, an hour or so away. Once it was aboard the trailer, I began to learn the greater complexities of putting the sheets on. Before we could begin to sheet the trailer, we had to hoist each heavy rolled tarpaulin onto the top of the load and then climb up after it. We then walked carefully along the top, unrolling the sheet as we went, starting with the back sheet, so that the front one would overlap and prevent wind getting under it. Watching Terry, I saw how he judged the sheet so that its rear edge just reached the floor of the trailer. We then unfolded the sheet and now I could see the reason for folding it so carefully. We dropped each double-fold over the side of the load and when we climbed down again, I saw that each side had fallen to an equal height. We secured the rear sheet with its ties, tucking the extra length of each side up over the rave as we moved along the trailer, so that the sheet was held just under the edge of the trailer. We pulled the rear corners of each sheet across the back of the load and made an envelope out of the rest, to form a neat, watertight package. Then we repeated the process with the front sheet. The third step was the optional flysheet, a single plasticised sheet that ran the whole length of the load and down its front and rear.

Finally came the ropes. Terry showed me how to slip the looped end of the rope to the first hook, take up a few coils and then throw it over the trailer. We then walked to the other side, pulled in the slack and tied the rope off using the drivers' 'dolly' knot, which could be pulled astonishingly tight. The procedure was repeated along the length of the trailer, using a series of ropes. An experienced driver could rope and sheet a forty-footer in about half an hour. That first week, I still had a way to go, but once I got the hang of it, I found it very satisfying to be able to rope and sheet a lumpy load so that the sheets remained neat and taut for hundreds of miles. More to the point, a well-sheeted load doesn't fall off.

Loading was slower than unloading, hence the generous fifty pence difference in our tip and load bonus payment. Of course, both jobs were faster with two drivers, and folding a sheet was easy with each of us holding a corner. Normally, however, I would be doing this alone, so Terry taught me how to fold the long tarpaulin by myself, working from the middle of each edge. I also had to be able to lift the sixty-odd pounds of sheet onto the top of the load. What with hauling on the ropes and lifting the sheets, I was going to be a lot fitter than I'd been as a student.

By the end of my first week, Terry and I had driven to Liverpool, London and Manchester, and sundry smaller towns. A couple of times, heading back south to Leicester, we'd called in at Hulland, high in the Derbyshire hills, to pick up a trailer previously loaded with concrete kerb or paving stones. This was such regular work for Walker's that they employed a 'shunter' at the concrete works whose job it was to load over a dozen trailers a day for the regular drivers to pick up. We'd leave an unladen trailer in the parking area and pick up a loaded replacement for the run back south to Leicester, ready to be delivered anywhere across the country the following day.

Uncoupling an artic semi-trailer is simple enough – once you know how. The crucial part is to wind down the 'landing' legs located towards the front of the trailer, to support its weight once the tractor unit is driven from under it. Terry impressed on me the results of failing to lower the legs – a trailer on its knees and the back of the tractor unit torn off. Everyone does it once, he said, but I determined right then that it wouldn't be me, and his warnings were so vivid that I've never yet landed a trailer on its nose. The next step is to uncouple the air hoses that supply the trailer brake systems and unplug the electric connection. These are universally known as 'susies', though I have never found a reliable reason why. Finally, you reach under the trailer and pull back the bar that locks the tractor unit's 'fifth wheel' to the hefty flanged pin protruding from a steel plate underneath the trailer. Coupling and uncoupling trailers quickly became a daily routine.

I spent two weeks as an apprentice, one with Terry and another with a dour but skilful driver named Bernard, and then I was on my own. I was given a Mk I Atkinson with a 180bhp Gardner engine as my regular vehicle and I was a long-distance lorry driver.

Walker's was a general haulage operation – we carried anything – and that first summer I hauled kerb stones, paving slabs, paper, soft drinks, hard liquor and, once, two forty-foot sections of crane jib. A typical day began at three or four in the morning, with a drive of several hours, arriving early enough to be able to tip a load and continue to the next loading point, or to Hulland to swap trailers. I found myself lucky to be able to tip and load once each day, which meant my daily earnings averaged £8.50. This was hardly generous, but I was happy to be driving and learning. I got used to reversing from a busy street into a narrow entrance while ignoring the impatient traffic I was holding up, and I became accepted by a fraternity of drivers who were always happy to give me advice as long as I didn't pretend to know what I didn't.

I soon found out that truck drivers had their own sign language, whose most basic element was a flash of headlights. In the days when trucks were relatively low-powered, they took an age to overtake each other and, particularly on a two-lane road, the passing driver was always anxious to get back on the right side of the highway as efficiently as possible. So the driver being passed flashed his lights as soon as the tail of the overtaking truck cleared his own, allowing its driver to steer safely in front of him with only a few feet to spare. The overtaking driver would switch his tail lights on and off twice by way of a thank you, though I later discovered that Continental drivers showed their appreciation by switching their indicators left and right, a style which gradually became fashionable in Britain. Flashing headlights towards an approaching driver might also be followed up by a gesture. A downturned thumb meant there were police, or some other hazard, ahead, while a gesture with two hands held palm flat, and moved up and down, represented a weight check round the corner.

In those early weeks of my driving career, the only aspect of the job I didn't relish, though it was undeniably interesting from a sociological point of view, was overnighting in 'digs'. Walker's base near Leicester was well placed in the English Midlands, so that on most days I managed to get home, or close enough, within my legal hours so that I could hitchhike home in the evening and back to my truck in the morning. I had hitchhiked half way across the world as a student, but now I had a guaranteed passport to a lift. All drivers in those days used standard logbooks to register their daily work and driving hours, and every driver recognised them. All I had to do was to wave my logbook at an approaching truck and its driver would be almost guaranteed to stop.

When I couldn't get home, there were digs. Nowadays, every long-distance truck has a sleeper cab, but in the '70s the vast majority of us had day-cabs and were still using overnight lodgings dedicated to drivers. My first experience of drivers' digs was in the notoriously rough Liverpool docks. I'd gone there with another Walker's driver and although he'd been unloaded and was able to head out of the city, I had to stay overnight to tip the following morning. My colleague directed me towards some digs he knew and left me with the parting advice not to go out to the pub without at least one other driver as protection. The warning was hardly reassuring, and I was so impressed by it that I attached myself to a small party of drivers before I headed out for a pint. In Manchester I sometimes stayed in digs at the vast Trafford Park trading estate, where we slept eight or ten to a room in unventilated dormitories. Drivers were assigned to the rooms according to the time we wanted to be woken, starting as early as 4.30am. Even the legendary Hollies transport café, off the M6 motorway near Cannock, may have served lightning-fast and brilliant breakfasts, but its rooms upstairs were nothing to write home about, with sagging mattresses, cheap nylon sheets and carpets made crunchy with age.

I took it all in my stride as part of the new world I was discovering. I was becoming part of a nationwide fraternity and I enjoyed being addressed by my function. Delivering kerb stones to a road construction site in South Wales, I took an obscure pride in being hailed by the foreman as 'driver'. I was even happier when it turned out that he wanted me to move some reinforcing mesh a mile down the new road, in return for a tenner in my hand. Perhaps best of all, I began to learn my way around a large part of Britain. I became familiar with the views from many miles of motorway and the routes through and around Liverpool, London, Birmingham and Leeds. After three months, I was by no means a fully-fledged professional, but I was getting there.

CHAPTER 3
GETTING THE HANG OF IT

Even though I made it home to Leicester on most nights, I seemed to be away from home for more than I would have been in a regular job. My wife, Jocelyn, had to deal with our small son, Ben, alone every morning and by the time I got home in the evening I was often too tired to be much company. I did take Ben with me a couple of times on short Saturday morning runs and I rarely worked on Sundays, but I could already see that driving and marriage weren't much of a combination. As it happened, however, my time at Walker's was only temporary, because Jocelyn and I had already decided to spend a year in Gloucestershire attending a residential philosophy course, run by my own father, that could scarcely have been more different from the job I was doing.

Walker's was surprised that I wanted to leave and I could see why. After a few weeks working with my outdated Mk I Atkinson I'd been wondering whether I might graduate to one of the newer Atkinson Borderers, the model I'd shared with Terry and Bernard. Instead, foreman Bill had suggested that I might be given a much fancier Volvo F88. The Volvos were so far advanced compared with either of the Atkinsons that the comparison was almost indecent. Instead of the cramped, unheated Atki cab, made of wood and fibreglass, which was, unbelievably, still Atkinson's current model, the Volvo had a large steel cab with a bunk bed behind the driver. It was quiet, insulated and warm in winter. It had a far more powerful engine – 230bhp instead of 180bhp – and as well as offering a much better driving experience, was fast enough to hold out the prospect of at least one more tip or load each day. Not only would the Volvo be much more pleasant to drive, it would probably have earned me more money.

Nevertheless, our plans had been made, and I left Walker's at the end of the summer and moved with Jocelyn and Ben to attend the course in Gloucestershire. In the company of over a hundred other students and staff, Jocelyn and I spent almost a year immersed in meditations, psychology and philosophy classes, and varied practical tasks from gardening to house-painting, around the large, converted mansion and sixteen-acre property in the village of Sherborne. The course was as great a departure from the work at A.M. Walker as Walker's had been from my university studies, but many of the meditation and people skills I learned in that year have served me well ever since.

I didn't take up driving again until the following summer of 1974 when, once again, I was in dire need of income. By then, the stresses that had long been apparent in our relationship had finally reached breaking point, and both Jocelyn and I left the course in the company of someone else. My new partner, Jane, had two sons, and together we all moved to Somerset, to a house we'd been lent by a generous friend until I began a master's degree in US political history back at Keele in the autumn.

The day after we moved in, I headed to the labour exchange in nearby Yeovil. Once again, my heavy goods licence gave me a rapid passport to a job, and I was sent across the town to see one Roger Bastable at Abbey Hill Vehicle Services. I drove my old Land Rover through Abbey Hill's narrow gateway and into a cramped yard with a number of ancient and draughty buildings along one side. I headed for the small office and asked for Mr. Bastable. "Roger's in the workshop," I was told, and I was directed towards one of the large doorways that opened into a dingy interior. As I approached, a young man appeared from the gloom dressed in a faded, light green brushed denim suit. He advanced with a rapid scuttling walk, head down and curly mane flying, hands thrust into his trouser pockets. He shook my hand and introduced himself in a softened Somerset accent. I don't remember much of an interview; instead, I seemed to be drawn seamlessly into a company that felt more like a family or a fraternity than a regular business.

Roger – I never heard anyone call him Mr. Bastable – was a year older than me and one of the most interesting people I met in my time as a driver. He was a born businessman, but he had a sense of humour and a generosity that made him fun to work for. When I met him, Roger already inspired an affectionate loyalty in his drivers, not least because he paid £1 an hour, which was better than the prevailing rate at the time, and compared very favourably with what I had been paid at Walker's the previous year. Some years later, Roger had built Abbey Hill Group into a major force in the car transport business, and Roger himself had become something of a legend, but this same generosity eventually got him into serious trouble. His company, by then numbering nearly 400 trucks – lost a major contract and he kept all his drivers for longer than he could afford to, with disastrous results for the business itself. Meanwhile, in the summer of 1974, the Abbey Hill fleet numbered fewer than twenty trucks, in an eccentric mix of vehicles. The line-up included a couple of old Leylands, a pair of new Dafs, various four-wheeled sixteen-tonners, a specialised long-wheelbase TK Bedford designed to carry caravans (it never did) and an ageing Mk V AEC Mandator, dating from the 1950s.

The vintage Mandator became my regular vehicle that summer. It was so old that it was rated at only twenty-six tons gross, instead of the prevailing maximum thirty-two tons, but it could still turn a profit and that was all Roger cared about. He was very relaxed about my taking the AEC home at night, leaving our old Land Rover for Jane to use, and I found a gateway near our temporary home that would accommodate the vintage tractor unit and its single-axled trailer.

I took a perverse pride in driving such a classic truck and Roger made no concessions to its age, nor to its 53mph top speed, when lorries were allowed to do sixty on the motorway. The Mandator and I made our stately way as far north as Manchester and as far west as Penzance, delivering all manner of goods. The AEC liaison was only ever going to be temporary, however, as I explained to Roger when I left Abbey Hill in early September, and set off with Jane and the two boys to look for a house near Keele University, where we would live for the year of my master's degree. Roger was sympathetic and told me I could be sure of a job if ever I wanted to return.

I was back in the familiar Potteries, but after more than a year of living in rural Gloucestershire and Somerset, the area seemed less than appealing – at least any area that we could afford to live in. After a dispiriting couple of days visiting rental agents in the city and, trailing Jane's two small sons, inspecting two-up, two-down miners' cottages in Scot Hay and Newcastle-under-Lyme, Jane and I decided to take a weekend break in my family's primitive cottage in North Wales, far to the west on the end of the Llyn Peninsula. The cottage, named Cadwgan (pronounced Cadoogan), was high above the sea on a saddle of land in the tiny village of Rhiw, a dozen miles west of Pwllheli, and overlooking the Irish Sea. Cadwgan was a two-roomed stone building, with a half loft above each room, running water only in a cramped outhouse, a chemical toilet and no electricity. All the same, it seemed wonderful in the mid-September sunshine and it dawned on Jane and me that we could live rent-free right where we were, and that I could commute home from Keele – some 150 miles – every other weekend. Only a woman as dauntless as Jane would have considered such an arrangement, with two children and a third – ours – visibly on the way, but she managed to make it work.

It was an eventful year, marked indelibly by the birth of our daughter, Laura, in early December, followed, seven days later, by the death of my father. This was a blow to both of us; not only was he my father, but he was also a teacher to both Jane and me, and he died while running another of the year-long courses we had completed the previous summer. His funeral, held at his residential college in Sherborne, was attended by several hundred people, including former students and friends from around the world. Jane and I, with our newborn daughter and the two boys, decamped to Gloucestershire to be with my mother and younger sisters until my university course resumed in January. Then we returned to Cadwgan and I resumed my fortnightly hitchhiking commute between Keele and the far end of North Wales. The following summer, with my exams and dissertation behind me, I again went looking for work.

Another degree, another labour exchange; this time in Pwllheli. The clerk was friendly enough but she had no driving jobs on her list, and she pointed out that no white-collar job was available to me since I wasn't bilingual. Even a bank clerk would have to speak both English and Welsh, not that I wanted to be one. Jane and I discussed what to do. There may have been no driving work available locally, but there was Roger Bastable and Abbey Hill, way down south in Somerset. Roger had assured me of a welcome any time, the money was good and I could start immediately. Moreover, I could live rent-free in my mother's cottage in Sparkford, which was near Yeovil and empty for most of the year, since she was living and working in Gloucestershire. With hindsight it seems deranged that I should have suggested working so far away, with little prospect of getting home regularly, but we needed the money immediately and Jane agreed, despite the fact that the boys were still under ten and our daughter Laura was only eight months old. I phoned Roger, who told me I could start immediately. We could afford only one car and Jane had to have it. Rhiw was in the middle of nowhere, five miles from any useful shop, and whenever I had returned from Keele it had been by hitchhiking. So I thumbed it down to Yeovil and once again started working for Abbey Hill.

Much had changed in the year I'd been away. The company had more than doubled in size, and the original cramped yard had been replaced by a large, airy workshop, sensible office and a long driveway wide enough to provide parking space for tractor units – the four-wheeled vehicles that pulled the articulated trailer. The end of the yard was a wide trailer park. On the south side was a vast field belonging to Westland, the helicopter manufacturer, and on the other side of the yard was Lock's Seeds, a farm seed supplier and one of our regular customers. Roger greeted me with his usual affability and I was immediately put to work.

Despite my untypical background, I was quickly accepted into the mix of madcap young men who ideally suited Roger's buccaneering style, and older, more experienced drivers. One of the latter, Bert Navey, took me under his wing and was always a friendly source of advice. Even Roger was impressed by Bert and his meticulous approach to general haulage. He was proud of Bert's driving skill and the care he took to maintain his truck in immaculate condition. I liked the fact that Bert had carried everything in his time and always knew how to secure an unusual load; knowledge he was happy to share. I thought I blended in quite well and I was quietly pleased to be accepted by the rest of the firm, but one day I was chatting to one of the other drivers and he said, "You were in Lock's yesterday, weren't you?" Yes, I had been. I'd taken three different four-wheelers across to the neighbouring Lock's Seeds to load them, ready for three of us to head west the following morning.

"How did you know?" I asked.

"Oh, I was in there just now and they said, 'that intelligent cunt' was in yesterday." It wasn't a compliment and it made me reflect briefly on whether I really had been accepted by the people I worked with. My higher education – which I never talked about – didn't make me a typical truck driver, but the truck-driving world seemed quite tolerant of variety. Years later, I even met a driver who had been three months from ordination as a Catholic priest, before giving up the ecclesiastical life in favour of driving. At Abbey Hill, I eventually discovered that I was not the only ex-private schoolboy working for the company, but the fact that I learned this only after several months showed that nobody cared one way or another. As long as I could drive well, and take care of all the aspects of the job away from the wheel, I was accepted.

Being a newcomer, I was swapped from truck to truck, and for a few days I drove a Commer four-wheeler with a two-stroke engine that had the alarming habit of belching burning red-hot exhaust from the pipe just below the driver's door. It was an impressive sight at night. In short order, however, I was caught up in a job that occupied all of us on the general haulage side of the business for many weeks. The summer of 1975 was one of unusual dryness, which set the stage for the record drought the following year, when reservoirs from Derbyshire to Wales receded so far that villages that had once drowned reappeared above the water. Meanwhile, the dry summer of 1975 still left West Country farmers in desperate straits. For lack of rain, the summer grass was so poor that farmers couldn't maintain their cattle, and this was particularly critical for their predominantly dairy herds. So the National Farmers Union stepped in. In those days the arable farmers of East Anglia, 200 miles to the east, were in the habit of burning all their straw – a practice that has since been outlawed – but in order to help their colleagues in the west, the NFU persuaded the easterners to refrain from burning. Instead, they would allow teams from the West Country to bale oat and barley straw so it could be transported west as emergency cattle feed. Apparently, the deal depended on the vast East Anglian fields being baled rapidly, because the arable folk were reluctant to lose even a day in their intensive cultivation schedule. Our part was to haul the straw westward as fast as possible and Roger put all his flatbed vehicles onto the job.

Abbey Hill was paid by the ton, while we drivers were paid by the hours we worked, and we put in a lot. The aim was for each of us to do three runs a week, which meant leaving Yeovil in the early hours of Monday morning and driving empty to some large farm in East Anglia, where we would arrive at around eleven in the morning. By the time we drove onto the hard, cracked stubble field, the baling crews would have made a good start and we'd then spend all day, working into the evening, to load six to eight trucks with straw bales, stacking them seven high. I learned to stack the bales from each end, and from the outside edge to the middle, so the final bales could be rammed into place and lock each layer together. With the bales seven high we were more than a dozen feet off the ground, walking around on the load as if it were home. Some firms loaded eight high, but the word went around among Abbey Hill drivers that we should stop at seven, which would give us clearance under most of the bridges back home.

We drivers worked together, in groups of three or four, loading each of our trucks in turn as the bales were hoisted up to us in batches of eight by a loading machine aptly called a 'Farmhand'. At one farm the bales were served up to us by three men using traditional long-handled pitchforks, which was impressive, but oddly incongruous in the general mechanisation of the overall operation. Roping and sheeting was a lot quicker with two men, because we could throw the coiled rope between each other, hurling it high in the air to get it over the lofty load. Some companies did without the sheets since there was never any sign of rain, but at Abbey Hill we preferred to play it safe and put on a single fly sheet, which also had the advantage of holding the bales together more securely.

By nightfall, our half-dozen trucks would all be roped and sheeted and we'd bring out our camping stoves to cook up a meal and brew some tea. There was no chance of driving to any café – even if one had been available – because our legal driving hours were up. We'd snatch a few hours' sleep in our bunk-free day-cabs and leave before three in the morning, in order to cross London before the city woke up; there was no M25 ring road in those days. By mid-morning, we'd be trundling onto a weighbridge near Salisbury to get a weight ticket that determined the payment for the load, and in the early afternoon on Tuesday we'd deliver to some West Country farm. Well before dawn on Wednesday, the eastbound routine would start again, and with a round trip fitting neatly into forty-eight hours, we managed three runs a week. We were being paid for at least a dozen hours a day for six days in seven. At £1 an hour, well above the local average, I was coining it, and getting fit into the bargain. Between the alternate days of loading and unloading, I must have been doing three or four hours' hard labour a day, with twice as many hours of driving.

By now, I'd been given a regular truck, an AEC Mandator that was a current model, unlike the vintage machine I'd driven for Roger the previous summer. AEC – the Associated Equipment Company – began life as the bus-building arm of the London General Omnibus Company in the late 19th century, before being established in 1912 as a separate truck and bus builder. Over the years, the company absorbed a number of smaller British truck builders, before being taken over itself in 1962 by its bigger rival, Leyland, with encouragement – or pressure – from the then-Conservative government. The current Mandator had a cab that some bright spark had dubbed the 'Ergomatic'. Whatever this actually meant, it was presumably coined to imply modern high-tech. So it might have seemed when the cab was launched on AECs and Leylands back in 1964, but by the time I was driving it, the design was showing its age, particularly compared with the European imports, such as Walker's Volvos, that were already changing the expectations of British drivers. As Abbey Hill ran some Dutch-built Dafs – complete with sleepers – I knew what a cab could be, particularly after Roger gave me one for a fortnight. As a Mandator driver, however, I sat low in the cab, next to an engine that took up far too much of the interior space. In fact, the cab was rather more cramped than the Atkinson Borderers I'd driven at Walker's, and those were hardly spacious. Naturally, being a 1960s British design, it offered nowhere to sleep, but the pattern of the straw job made it impossible to sleep in digs, even if I'd wanted to, and I soon got used to sleeping in the cab and cooking my own meals. Lacking a bunk, I used to put a board between the tall engine cover and the passenger windowsill, which I kept in place with two slim brackets slipped down beside the window glass. I put my small suitcase on the driver's seat and lay a sleeping bag across the whole ensemble. At six feet three inches tall, I could just about stretch out across the cab, but there wasn't much room to spare. Nor was there much privacy, though I did hang a sheet across the sun-blinds to make a rudimentary curtain across the windscreen. In time I replaced this with all-round curtains, and the cab could seem almost cosy, though I never really slept properly.

Even though it was still two years before I become a Continental driver, where self-sufficiency was the norm, I was happy to acquire the habit of overnighting in the cab. Even with the discomforts of the Mandator it was more convenient, and probably more hygienic, than some of the digs I'd used when I worked for A.M. Walker. And 'cabbing it' saved money. We were paid a modest, tax-free night-out allowance and it made sense not to spend it on lodgings that were functional at best.

The Mandator may have been cramped, but it had a wide, single-piece windscreen, which was an improvement on the split-screen Atkinson I'd driven two summers before. Beside me, the twelve-litre, six-cylinder engine was relatively quiet and the six-speed gearbox simple to use, if rather slow through the gate. It was still a non-synchromesh box, but double declutching had long since become second nature to me, to the extent that when I later started driving trucks with synchromesh gearboxes, it took me weeks to unlearn the habit. And although the Mandator had its limitations, it was powerful for its day; at any rate, it made easy work of the straw loads, which averaged about eight tons, less than half the truck's capacity.

The emergency straw operation gave me two months of high-energy work and by the end of it, I'd learned a lot. I still assumed that all the other drivers knew more than I did, which may have been a fair assumption at the time, but I had gained new confidence in myself as a driver, helped by the camaraderie of loading with as many as half a dozen other drivers on any particular farm. Apart from learning how to stack straw bales so they would stay in place at speed, I also got used to manoeuvring through narrow lanes and tight gateways. The contrast between the farming cultures of eastern and western England was easy to appreciate from behind the wheel, with the added trucker's advantage of being able to see over walls. The arable fields of East Anglia had long been denuded of hedges, making vast areas of cultivation. Access to these was usually straightforward, and we were often helped by having large areas of concrete hardstanding, left over from wartime airfields. In the West Country, by contrast, I often found myself navigating narrow lanes and hoping, as I was funnelled down them, that there was actually a farm at the end, with room to turn around.

It was one of the best summers I can remember as a driver, though not without its hazards, even if we did survive climbing around a stack of bales a dozen feet high. Roger had impressed on us the importance of not tossing cigarette ends out of the window because they were likely to lodge in the straw behind, where the wind at a 60mph cruising speed might easily fan the fag-end into flame. During that summer I must have seen half a dozen burnt-out wrecks along the road, whose drivers had presumably not heeded similar warnings. None of us would park in London, either, once we'd heard of a truckload of straw being torched as a prank.

The work fostered an unusual camaraderie among drivers and farmers at both ends of the route. Although we'd be stuck in the fields for the evening, with no means of running down to the pub and obliged to cook for ourselves, we sometimes got lucky. One evening a farmer fetched us home in the back of his van, which he then lent us to go to the pub for an hour while his wife cooked us supper. At other times, if a pub was within walking distance, we'd cook our own meal and then head off for a pint or two, and often meet some of the men who'd been loading us. I remember one Norfolk farmworker claiming kinship with my Somerset colleagues because, he maintained, their accents sounded the same. As a neutral from the Home Counties, I wasn't so sure, but the sentiment was sound.

In the West Country, I found myself surprisingly popular. When I'd been delivering twenty tons of fertiliser in bags, I'd noticed how reluctant farmworkers could be to help unload, and how many of them seemed to find some important job to do elsewhere. Sometimes I'd had to unload all 400 bags unaided. One time this happened I was with an Abbey Hill colleague who had another twenty tons, and he gleefully suggested that we stack the fertiliser in the barn, as directed by the departing farmhand, but in front of a tractor so no one could use it without moving the fertiliser first.

Oat or barley straw was another matter and I've never felt so appreciated as a driver. One Dorset farmer shook my hand vigorously when I arrived with his load of straw and said, "Thank God you're here. I was going to get rid of half my herd tomorrow, because I've got nothing to feed them on." And it was common to be given tea and cakes when the unloading was finished, sometimes with the farm family making it a party. Once I had to deliver to a certain Sonny White in Hardington, a village near Yeovil. Sonny was famous for his 'scrumpy', the potent local cider, which he sold from what looked like a semi-official pub in his front parlour. When Roger heard where I was delivering, he came along for the ride and pitched in with the unloading. I soon found out why. With the trailer half empty, Roger and I took a break while Sonny disappeared into the house. He emerged after a couple of minutes carrying a tray loaded with pint mugs of scrumpy. What with the heat and the work, the pints were gone in seconds, and the refills went almost as fast. It was only when we started working again, and I found myself reeling across the stacked bales, that I realised how strong the cider was. It was one of the more hazardous moments in my driving career and the truck wasn't even moving. Roger, of course, thought it was hilarious.

As the summer, and the straw job, ended, I reverted to more conventional general haulage work, sometimes carrying folding or rolling garage doors from Garador, a Yeovil-based subsidiary of helicopter maker Westland, and often running up to the ICI plant at Avonmouth to pick up another load of fertiliser. These we stacked by hand, but the work was easy, since each hundredweight bag was delivered on a conveyor, which extended to the front of the trailer and steadily retracted as we loaded, so that we had only to pick up each bag and swing it into place.

Unloading, as I've said, wasn't so pleasant. For one particular week, I did one twenty-ton load of 'Nitram' fertiliser every day from Avonmouth to a large farm hidden down a narrow, winding lane in Dorset. It was the owner of the farm himself who helped me unload the 400 bags each day; apparently his dairy man was too grand to hump fertiliser bags and, as usual, the other farmworkers had scrambled to find better things to do. During a break towards the end of the week, the farmer began musing on our situation. "It's not right," he said. "To be competitive, I've got to put this stuff on the fields, even though it's not good for them, and you've got to bring that wagon down lanes that are much too small." His attitude to the bagged fertiliser was summed up in the general term used across the West Country. Proper fertiliser came from the back end of cows; what I was carrying was known as 'artificial', as in, "You'm bringing another load of artificial," pronounced with a roundly rolled 'r'.

I enjoyed general haulage for its variety. I could be carrying fertiliser one day or garage doors the next, and one day I was sent in to load at W.D. & H.O. Wills' cigarette factory in Bristol. The load consisted of pallets of unused cigarette packets that were being sent to Kent to be recycled. When I asked why, I heard that Wills had launched a new brand with a gold pack that looked too similar to the rival Benson & Hedges. Gallagher, the maker of Bensons, had sued Wills and won. Wills' new line was stopped by court order and all the pre-printed packs were due to be pulped. And so one minor result of this clash of the tobacco titans trickled down to me. As it happened, I didn't feel like a neutral in this dispute. My brother, Ben, was then working as an assistant to a highly successful London photographer who shot many of Benson's iconic advertisements, so I was pleased to see the brand prevail.

The Wills plant was a series of forbidding red-brick buildings, blackened with age, that towered over the yard where I was to load. As I waited, another driver approached me and told me to make sure I got my free cigarettes when I left. This was good news, since I was a smoker at the time and, looking at the sprawling factory around me, I expected Wills to be generous. The pallets of light and mobile card took careful sheeting and roping but finally I rolled up to the security gate with my loaded truck, where the security guard handed me a small pack of ten Embassy – one of Wills' workaday brands. Perhaps the company was feeling the pinch after the court case, but I had hoped to get at least a pack of twenty.

Within the variety of general haulage, there was the occasional oddity. One day, Roger sent me into a nearby factory in Yeovil to pick up a piece of crane machinery that was over twelve feet wide, half as wide again as my truck. I had to carry this only as far as Bristol, but the width meant I needed a police escort. A patrol car duly turned up and one of the two cops gave me a sheet with a long list of conditions, which I'd have to sign. As I began to read it, the officer cut me off.

"You know what it means, don't you?" I muttered something or other, and he continued, "It means that if anything goes wrong, it's your fault." That was hardly reassuring, nor was the idea that for the whole trip I'd be under the watchful eyes of the police. The officer told me to keep moving, and he and his colleague would clear the road ahead of me. The crane component was relatively light – six or seven tonnes – so I could make good speed. The cop returned to his sleek police Rover and sped off. As I rounded the first bend on the Yeovil street, I saw the flashing blue lights and the gratifying sight of a line of cars pulled to the side of the road. A double-decker bus had even mounted the kerb to make way for me. Once I was past this bottleneck, the police roared on to the next obstacle and so it continued. Every time there was a potential hold-up, traffic lights or a roundabout, other traffic would be held back to allow my truck free passage. I could learn to like this and I'd never had such an easy run through Yeovil. In fact, I covered the forty-odd miles to Bristol faster than I'd ever done. On the outskirts of the city, a second patrol car was waiting to clear my way to my final destination, and as I turned carefully into the customer's yard, just easing the wide load through the gates, the cops simply waved and drove off, with a valedictory toot of their horn.

I may have been enjoying my time at Abbey Hill, and learning a lot, but I was also working six days a week, and it was a struggle to get back to Jane and the children in North Wales. Once I was making a Friday delivery to the town of Rhyl, on the north Welsh coast, and managed to leave my truck for a day and a night, and hitchhike the eighty-odd miles to Rhiw to spend a truncated weekend with the family. But for most of the time, our relationship was conducted by phone, and the occasional anguished letter. When I wasn't actually working, it was a lonely existence, but I told myself that I was being responsible and earning us all a living. This was true as far as it went, but it was also true that for most of the time I was completely caught up in my life at Abbey Hill and on the road.

My mother's house in Sparkford had one inestimable advantage – it was next door to the village inn. As well as providing a couple of good bars, the Sparkford Arms also offered proper food, which was something of a rarity for a country pub in those days. On Sundays, when the restaurant closed after lunch, I'd walk next door and pick up a loaded plate of leftovers from the kitchen, for which I paid considerably less than the punters in the dining room. The rest of the time I cooked for myself and sometimes, on a Sunday evening, Roger would come over for a home-cooked curry. As I got to know him better, I discovered that he had begun buying and selling cars as a teenager, before he went to Kent University in Canterbury, where he took a degree in economics. While he was still at university, Roger continued trading and one day he came across a small, five-car transporter, which he promptly bought. With it, he started hauling imported Fiat cars from the nearby Dover docks and delivering them to London. When he graduated, Roger returned to his native Yeovil and his business grew rapidly, with a mix of car transporters and general haulage trucks, but he retained an interest in economic theory, even as he was proving more than a little adept at putting it into practice. Later, when his truck fleet had achieved national prominence, Roger still took time out to teach a course in economics and business at Yeovil Technical College.

When I later moved from general haulage at Abbey Hill to car transport, I once spent a week delivering Japanese Mazdas out of Newport Docks in South Wales. One evening, as I was reloading my transporter, Roger showed up after a meeting with the Mazda depot manager. He helped me load my seven cars and as we finished, he surveyed the scene. Hundreds of Mazdas were lined up in truckload batches across the docks, all pointing inland. In a neighbouring compound stood acres of British-built Rovers, all facing the water, ready for export.

"The capitalist system is crazy," Roger mused. "Look at them, what a waste. All those cars going out and all these others coming in; it's so inefficient." He paused and laughed. "Still, it's making us all a living."

Roger was always in motion, whether scuttling around the yard, buying drinks for a close coterie of drivers after hours, or hard-charging between business meetings in his car of the moment. When Abbey Hill hit the big time and then collapsed in the aftermath of a major lost contract, Roger sold the company off at a bargain price and started over as an importer of oddball cheap cars from Eastern Europe. By then I was working as a journalist, and Roger was a regular source of quirky stories that I published in *Car* magazine and even in the then-successful *Independent* newspaper. When I finally left the magazine business in 1998, Roger's latest venture – a return to car transport – was almost my last feature as a full-time journalist.

One reason for his early success was that he never turned down an opportunity. When I first knew Roger, his own car was a souped-up Ford Mustang GT, which he used to blast down the rural roads of Somerset. Knowing that he still bought and sold cars on the side, I once asked whether he'd ever part with the Mustang, since he clearly enjoyed it so much.

"Of course," he said, "if the price was right." Evidently somebody's was because, within days, the Mustang was gone.

One of Roger's wackier wheezes in the early days was an arrangement with ICI to deliver a trainload of fertiliser to Yeovil Station on a Friday evening, which we would have to unload onto trucks and deliver by Sunday night. Four or five hundred tons of fertiliser meant twenty or thirty truckloads, and it was always a rush job. If the train wasn't cleared on time, Abbey Hill would have to pay demurrage charges. Ignoring the fact that we were supposed to be having our weekly break over the weekend, most of the drivers would show up at the station early on the Saturday morning to load their trucks with 400 bags of fertiliser and deliver them to nearby farms in Somerset and Dorset. To boost the workforce, Roger would round up likely lads from the pub and even his own father, a retired Yeovil bus driver.

It was no joke hoisting the hundredweight bags off the floor of the traditional wooden railway wagons and carrying them out to our trailers parked alongside, but we managed to make it fun and we clocked up a considerable amount of overtime in the process. Once a truck was loaded, two or three of us would pile into the cab, roar off to the farm, unload as fast as we could and hurtle back to Yeovil Station. We'd work until after dark and usually end up in the Plucknett Arms, near the yard, and better known to us as Abbey Hill's Plucknett office.

Another of Roger's schemes ended in disaster, at least for me. I drove into the yard one evening to find a large, brand-new tipping trailer parked in the middle of the compound. It was destined for me. Yeovil was a few miles south of the A303 trunk road to the south-west, where the small town of Ilchester was finally getting a bypass. Roger explained that the bypass needed truckloads of infill material to be hauled from nearby Ham Hill quarry and I'd be swapping my flat trailer for the tipper for the next few days. I'd never driven a tipper before, but as soon as I saw it, I knew this trailer was all wrong for the job. It was a thirty-foot, alloy-bodied bulk grain carrier, with sides too high and too light for rubble.

Roger had recently hired an experienced ex-driver as a transport manager, who quickly showed me how to operate the tipper controls and the donkey engine mounted at the front of the trailer to power the hydraulics. Under his supervision, I fired up the donkey and raised the trailer body to its full height on a single, five-stage hydraulic ram. Fully extended, the body looked intimidatingly tall, and the trailer's twin red chassis rails looked strangely naked without the body sitting on top of them.

"Whatever you do," said our new manager, "make sure the trailer and unit are in line before you tip, or you'll lose the lot." I knew exactly what he meant; a tractor unit's fifth-wheel table is quite stable laterally, but it's designed to tilt up and down fore and aft to allow for independent vertical movement of the trailer. The greater the angle between the tractor and trailer, the more that tilt becomes a liability, as it allows the trailer plate to tilt to one side.

Roger explained that we were being paid by the ton and added that I couldn't be prosecuted for overloading if I was heading for the nearest weighbridge, which in this case just happened to be at the destination construction site on the bypass. So, he pointed out breezily, I could load as much as I wanted. I wasn't convinced, but he was the boss. In retrospect, I realised that Roger probably knew as little about tippers as I did.

I was on the top of Ham Hill as dawn broke the following morning. It was a cold start and I shivered with a combination of temperature and a nervousness brought on by the growing realisation that I had entirely the wrong vehicle for the job. A couple of experienced tipper drivers, with their compact twenty-four-ton six-wheelers, watched me pityingly as I approached the driver of the bright yellow JCB bucket loader. He wasn't too happy. "The trailer's too tall for me to reach," he told me. "You'll have to go down into the quarry."

Gingerly, I crawled the Mandator down the dirt haul road, with the big empty trailer banging and booming behind me, and lined up along the quarry wall, with the loader above me. Dirt and rubble started crashing into the trailer and, encouraged by Roger's injunction to load as much as possible, I kept on waving for more until the loader's nerve finally broke. I climbed into the cab and set off up the haul road, which was definitely not designed for artics. At one point the only way I could get the trailer to clear a major rock was to drive onto a stretch of dew-wet grass and, of course, the wheels started spinning. A differential lock might have helped, but the AEC didn't have one.

I made several fruitless attempts to get past and finally decided to jettison some of the cargo. I was too far up the narrow haul road to reverse all the way down, but the only way to tip the trailer with the rig in a straight line, as I had been warned to do, would have been to tip it behind me, thereby blocking the haul road. That would have made me decidedly unpopular with the quarrymen. Carefully, I reversed into a small opening just before the offending rock, but there wasn't room to straighten the AEC under the trailer. I debated with myself and finally decided to raise the tipper only a little way. Had I been more experienced, I'd have known that sticky rubble wouldn't shift from a partly inclined trailer, but I was about to learn. I fired up the donkey engine that powered the tipper's hydraulics and took hold of the operating levers at the front of the trailer chassis. Very carefully, I extended the ram by three of its five sections, but the load stayed right where it was, with the trailer swaying slightly, but unnervingly, on its single ram. I tried improvising, raising the ram and shutting it off again rapidly, trying to bounce the body enough to dislodge the muck, but it remained stubbornly stuck.

Finally, I decided to inch it up a little bit more, but it was all too much for the flat-road grain trailer. With a gathering roar, the whole thing fell away in front of me, dragging the tractor unit round and crushing the passenger side of the cab, so that the roof was forced down onto the base of the passenger seat. The Mandator's cab was a write-off and its rear wheels were three feet off the ground. The trailer body was half twisted off its chassis, but even now the load had scarcely moved; some had spilled out to the side, but the rest might have been glued inside the body. I was more numb than horrified until I realised that if the trailer had come the other way, I'd have been buried beneath it. There was nothing I could do, so I trudged up to the top of the quarry, where one of the six-wheeler drivers offered to drop me off at our yard, only a few miles away.

I walked into Abbey Hill's portable office building and stuck my head through the drivers' window. By chance, both Roger and the transport manager were there, and both were surprised to see me.

"I think I'd better give in my notice," I began.

"Go on, what've you done?" Roger asked.

I explained about the trailer, and in short order all three of us were in a car heading for Ham Hill. Roger drove down the haul road until we reached the remains of the truck. His only comment was, "Bloody hell, George." He was remarkably cheerful, considering I'd just destroyed his tractor unit and the new rental trailer and, yes, this would have been its very first load. We had a quick discussion and decided to return with the firm's newly acquired ex-military Humber wrecker, which wasn't big enough to pull the truck, but did prove sufficiently powerful to roll it back onto its wheels, after we'd shovelled out most of the load. The Mandator looked a sorry sight but, amazingly, its engine still ran. I could drive it too, though the roof had been crushed down so far that I had to crouch beneath it. The whole rig leaned like a drunkard, but with the wrecker ahead of me as an escort, I nursed it back to the yard. Roger said nothing about my notice. It was a Wednesday and the next morning I was sent way up north-east to Hull, to deliver a Land Rover 'on wheels', in the company of fellow driver Jesse Pockson, whose car transporter was carrying six more Land Rovers.

"You'd better go home after that," Roger said, "and give me a call on Saturday." We delivered the Land Rovers the following evening and, armed with my driver's logbook, I hitched right across the country in a day, from the east coast to the western tip of Wales. I'd never been so glad to get home, but I wasn't sure whether I still had a job. Amazingly, I did. Jane and I had hardly begun to consider alternatives when I heard from Roger on the Saturday that the workshop had already fitted a new cab to my truck and it would be ready for me on Monday morning. On Sunday, I hitched back south and went back to work as if nothing had happened, but at the same time I lost the chance to move back home.

CHAPTER 4
CAR TRANSPORT

Shortly after the trailer incident, Roger told me he was switching me and my Mandator to car transport. I wasn't keen on the idea, since I enjoyed the variety of general haulage, but I had no choice. The rates for carrying cars were far better than for general haulage, and in a matter of months, the whole of Abbey Hill's growing fleet had been converted to couple with a car transporter trailer. Technically, this simply meant fitting a hydraulic pump to the tractor unit to operate the mechanism that raised and lowered the upper of the car trailer's two decks. Nowadays, car transporter trailers are very complex, with several independently moving platforms, but in those days they consisted of a fixed lower deck and an upper deck that tilted as a single piece for loading and unloading. The conversion may have been simple for the truck, but it was a whole new field for me.

I now had a single-axle MkII Hoynor car transporter trailer, able to carry seven large cars and, at a pinch, eight small ones. At the time, a few big established car transport companies controlled delivery of all the domestic car production, but Abbey Hill built itself up nicely by catering to the importers. We loaded Citroëns from Poole, Mazdas from Newport, Fiats from Dover and Avonmouth, and a variety of domestic loads as subcontractors to the big boys. We also carried returned rental cars in what became an important niche business for the company. I learned how to chain down cars so they wouldn't bounce on their suspensions, which was particularly tricky with the famous Citroën 2CVs, which we drivers called 'humpies'. These were so softly sprung that they required three or four chains to keep them in place, where a bigger but more conventional car might need only two. We typically loaded cars from dockside compounds, where they would be lined up in truckload batches of seven or eight, depending on the transporter they were destined for. We drove each car up the steep ramp formed by the lowered top deck, which was pivoted near the front and lowered to the rear, so that the front car ended up almost twenty feet in the air, until the deck was returned to its normal position, with a running height (including cars) of about fifteen feet.

I'd always thought of car transport as a rather lightweight job, compared with the manly rigours of general haulage, but I soon discovered my mistake. I'd imagined that transporter drivers had only to drive the cars on and off, but naturally it wasn't so simple. First we had to work out the order of loading, so that in a multi-drop load we'd be able to dispose of the early cars first. This, however, was complicated by the small matter of fitting them onto the trailer decks in the first place. The usual form was to reverse the first car to the front of the upper deck so the wheels were touching the stops at the end of the deck, leaving the rear of the car overhanging the front of the truck. This gained us a few inches of space along the whole top deck. On a wet or freezing morning, this could be an adventure in itself, as was the business of walking back down the slippery ramp – no safety rails in those days – to fetch the next car. With the top-deck cars in place, I'd return the upper deck to its horizontal travelling position and walk up the lower deck beneath it to secure the cars in place. Each deck was equipped with a number of short chains on ratcheted spools, which we hooked to the chassis of the cars and tightened down with a small bar. It was a surprisingly messy job and it was worth losing the time it took to scramble into a pair of overalls. With the top deck secured, we'd load the bottom deck and chain the cars with ratchets at each side.

We seemed to always be in a hurry, and I'd find myself making endless calculations and adjustments as I drove, working out when I would reach each drop, if I was delivering to several dealers, and estimating whether

I'd be in time to get another load on that evening. There was no pressure from the company, at least none that I was aware of, and we were paid by the hour, not by the car, as were drivers in the big unionised firms. Instead, the speed came from our own professional pride in getting as much work done as we could in the time that was available. It was a full-on job, but it wasn't for lack of sleep or rest that, at the wheel of a car transporter, I had my closest call in my whole career as a driver.

It was mid-morning and I'd just finished a large, leisurely breakfast at the famous Hollies transport café, just off the M6 motorway near Cannock, twenty-odd miles north of Birmingham. I'd rejoined the southbound M6 motorway, the Mandator rolling easily with a load of seven bright new Fiats. I wasn't aware of being tired and I'd just had a break, but suddenly I woke up to find a row of cones directly in front of the truck. I was still travelling at 60mph and had moved onto the elevated section of the M5 that crosses for several miles above houses and factories on the west side of Birmingham. The road ahead had been coned off for roadworks, leaving a single lane to the left, but I couldn't move over because another articulated truck was right next to me. In the time-shift that attends disasters, I had time to notice that the truck was a green Guy Big J with an unladen flat trailer, and to realise there was nothing I could do to avoid the cones, which I sprayed in all directions as I hit them. I was braking as hard as I could, and as the other artic forged ahead, I switched lanes and tucked in behind it. I was now more awake than I'd ever been and I looked over the parapet to the fifty-foot drop below. I realised that, had I crashed, it would have been a headline story on the TV news, as most of my load of cars would have rained down on the buildings below, followed by the Mandator and me. I was still shaking when I approached Frankley service station a few miles ahead. The Big J driver must have seen my indicator in his mirror, because he veered onto the slip road ahead of me and we both pulled up in the truck park. As I climbed down from the cab, he was already storming towards me.

"What the hell were you doing? You almost hit me."

"Sorry, pal," I confessed. "I fell asleep."

"Oh… well," he said, his anger instantly deflated; we both knew it could happen to anyone. But now he was curious.

"Didn't you see any of the warning signs?" I hadn't. "There were signs at 600 yards, 400 yards and 200 yards. You didn't see any of them?"

"Nope."

"Boy, you were lucky."

We parted amicably, but as I continued southwards I realised that I must have driven for several hundred yards with my eyes closed. 'Lucky' didn't begin to describe it.

That may have been an unusual moment of drama, but car transport had already shown me new hazards that I had scarcely noticed on general haulage. As a transporter driver, I had to develop a new awareness of bridges and trees. A loaded transporter stood at least fifteen feet high and any bridge marked lower than that had to be avoided. If we were in any doubt, we would stop just short of a bridge – and to hell with the traffic behind – climb to the top deck and sight along the tops of the cars for clearance. The first time I did this, I was surprised by how nonchalant I felt, even as I held back a growing line of traffic behind me. As I grew in experience, of course, I learned where the obstacles were and how to avoid them, but in narrow urban streets, the trailer itself was a hazard. To maximise the loading length, the top deck extended all the way to the front of the cab, with the front car usually overhanging a couple of feet beyond that. The snag was that the fifth wheel, around which the trailer pivoted, was back behind the cab, so that as the whole rig turned a tight corner, the front of the trailer would describe a much wider arc and risked catching on streetlights or other obstacles. This could sometimes be amusing, and for some reason I particularly remember turning a corner at traffic lights in Crewe and watching the alarm on the face of a car driver as the front of my trailer, plus cars, sailed over the top of him.

It wasn't always so easy. One winter's night, I was sent to the town of Ottery St Mary in Devon with a load of Mazdas. This was the first time the company had sent a transporter to the Ottery dealer; previously, cars had been delivered on wheels, one or two at a time. It was dark by the time I reached the town, and in the centre the road divided around an old market building, leaving a one-way street on each side. I slowed the AEC to a crawl and inched around the narrow corner of the building, taking just as much room as I needed for the single trailer axle to clear the kerb. I knew that the trailer overhang, with the front car sticking out still further, must be getting pretty close to the buildings on my left, so I stopped for a quick inspection. Sure enough, as I walked around the front of the truck, I saw that I was about to insert the front car through the first-floor window of a small hotel; I'd stopped just in time. It was around five in the evening and I was in the midst of what passes for a rush hour in Ottery St Mary, which meant that several cars were already lined up behind me. I managed to persuade them to back up a little to allow me space to reverse and try the corner again, but there was no way through. A normal articulated truck would have had no trouble, but the transporter's overhang made it impossible. Once again, I had to tackle the car drivers behind me, this time to persuade them to allow me enough clearance to reverse right out of the one-way street. With headlights on main beam, I drove the wrong way down the one-way street on the other side of the market, forcing oncoming cars to give way. A fully laden transporter looks impressive and intimidating when it's coming towards you where it shouldn't. The cars moved and the Mazdas made it to the dealer in one piece.

If bridges and buildings were at least predictable, trees were a different matter, and I had to be constantly alert, on an ordinary road, for trees that could do thousands of pounds-worth of damage to top-deck cars. One evening, I returned to the yard to discover the workshop fitters welding a guard rail around the top deck of an old transporter trailer. Roger was highly excited. He explained that the company had just won a large contract to transport several thousand Citroëns from the port at Poole – where they arrived from France – to a huge field in nearby Crewkerne, where we would store them. The route was about fifty miles and our transporters would be shuttling between Poole and Crewkerne for weeks. The snag was the trees growing along the road between Crewkerne and Dorchester, which accounted for about half of the route. Roger's solution was to cut them back on the side of the road we'd be using when our transporters were loaded. In typical insouciant style, he didn't intend to ask permission; instead, he sent a small crew armed with chainsaws on the top of the converted transporter to hack off any trees that might cause us a problem and, being Roger, he got away with it.

As was the practice in most firms in those days, I received no formal training in the operation of a car transporter, beyond a perfunctory introduction to the controls for the hydraulic system that operated the top deck. The rest I learned from my colleagues when I met them at various loading points around the country. But even when I had mastered the car transport business, I never really took to it. It is true that I enjoyed the sight of my truck fully loaded with bright new cars, particularly under lights at night, but the real drawback was the constant jousting with the car dealers to whom we delivered.

Our job was to check each car before we loaded it and note any damage, however slight, that we could find. The damage sheet would be signed before we left our loading point and the dealers, when we reached them, took great delight in finding any blemishes that we drivers hadn't noticed, because then they could charge Abbey Hill for the damage and make themselves a little on the side. It made the job very stressful, and not only because I am not meticulous by nature. We often loaded in the dark, under floodlights, when the chances of spotting minor damage were considerably restricted, particularly if the cars were covered in a protective wax.

Chiselling dealers weren't the only uncongenial aspect of car transport; it was generally lacking in social contact and sometimes downright lonely. Dealers didn't count, for it was hard to feel friendly towards someone whose aim was to find fault where none existed. With general haulage, I'd grown used to finding company when loading and unloading. Even at ICI's vast and impersonal fertiliser plant in Avonmouth, where 400 bags of fertiliser would be delivered to my trailer with metronomic efficiency, there'd always be an ICI man to help me stack them, which meant a few minutes of social life, even if all we did was complain about the job. Unloading, too, often meant an opportunity to meet someone new.

There's also something about hard physical work that can create a bond between total strangers in a matter of minutes. I'd discovered this in my very early days at Walker's, when I once delivered a twenty-ton load of paving stones to a building site in the centre of London. It was a searingly hot day, and a single Irish labourer and I worked flat out to unload and stack the several hundred paving slabs. When he signed my papers, at the end of a strenuous hour, we shook hands and exchanged a look in which we both recognised that our hard work together had created a connection between us. It was a momentary contact; we didn't speak of it and I never saw him again, but the incident taught me that people can be linked together through physical effort in a way that no amount of conversation can manage. I'd seen the principle repeated in numerous situations since then, from the philosophising farmer in Dorset to individuals to whom I'd delivered garage roller doors.

Even a forklift driver, bringing twenty pallets to my trailer, needed to exchange words about where to place each pallet, or simply to pass the time of day, but loading cars was quite different. I'd be directed out to the lines of waiting vehicles and start loading, usually working flat out so as to be away up the road as efficiently as possible. There was little time for chat and usually no one nearby to talk to amid the sea of cars. So although I learned how to do the job, I never really liked it, while dicing with dealers took most of the joy out of deliveries.

The combination of my dissatisfaction with car transport and the sheer idiocy of living so far from my family came to a head shortly after the Christmas of 1976, when I'd managed to get home for a few days. With hindsight, I wonder why Jane and I didn't simply move to Somerset, where the work was, but we never discussed it. On the practical side, we had a home that we owned, since my mother had some years ago transferred Cadwgan to my brother and me, so that although the cottage was primitive and cramped, it was rent and mortgage-free. Beyond that, Jane and I both loved the far end of the Llyn Peninsula and the boys were already fluent in Welsh, so instead of moving the family south, I moved back to Wales to take my chances.

Years later, I sometimes speculated where I might have ended up had I stayed with Roger Bastable. Only seven years later, in 1983, after I'd begun working as a journalist for *Truck* magazine, I went to Yeovil to interview him. Abbey Hill Group had grown in the intervening years into a vast organisation employing nearly 1000 people and running almost 500 trucks. Many of the drivers I'd worked with in the early days were now in senior management jobs. My old driving mate, Jesse Pockson, was national contracts manager and the former workshop foreman had become managing director. Roger himself flitted around the country in a helicopter, checking in with his nationwide network of depots, while still finding time to teach economics at Yeovil Tech and front a retro rock band called Rave to the Grave. Had I remained with Roger, I would probably have been promoted to management myself. It might have been an interesting ride, but if I'd stayed I would never have become an international driver, which was my ambition from the very start. Nor would I have ended up working for a firm that was typical of old-time family haulage companies across the whole of Britain, whose era was already coming to an end.

CHAPTER 5
LOCAL SERVICE

I'd been away from home for many months, with only occasional visits. As I'd done so often before during my MA course at Keele, I hitchhiked back to Pwllheli – our nearest town – where Jane met me in a pub to drive me the last eleven miles to our remote hilltop village. Although I had enjoyed myself as a driver for Abbey Hill, and earned a regular and reasonable living, in terms of my family I'd wasted a year. Now we all had to adjust to the idea that I was home to stay, as long as I could find a way to earn a living. At first, the knowledge that I was home indefinitely, with no deadline for return to Abbey Hill, made my homecoming feel like a holiday. I began to fit back into the family, and for once there was time for Jane and me to get past the awkwardness that had attended my previous fleeting visits. All the same, we couldn't afford too much time before I had to go looking for work.

Within a few days, I was back full circle at the labour exchange in Pwllheli. This time, however, I didn't even think about white-collar work, which by now held no attraction at all. My time at Abbey Hill had made me comfortable and competent in the role of truck driver, and that was the work I wanted. Besides, in the furthest reaches of North Wales, where Welsh was the first language, my inability to speak it was no barrier in a job where I'd spend most of my working day alone, regularly running to and from England. To my surprise and relief, there was a vacancy for a class one driver at John Williams (Red Garage) in the relatively nearby seaside town of Portmadoc – or Porthmadog, to give its proper Welsh name. As far as I could make out, Williams Transport was the nearest haulage company to my home that was running artics on anything like long-distance work. I drove the twenty-five miles to Porthmadog and drew up in front of Red Garage, which was fronted by a 1950s-style car showroom, dedicated to Ford.

The business had clearly seen better days. The display room was empty of cars and the Ford oval was a fading blue. There was little sign of life and no eager salesman ready to persuade me into the latest Cortina. Instead, a single door beside the display window opened onto a steep and narrow staircase leading to the transport office. Here I met Miss John, a solidly built, forty-ish woman who turned out to be the traffic clerk and general factotum. Miss John – I never used her first name in eighteen months of working for the firm – took me into a back office to meet Tudor Griffiths, nephew of the overall boss, John Elfed Griffiths. Tudor was an affable chap and, I discovered, the family member who had overall responsibility for the transport side of the business. He gave me a short interview and sent me half a mile inland to Tremadog, where the company's trucks were based. I was told to ask for a Mr. Parry, who would appraise my driving.

Tremadog's main street was tucked under a high granite cliff, which looked over a terrace of slate-grey houses. On the opposite side of the road, I found a narrow yard whose unpaved surface was stained black with oil. On one side, against a high wooden fence, was parked a single flatbed trailer and on the other, a thirty-foot tipping trailer, with its body partly raised. That left a space of about two truck widths, giving access to an ageing workshop, with doors tall enough to accommodate a thirteen-foot-high box-van. The sliding door was open, revealing a dimly lit interior with the usual detritus of an old commercial vehicle workshop, and I felt as if I'd stepped back into the 1940s. An ERF tractor unit was reversed into one side. It was an LV, forerunner of the A Series that was then ERF's current model, and also represented in Williams' colours. A badge on the grille revealed it to be powered by a Cummins engine, built in Scotland by the American diesel engine giant.

In the far corner, a figure in greasy, dark blue overalls was reclining on the top of a massive, ancient cast-iron radiator. He swung his legs down as I approached and I saw a man in his mid-twenties, about my own age.

"I'm looking for Mr. Parry," I told him.

"Believe it or not, that's me. My name's Gareth, but people just call me Parry." We shook hands and I explained that Tudor had sent me for a driving test.

"We'll take the tipper," Parry announced. "Have you ever driven one?"

"No," I lied. There was no way I was going to talk about the incident at Ham Hill quarry the previous year.

"Well, you'll learn easily enough," said Parry, laconically. He climbed aboard the ERF and fired it up. The Cummins emitted a loud, barking roar as he reversed the unit out of the workshop and trundled it backwards under the tipper trailer. He hooked up the susies and dropped the tipping body back onto the chassis as I wound up the trailer legs, and we were ready to roll.

The ERF was taller than the AEC I'd been driving at Abbey Hill and I liked the improved view. Back in my time at Walker's, who were diehard enthusiasts of Gardner engines, I'd been taught to be suspicious of Cummins, but I soon discovered that there was nothing wrong with the American engine except the horrendous racket it produced in the cab. No British truck was quiet in those days, but the AEC had been among the best of them. In comparison, the Cummins-ERF was a shock. In the first few days of our partnership, I plugged my ears with cotton wool but, for better or worse, I soon got used to the roar and even came to enjoy it, so I abandoned the practice. Meanwhile, I had to pass Parry's test, which was a perfunctory affair. Once it was clear that I could navigate in a straight line and reverse around a corner, I was in.

Williams was a traditional haulage firm whose work was centred on the economic life of the surrounding community. It had an old-fashioned hierarchy, in marked contrast to Abbey Hill, where the boss was 'Roger' to all and sundry. Mr. Griffiths, whom we only called John Elfed (pronounced John Elved in Welsh) behind his back, was a remote figure I never got to know. His company had once been a power in the land, with several dozen tippers and a number of coaches in the colours of Williams' subsidiary, Creams. These coaches were now used mostly for summer tours around North Wales and Anglesey, with one or two on local contract as school buses. The tipper fleet had diminished with the decline of local quarries and undercutting by local owner-drivers. The only dedicated tippers left in the line-up were a sixteen-ton four-wheeled Guy Big J and a twenty-four-ton ACE Marshall six-wheeler, neither of which had a regular driver. If the fading offices had suggested a company in decline, the limited lorry line-up confirmed it.

Despite being the only Englishman – a *saes*, in Welsh – in the company, I seemed to fit in straightaway. I was the third of three artic drivers and as the last man in, I was given the older LV ERF of my brief road test, with its cacophonous Cummins. At first, I drove to and from work in our family car, which left Jane stranded at home, but once I had my feet under the table I was allowed to take the tractor unit home, because most of our work came from a couple of miles north of the coastal town of Pwllheli, closer to our home than the Williams' yard.

Williams had two main customers: Spiller's farm feed mill at Four Crosses (now better known by its Welsh name, Y Ffor) and the nearby South Caernarfon Creameries (SCC) in Chwilog. I'd usually leave a trailer overnight at one or other customer, or park it on the quayside in Pwllheli, ready to pick it up for an early morning run to some destination in England. The creamery was a local farmer-owned cooperative that sold milk locally and made cheese for 'export' to England. Williams played the traditional role of a local haulage company, serving the needs of its immediate neighbours. Even though Jane and I had been based in Wales for two years, I'd spent most of that time away from home. Now I found myself not only living full-time on the Llyn Peninsula, but also playing an integral part in the economic life of the area, which was surprisingly satisfying. So was the largely unspoken recognition of my neighbours that what I was doing was useful. I found myself carrying all manner of supplies into the area, from coal and the raw materials for animal feed, to earthenware pipes for land drainage. And as an outward load, I almost invariably carried twenty-ton loads of cheese, made from the milk of cows grazing in the fields around my home. This was a world away from the impersonal life I'd led as a car transporter driver and a much happier one.

My two fellow artic drivers were based near Porthmadog, but my truck became a familiar sight on the narrow roads west of Pwllheli, since I drove the tractor unit to and from our village of Rhiw on most days – apart from the one or two nights a week that I spent away from home. On most mornings, I'd leave home as early as four in the morning, trying in vain to keep the ERF's raucous engine down to a reasonable rumble as I crept through the sleeping village. The Cummins must have been everyone's daily wake-up call, but they never complained; I was doing a job that everyone recognised as necessary and when I returned in the evening, I'd get a wave from people I scarcely knew.

I even got to know one truck-mad teenager, Dylan Evans, whose house I passed on my way to and from home. I can't remember how we actually met – perhaps I pulled over to talk to him after I'd seen him wave so often – but the upshot was that he came with me for a couple of runs, once as far as the English Midlands. As soon as he could, Dylan learned to drive a truck – perhaps inspired by the sight of the various artics I drove past his house – and eventually became a successful owner-driver. More than three decades after I moved away from Wales, I returned to write a magazine article about him, and he could still remember details of my trucks that I had long since forgotten.

Meanwhile, at Williams, we three artic drivers swapped jobs and trailers frequently, and in my first week I followed Ray, one of my new colleagues, to a large grain mill in Liverpool, where we both loaded tipping trailers full of grain screenings – the chaff left behind after milling – which formed the base raw material for Spiller's farm feeds. With my one previous experience of tippers having ended in disaster, I was somewhat wary of them, but at least loading should be risk-free. Arriving in Liverpool, we drove onto a large weighbridge to get the trucks' unladen, or 'tare', weight and then took turns to reverse into a dusty shed and under a gantry from which the screenings would tumble into our trailers. Williams was paid to the nearest ton and our aim was to get more than 16.5 tons into the tipper body. This wasn't as easy as it sounds because the bulky screenings soon filled the trailer, leaving it still well below the target weight. "No problem," Ray told me. The trick was to accelerate the truck as fast and as far forward as we could within the confines of the shed and jam on the brakes, causing the screenings to settle – a process called 'shunting'. A reverse shunt would compress them further, but even that wasn't enough. To ensure we'd get the last paying pound on board, we then waded to and fro across the top of the load in our wellington boots, trying to tramp it down still further. We then topped off the load with another ton or so, still controlling the chute ourselves.

By the time we pulled the sheet across the load, the screenings were heaped up along the centre line of the trailer and we were covered in dust. We drove out into the daylight and onto the weighbridge, which showed our efforts had been worth it; both of our trucks would be paid for seventeen tons. That was my only training on tippers, but discharging them was considerably less hazardous than my quarry experience at Abbey Hill. Back at Spiller's feed mill, we tipped on comfortingly level concrete and into an underground hopper, from which the screenings were carried into a vast storage bin by an augur whose principles dated back to Archimedes' screw, which I remembered from junior school.

Not all our tipper work was risk-free, however. From time to time I was sent to the English Midlands to pick up a load of coal, which in those days was still being mined in quantity all across the country. Lines of trucks were weighed, loaded and despatched with quick efficiency, and I enjoyed being just one small part of the whole grimy business. Back in North Wales, one of our delivery points was to a small coal merchant located high up the side of a mountain that fell away to the sea on the further side. The approach road was so steep that I had to tackle it in 'crawler' gear, the bottom ratio in the ERF's nine-speed gearbox. Moreover, the lanes were sufficiently narrow that I couldn't turn into it from the 'main' road, but had to approach it from a crossroads, barrelling at full power over the other road to maintain momentum, and hoping that nobody was coming the other way. Once I'd ground my way up the steep lane, my troubles had only just begun, since the customer's yard was on a slope. So, before I could risk tipping the trailer, I laid down a row of heavy railway sleepers on the lower side of the slope and reversed all the downhill wheels of both tractor unit and trailer onto them. This levelled the whole rig enough to raise the tipping body safely, but it didn't help that the yard, perched high up and very close to the sea, was frequently raked with wind, so that the trailer body swayed alarmingly. By now, I'd learned a good deal about how to handle tippers of all kinds, but I was always relieved to see the hydraulic ram telescoping safely together at the end of each discharge.

Another occasional load was from a specialist, high-grade coking plant in South Wales. This involved a beautiful but challenging drive through the mountainous heart of Wales, from the north to the south of the Principality. It was at this coking plant that I had an unexpected encounter. I was waiting in a line of trucks while some technical hitch in the loading bays was ironed out. To while away the time, I climbed up to a gantry, from which I could see most of the plant spread out, and there I met a middle-aged manager in a white coat and safety helmet, making notes on a clipboard. I asked him about the plant, and what made it special, and he told me that before nationalisation it had belonged to Powell Duffryn, one of the major private coal companies.

"Oh," I said. "My father used to work for Powell Duffryn in their research department." In fact, he had been the company's director of research. The man eyed me curiously.

"What was his name?" he asked.

"J.G. Bennett."

"I remember him well," he said and told me that he'd worked under my father as a young man. "What does he think about you being a lorry driver?" I explained that my father had died, but that he had never objected to me working as a driver; in fact, he rather enjoyed the idea. We continued chatting for a few minutes and I learned that the plant was unique, and produced a special form of coke that Powell Duffryn had developed; perhaps my father had had a hand in it. Then, down below, I saw the line of trucks begin to move towards the loading area. I said a hurried goodbye, before scrambling down to the ground and taking my proper place behind the wheel.

From time to time, I was sent to the English Midlands to load coal in the AEC Marshall six-wheeler. The Marshall had the same cab as the Mandator I'd driven for Abbey Hill and the same stately six-speed gearbox. This was so slow between ratios that it was said you could have a wash, shave and haircut while you were shifting, but the six-wheeler was still fun to drive for a change, and lighter and niftier than my regular artics. On the coal runs I was entering a world that is all but forgotten, but in the mid-1970s, coal mines still flourished all across the Midlands, with their attendant industry, grime and lines of lorries waiting to spread the fuel all over the land. No one denigrated coal in those days, because the link between burning it and climate change was yet to be made. Or if it had been, people as a whole hadn't heard. The ground around a pithead was always black and so it was under the hoppers that delivered coal into our wagons. I didn't mind waiting in line because it was an occasion for socialising. Truck drivers may have a solitary streak, which suited me fine, but most of them make up for lost time when they get among their colleagues. Very often I found myself chatting to a driver I would probably never see again, but it made little difference; whoever we worked for, we had a great deal in common. If we ran out of topics, we could always moan about the wait, though delays never really bothered me; if you haven't got patience, you'll never make it as a driver. Moreover, since I was paid by the hour, delays made me money, though occasionally they threatened to use up all my available legal driving hours. This was a threat I ignored once I was safely into the Welsh hills, where I assumed – apparently correctly – that I was beyond any ministry enforcement.

I didn't even meet my fellow drivers at Williams very often, despite the firm's small size. Every evening, Miss John would give us our jobs for the following day, but we'd generally come into the office at different times, so the people I got to know best were the ones with whom I loaded and unloaded at Spiller's and the SCC cheese factory. I was in and out of Spiller's so often that I got to know not only the men who worked there but also the dynamics of the company, which was irritatingly hierarchical and determinedly outdated. The twenty-odd manual workers laboured in the mill buildings, grinding and mixing various types of feeds, and either bagging them or loading them into Spiller's own sixteen-ton bulk delivery truck. It was hot, dusty work and though I often brought in bulk screenings in the tipping trailer, I also brought screenings in sacks, under ropes and sheets, which I had to help unload. Come tea break or lunch time, we repaired to a dingy restroom, equipped only with a kettle, to eat the sandwiches we'd brought with us. Across the yard, the half-dozen salesmen and administrative staff sat down in the staff dining room to eat a meal specially cooked for them on the premises.

A few months after I'd started, a dispute arose that threatened to lead to a strike. I happened to be in the primitive restroom when the manager came to address the manual workers about their proposed stoppage. "We're all in this together," he declared and I thought how hollow this sounded, given the separate lunch arrangements for the white-collar staff. A couple of years later, as a Continental driver, I visited a French firm of similar size. When the owner went out to lunch with two of his yardmen, he invited me, a mere visiting driver, to join them. I remembered the separation of workers and management back at Spiller's, and the difference underlined just how antiquated labour relations could be in Britain.

One of our regular jobs was loading cheese at SCC early on a Monday morning. The cheese came aboard my trailer in forty-pound boxes, via an ancient, rattling conveyor. My job was to stack the cheese onto the pallets I'd laid out along the trailer, fifty-six cases per pallet so that each one weighed a ton. Manhandling over 1100 cases was a useful morning workout, followed by the task of sheeting and roping the whole load. Nowadays, any perishable load is carried in a refrigerated trailer, but in those days, sheets and ropes were still very common, even for foodstuffs. Hand-loading was slow and inefficient, and after I'd been with Williams for a year or so, SCC finally saw the light. For a couple of weeks, I regularly backloaded new pallets from Manchester and SCC bought a brand-new forklift truck, which was given to the yard foreman to drive. At first he was so tentative that it took him as long to load twenty pallets as it had for me to stack cheese on them by hand, but when he did learn to use the forklift properly, loading became a good deal quicker, even if it did deprive me of a regular exercise routine.

I normally returned to Williams' yard by late morning and I soon discovered that my colleagues generally considered this a day's work. They preferred to wait for the following morning before heading to our usual destination, the national distribution centre for British Home Stores (BHS) at Atherstone, in the heart of the English Midlands, so they could do the round trip in a single day and avoid a night away from home. After the headlong style of Abbey Hill, this seemed positively lackadaisical, and besides, our family's bank balance needed me to work all the hours I could. So instead of running some local job in the afternoon, I preferred to set off for Atherstone immediately, and arrive there in the late afternoon or early evening. Not only did this give me more hours, but it meant I'd be paid the modest tax-free night-out allowance as well. From Williams' point of view, it was a bargain, because I could tip, reload and sometimes deliver the backload on the Tuesday, thus doing three days' work in two.

Although Atherstone was only 150 miles away, the trip took around five hours, since it involved climbing up into the hills of Snowdonia, and the whole distance was on regular roads with no sign of a motorway, except when I crossed the M6 near Cannock. Outside BHS, I parked up at the gates and spent the night in the cab, cooking myself a simple meal on a single-burner gas stove and reading by the cab's dim interior light. I resisted the temptation to go out to the pub because we needed every penny back home.

The BHS site was enormous, with dozens of loading bays along each wall of the central warehouse. Once the gates were opened, I drove into the yard, removed the ropes, and waited with the sheets in place before my turn came to reverse up the loading bay door. Now I pulled the sheets off and a warehouse man with an electric pallet carrier trundled each pallet from the trailer, while I folded the sheets on the ground and coiled my half-dozen ropes. From BHS, I was usually sent to pick up a load of agricultural supplies for some farm on the Lynn Peninsula. Sometimes this was a load of animal feed from Rumenco, at Burton-on-Trent, where loading was satisfyingly swift. I was told that the company's star forklift driver had won a national championship and his artistry was a joy to watch, not least because he was so fast that I could be in and out of the Rumenco yard in well under an hour, including the time taken to sheet and rope the load.

Another regular backload could scarcely have been more different. Red Bank, at Measham in Derbyshire, manufactured clay field-drain pipes, and a load might consist of several thousand short pipe lengths, about eighteen inches long, which farmers would lay end-to-end in trenches for land drainage. Instead of watching a forklift deposit a pallet of pipes onto the trailer, I had to load and unload them by hand, which was slow and backbreaking work. With Red Bank's loaders as an example, I learned to handle the pipes four or six at a time, and to throw them off the trailer to the farmer and his workers at each destination. I got so slick that one farmer insisted we swap places, so he could stand on the trailer and throw the pipes down to me, and I would appreciate how much harder it was to catch than to toss them.

Occasionally I'd be sent to east London with a load of cheese, and compared with regular runs to Liverpool and the Midlands, this 250-mile trip was an excitingly long haul. It also gave me the chance to visit my brother and his wife for the evening, and I'd park my fifty-five-foot truck outside his house in Maida Vale, taking up several parking meter spaces in the process. You'd never get away with that now, with all the restrictions on trucks in central London that have accumulated over the past forty years.

Nearer home, I could hardly have had a more beautiful workplace, and I often reflected how lucky I was to work at the far end of north Wales and to enjoy year-round scenery that tourists saw for only a few days each summer. The north-coast route to Liverpool and onwards to the Fylde – that strange coastal area north of the city – was always a pleasure, particularly since I was often driving it as the sun rose. The old road – now replaced by a soulless dual carriageway – took me through the medieval towns of Caernarfon and Conwy. As it continued eastwards along the coast towards Liverpool, the route offered fine views of the sea that were available only to someone sitting high in a truck cab. Stone walls lined most of the roads of North Wales, and for car drivers, severely limited their view, but not mine; whichever truck I drove, I could see to the horizon. Journeys to the English Midlands, or to South Wales, also took me through ancient and heart-stirring scenery. Perhaps my favourite stretch was the twenty miles of moorland road between the village of Trawsfynydd, with its intimidating nuclear power station, and the town of Bala on my route to England. The road skirted the southern edge of the mountains of Snowdonia, and after a long climb up from the estuarial plain behind Porthmadog, I made a left turn towards Bala, and twenty miles of dramatic scenery and changeable weather that could occasionally be challenging.

One winter's evening I was returning home and by the time I reached Bala, it had begun to snow quite heavily. I took the turn towards Trawsfynydd and pulled over under the sodium street lights to consider the situation. Ahead were twenty miles of tricky road and I had neither winter tyres nor snow chains. I had just decided to park in Bala for the night when a snow-plough came past, discharging reassuring grit onto the snow, so I changed my mind and set off behind it. The snow-plough and I drove slowly and steadily in tandem up the long climbing road to the middle of the moor and I was beginning to congratulate myself when the plough pulled off the road, reversed into a gateway and returned the way it had come. There was no room for me to turn my considerably longer truck, so I had no alternative but to continue along the unploughed road. In those days I had relatively little experience of snow driving and I crept carefully along the road I knew very well, but that had now been made unrecognisable by the weather.

As the months went by, I gradually moved up the small hierarchy at Williams, at least as far as truck choice was concerned. One of the two original artic drivers decided to leave and I was promoted to the newer, and marginally quieter, A-Series ERF, with its more powerful 220hp Cummins. When the second driver left, I was offered my choice of trucks and went for the impressive Scammell Crusader, a tall and purposeful machine that made me feel like a king of the road, at least on the narrow roads of North Wales.

The Crusader first appeared in the late 1960s, as Scammell's answer to the European imports that had challenged the British truck establishment so successfully and would eventually wipe them out. Scammell had once been an independent company, but was now part of the sprawling and ineptly managed British Leyland group. Scammell was best known for its heavy haulage trucks, but the Crusader was developed as a standard tractor unit, primarily to suit the nationalised transport company, British Road Services. That was probably why, although the Crusader looked radical by British standards, it was still a broadly conservative machine. Mainly this was because its cab was still a non-tilting design, which even parent company Leyland had abandoned, but also because the cramped sleeper option – itself a rarity – was so obviously an afterthought.

I loved it, all the same. The Scammell's tall, angular cab gave me a commanding driving position and I could not only look over any roadside wall, but I could also look down on most other drivers. Naturally my Crusader had only a day-cab, but it was much wider and more spacious than the ERF I'd been driving before. I built myself a wooden bunk, which I hinged off the back wall, and this, combined with the low engine cover, gave so much space underneath that another person could sleep across the seats beneath it, allowing me to take friends or children on occasional overnight trips.

Power came from a 220hp, twelve-litre Roll-Royce six-cylinder engine, which was quieter than either of the Cummins I'd been driving before, but still had a distinctive, if more muted, bark to it. The nine-speed Eaton-Fuller gearbox was the same as in both the ERFs and a pleasure to use. This was a 'range-change' transmission, which, from the driver's point of view, meant a standard four-slot gate, such as you used to find in any car. In this case, however, once the truck had reached fourth gear, the driver flipped the range-change switch, which swapped the gearbox's final drive to a second, higher gear, giving a higher ratio for each of the original four stick positions. The ninth speed was a very low-ratio 'crawler' gear, for getting out of trouble on the steepest gradients. As with most gearboxes at the time – and all those fitted in British trucks – the Fuller was a 'constant-mesh' design, with no synchromesh, so I still had to double declutch for every gear. With practice, however, it was possible to change gears without using the clutch pedal at all, by ensuring that the road speed and engine revs were perfectly matched as I moved the lever.

The Crusader's cab was so wide that in some places on my regular routes I had to make special allowances for it. The first was along the half-mile causeway that led eastward out of Porthmadog. This was part of a sea wall that also carried the famous narrow-gauge Ffestiniog Railway, but the road was cramped by a high wall on one side, against which it was easy to break a mirror. The causeway was easy enough to negotiate, until I met one of Crosville's public buses coming the other way. After a couple of tight encounters, in which a Crosville driver and I took several minutes to inch past each other, we took to waiting for each other at one end of the causeway, with whoever arrived first taking priority. The other tight squeeze was at the medieval town of Conwy on the North Welsh coast. Here the main road still passed through the medieval town wall, but negotiating the original stone arch with a forty-foot trailer, and the tight turn that preceded it, meant mounting the kerb with the Scammell's nearside front wheel and folding in my driver's side mirror arm to fit through the gap. When, decades later, I found myself teaching schoolchildren about medieval towns and castles, with Conwy as a prime example, I couldn't help smiling when I remembered taking a thirty-two-ton artic through the town's ancient gate.

For several months, the Crusader became my family's only means of transport. Our car had been wrecked when a local old lady drove out of a gateway into my path. Our own, minimal, insurance didn't cover repairs and while we waited to find a suitable old banger to replace our lost Cortina, we used the Crusader for our weekly shopping and pub trips to the nearby village of Aberdaron. The boys could scramble into the cab themselves, but our daughter, Laura, not yet three, needed help. Technically, I shouldn't have been driving the tractor unit at all during my weekly break, but our local copper was one of the best and turned a blind eye.

My time at Williams made me into a competent all-round general haulage driver. I carried everything from our regular loads of cheese to a load consisting simply of three six-ton blocks of granite, which I drove carefully down a dirt track from a small mountainside quarry, before hauling it off to Derbyshire. On another occasion I was sent to a Ministry of Defence establishment in Cumbria to collect a narrow-gauge steam engine and assorted rolling stock. The site was an MoD depot and at the gate I had to sign a declaration that I was carrying nothing inflammable, and after a cab inspection by the guards, I had to leave my cigarettes, lighter and camping stove at the gate. When I realised where I was, I was only too happy to agree. The site was a munitions store and the narrow-gauge train had been used to carry explosives between the sensibly spaced-out storage bunkers. The locomotive and rolling stock made an unusual load and, once they'd been craned on board the trailer, I chained and roped them particularly carefully. On the road they turned heads, too; everyone likes small trains. In mid-summer, I was sent out to central Snowdonia to rescue two farmers who had attempted to carry hay from England on a pair of sixteen-ton four-wheelers. When I got to them, their two trucks were leaning drunkenly together, both their loads having shifted dangerously sideways, so they were held up only by each other. Together, we restacked all the bales onto my truck and I completed the delivery myself. As I left, I couldn't resist suggesting that they should leave their haulage to the professionals.

Working at Williams made me recognisable among customers and farmers who were connected – as most of them were – with SCC. It also brought me into a loose association of people connected with the North Wales transport scene. From time to time, if my own truck had to be left in the Porthmadog yard, I would use the firm's sixteen-ton Guy Big J tipper as my personal transport home. The four-wheeler was fun to drive for a change. At the time, Jane and I were remodelling one room of our little stone cottage and we needed a load of gravel to make concrete for a new floor. I borrowed the Guy for the job and drove to the local quarry to buy ten tons of aggregate. As I drove the empty tipper onto the weighbridge to check its unladen weight, I told the operator I was picking up a load for myself and I'd be paying cash. When I'd loaded my ten tons, I returned to the weighbridge in the usual way. The operator clocked the weight and then asked, "It's definitely just for you?"

"Yes," I told him. "I'm putting in a new concrete floor at home."

"You're all right, then," he said. "Just go; don't worry about paying." I didn't know the man, but he knew the truck, and as its driver I was just part of the local transport fraternity.

As my first year with Williams came to an end, Jane and I were invited to the firm's annual Christmas celebration. Since our family finances were completely dependent on my truck driver's licence, I approached my first Christmas at the firm determined not to be caught for drinking and driving in the prime season for prosecutions. I therefore decided not to touch a drop of alcohol at the party, so I could drive the twenty-five miles back home with impunity. Jane had no such inhibitions.

If I'd become used to the company's old-fashioned ways, the Christmas 'do' reminded me just how different life was in rural north Wales compared with living in London, or with Abbey Hill in Yeovil. A day earlier, Miss

John had given me a roguish grin as she handed me my wage packet. "You'll notice a little more in it this week," she told me. I opened the envelope and, for the life of me, could see nothing unexpected. Finally, she had to tell me that John Elfed had put an extra fiver into my wages. That was less than ten per cent of my weekly take-home pay and I had to struggle to look impressed. When Jane and I arrived at the do, Miss John told us that John Elfed would be paying for our first drink and, once again, I strove to look suitably grateful.

This party was a rare opportunity to wear good clothes. Our usual attire at home was jeans and thick baggy sweaters, so when Jane put on the little black number she'd bought through a mail-order catalogue, I couldn't take my eyes off her. Neither could the other men in the firm, particularly since she propped up the bar with the rest of us and proceeded to knock back double gin and tonics. At first, I didn't notice anything unusual about this, until I realised that all the other wives were sitting in a row on the other side of the room, sipping nothing more threatening than Babycham. The nearest we got to formal introductions was when one of my colleagues waved vaguely towards the row of women and told me, "That's the missus over there." I smiled in the same general direction, exchanged a wave and that was it; we turned back to manly conversations at the bar, Jane included.

After dinner – the standard Christmas menu – John Elfed stood up to make a short speech and award a gold watch to one of the car mechanics for completing twenty-five years of service. To my left, one of the older coach drivers leaned over and confided proudly, "In two years, I'll be getting my second gold watch." On my right, Parry whispered, "The day before I get mine, I'll shoot myself!" I couldn't see either of us lasting that long.

I stayed another six months, but for a few weeks my regular routine was broken by Williams' decision to buy a new truck. As was common practice, the firm surveyed the market by running a series of demonstrators. These were trucks loaned for a week by various dealers, and as I had now become the senior artic driver, I was given them all to test and compare. I carefully kept track of fuel consumption and the weight of each tractor unit, which would affect how much load we could carry and be paid for.

I drove half a dozen new demonstrators, including a TM from General Motors' British subsidiary, Bedford. This was another failed attempt to match the Europeans, with a noisy and gutless 206bhp two-stroke V6 engine that wouldn't have pulled the skin off a rice pudding. The one I really wanted was a high-powered Ford Transcontinental, which Ford had just launched as a serious long-hauler. Rumour had it that Williams could get the Transconti at a serious discount because of the company's Ford car dealership. We drivers hugged ourselves in anticipation. The Transcontinental was even taller than the Crusader and in a world of stone-walled roads, height was definitely an advantage. It had a full sleeper cab, a 270hp Cummins and tremendous street cred. My second backload with the Transconti was from Rumenco, the farm feed manufacturer in Burton-on-Trent. It was a disaster. Over the weighbridge, the Ford was so heavy I lost two tons compared with the load I could put behind the Scammell. However much I liked it, there was no way I could endorse a truck that might lose us ten per cent of our revenue every trip.

As for my recommendations and careful fuel consumption records, I might as well have not bothered, for Williams' management never thought to consult a mere driver about the final choice. In the end, they bought a newly launched Seddon Atkinson 400, which we hadn't even tried. It was a decent, modern truck and, with a 250hp Cummins, more powerful than any of our existing line-up. In some ways, I still preferred the Crusader; it had more character, and a larger and more imposing cab, but I still moved over to the more powerful Seddon Atki. After all, everyone likes a new truck, and it certainly helped me when I went looking for another job and the next step towards my ambition to be an international driver.

CHAPTER 6
BAPTISM BY BREAKDOWN

As long as I'd thought seriously about trucks, I'd wanted to drive one abroad. When I'd worked for Roger Bastable, I'd entertained the hope that he might venture Abbey Hill's trucks across the Channel, but it had become clear that he found car transport more congenial than continental work, and it was almost certainly more profitable. From my vantage point at the end of the Llyn, the nearest international operator was actually quite close by, in Pwllheli. The snag was that Caelloi, as it was (and still is) called, was an international coach company. For a while I considered taking a coach driver's test and applying to Caelloi for a job, but I was never very serious about carrying a cargo that could talk back to the driver, even if it was able to load itself unaided.

Instead, I began to notice trucks belonging to Cadwallader, a company based in Oswestry, on the English border and just off the A5 trunk road that I used regularly on runs to the Midlands and London. Cadwallader ran white fridge trailers and box vans, on which were emblazoned a large pair of Union Jack flags and the words *UK Continental*. I later learned that the firm was owned by two brothers, Gordon and Russell Cadwallader, who were pioneers in international refrigerated transport. By the mid-1970s, the company was a major player in international haulage, and the striking livery of G&R Cadwallader was recognisable all over Europe. When I joined the company, Gordon seemed more involved with the technical side of the business and the trucks themselves, which, at the time, numbered at least 150. Russell, on the other hand, was definitely the front man and was almost as well known as his trucks, at least in name. Once I'd begun to work for Caddy's – as everyone called the company – I often heard drivers from other firms, ferry personnel, customs agents and customers ask after Russell, always using his first name. Or, if I made some mistake, a driver who couldn't have known him personally would say, "Ah, Russell won't like that."

It was a far cry from Cadwallader's first steps into haulage in the 1950s. Having left school at fourteen to work as a farm labourer, and later as an agricultural engineer, Russell bought his first truck in the late 1950s. From his base in Oswestry, he delivered canned food for Heinz all over North Wales. When he then found new work with British Steel, he persuaded his brother, Gordon, to join him so that he could service the contract properly. Cadwallader soon moved into refrigerated transport, eventually hauling beef and lamb from abattoirs all over the UK to destinations across the Continent. Customers included FMC, then the largest meat producer in Europe, while within the UK, the company hauled for clients including Lever Brothers and margarine manufacturer Van den Bergh, both part of the giant Unilever group, as well as British Steel.

As I soon appreciated, the brothers employed a highly competent team of transport managers, on both UK and continental work, but they kept their ears to the ground. I remember meeting Russell one winter afternoon as he returned from Oswestry cattle market and listening to him lament the low prices the animals were fetching. It would result in a shortage of work in the spring, he said, and some months later, he was proved right.

All this I learned long after I had joined the company; first, I had to persuade them to take me on. Some months after Williams assigned me to the new Seddon Atkinson, I decided to pay Cadwallader a visit. I made sure the load I was carrying was immaculately roped and sheeted and, on a run home, diverted through Oswestry. Cadwallader's yard seemed enormous by comparison with Williams, with lines of trailers and a few tractor units parked across from a large, two-door workshop, with a low office block attached to the side. There was even a full-sized truck wash near the entrance to the yard, a sign that Cadwallader took pride in its vehicles' appearances, and had enough trucks to justify the expense of having its own wash.

I drove into the yard and took care to park neatly in line with the company's own trucks. Somewhat self-consciously, I crossed the yard to the office block and presented myself at one of the two drivers' windows. Through it, I could see a large transport office, with an extensive chart on the opposite wall, marked with rows of vehicle registration numbers next to destinations as far apart as Frankfurt, Rome and Paris. This was what I wanted.

A genial man in his late thirties or early forties detached himself from his desk and stepped across to the window. He introduced himself as Mike Goffin, one of the two international transport managers, and I explained that I was looking for work as an international driver. He ushered me through to the office and gave me an interview, interrupted by phone calls from what I deduced were various drivers dotted around Europe. He asked me to fill in my details on a printed form, which he then filed. I told him that I spoke French but, somewhat to my surprise, he said that made little difference to my prospects. On the other hand, he had commented on my Seddon Atkinson, and noticed from its registration number that it was almost new. Effectively, the newness of the Seddon was my only reference; presumably the fact that my present employer had entrusted me with a pristine vehicle counted for something. I was introduced briefly to Gordon Cadwallader and was told that they'd be in touch when a vacancy arose.

Three months went by but I heard nothing, and by late spring I realised that Cadwallader had forgotten me. Once again choosing a day when my truck looked particularly tidy, I returned to the company's yard. Again, I reversed neatly into the line of the company's vehicles and presented myself to Mike. "Oh," he said. "You'll have to keep nagging us if you want a job!" With my customary diffidence about my qualifications, it hadn't occurred to me to badger him, but from then on I called in almost weekly. Much later, when I'd been with Cadwallader for several years, one of my friends in the workshop, Lenny Evans, told me that my careful parking had not gone unnoticed. Gordon had remarked to him, "You see that bloke over there? He always parks his wagon tidily."

Within a few weeks, I was greeting the transport managers by name; apart from Mike, there was Tony Ellis, the UK traffic manager, and Phil Spittle, the second continental manager, an energetic and creative organiser of vehicles who became a long-term friend. One day, Phil told me, in what I came to recognise as his terse style for delivering instructions to drivers, "Give your notice in; you can start next week. Give us a call on Friday." Mike added that I'd spend the first two weeks on UK work, until I got used to the firm, and then I'd be sent abroad. I couldn't get back to Porthmadog quickly enough, and as soon as I arrived, I hurried up the steep, dark stairs to the transport office and told Miss John I was leaving. She was sorry to hear it, but Williams and I parted on good terms, and in some ways I was sad to leave myself, because I'd enjoyed working at the small family firm and I'd appreciated being part of the economic life of my own community. I was also home often enough to have a social life, and to enjoy the sense of place that came from the landlord beginning to pull my pint as soon as I entered our local pub. Nevertheless, I was in no doubt about the move; Cadwallader represented a step up in my driving career and, far from incidentally, I would be earning twice as much money, as long as I was prepared to spend many nights away.

This was a serious consideration, since financing a family of five on an average of £55 a week wasn't easy. Jane and I had already discussed this, though I realised much later – far too late – that I never asked myself whether it might be better for all of us if I continued to come home regularly, even if it meant constantly flirting with overdrafts. At the time, however, we agreed that higher income was the most important consideration in our cash-strapped family. Neither of us really thought through what it would mean for me to be away for weeks at a time, and the truth is that I was too interested in the prospect of international work to take proper account of what Jane and my family might really want or need. Nor did I realise that the long periods of separation would finally prove fatal to our relationship.

My last day at Williams ended early and Jane came to pick me up from Porthmadog. As instructed, I phoned Cadwallader and Phil told me to come in the following morning, with overnight gear, ready for a trip to Basel in Switzerland. So much for two weeks' probation in the

UK. That night in the pub I told my friends that I was off to Switzerland the following day. In the past they'd been impressed when I was going to London, for some of them had scarcely been as far as Liverpool. Switzerland was almost too exotic to contemplate, and later, when I began driving to Dubai and Saudi Arabia, they had nothing to say on the subject; such lands were simply beyond their ken.

Jane and I set off early on the Saturday morning on the ninety-mile run to Oswestry. The distance underlined the fact that I'd be coming home quite rarely and it was a sober journey. The rain didn't help. We later bought a second car for my commute, a Citroën 2CV that my brother imported for me from Holland, but right now Jane would have to make the long round trip to Oswestry every time I got that close to home. Now I unloaded my small suitcase and sleeping bag, and Jane and I parted in the unromantic drivers' car park behind Cadwallader's workshop.

In the office, Phil gave me rapid instructions about the paperwork I'd need for the run to Basel. At the time I thought this was a long haul, and indeed it was compared with my regular runs to Atherstone and Liverpool, but I later came to see Switzerland as a comparatively local trip. This first time I would travel with 'Alan', an experienced Continental driver whose real name I have long since forgotten, who would show me how to deal with borders and ferries, and how the paperwork should be handled in practice. Alan was driving a sleeper version of my Seddon Atkinson 400, but I was assigned to an MW-model ERF, a version built for export that had since been converted to right-hand drive following some unspecified accident. Both of our trucks were powered by the 240hp straight-eight engines introduced in the early '70s by the legendary Gardner engine company – based in Manchester – in an ultimately doomed attempt to match Cummins and the European imports.

Behind the Gardner was a thirteen-speed Eaton-Fuller gearbox. This was vaguely familiar, since it was based on the nine-speed transmissions I'd been driving at Williams. The difference was that the top four gears had a 'splitter', which doubled the number of ratios above fourth gear and allowed more precise gearing over a range of driving conditions. Nobody bothered to show me how to use this; the last and only formal driver training I ever had, once I had my licence, was those distant couple of weeks with two experienced drivers back at Walker's. Nevertheless, it didn't take many miles for me to work out how to use the thirteen-speed Eaton, and it became – and remained – my favourite transmission, even compared with the slick sixteen-speed gearboxes I later discovered in various Volvos. The ERF was four years older than my Seddon Atkinson at Williams, but I didn't care; it had a full sleeper cab and my days of dossing across the seats were over. On the other hand, the trailer and the load were slightly disappointing. I'd imagined myself hauling a fridge trailer, making roping and sheeting a thing of the past, but instead both Alan and I had sheeted flatbed trailers, each loaded with three steel coils totalling twenty tons.

Together we set off for Dover, where we were booked on a ferry to the Belgian port of Zeebrugge early on the Sunday morning. The aim was to cross Belgium and wait at the French border near Arlon until 10pm on Sunday evening, when France's Sunday ban on truck traffic would be lifted. Alan and I parked on the docks for the night, joining the lines of trucks waiting for the morning ferry. He showed me where to get my export papers stamped, but generally wore his responsibility as a guide so lightly that before we'd reached Brussels he'd left me behind. It was dark and raining as I grappled with the Brussels road signs, looking in vain for directions to Liege. I'd forgotten that Belgium is determinedly bilingual and it was only after several U-turns and wrong directions that I realised that Liege and Luik were the same place. When I did finally reach the French border, Alan had been resting there for a couple of hours, but as the new boy I hid my irritation.

Promptly at 10pm, the border opened and, with our French transit permits stamped, we were on our way. The route led over the 3000-foot Bonhomme Pass, which we climbed in the dark, and it was dawn by the time we reached the Swiss border at Basel. It took an hour to clear customs, which seemed unnecessarily slow, but I later learned was positively slick compared with customs in Dover or Italy. Alan and I parted to make our separate deliveries, and although we planned to meet for our return, it was actually months before I saw him again. Instead, I made the return trip alone and learned a good deal more than I would have done if he'd been with me.

I swiftly disposed of the steel coils, hoisted off the trailer by a crane in three easy lifts, and set out to pick up a load of chipboard from a factory a few miles outside Basel. The plant was vast and there were at least a dozen trucks in the loading area, from a number of European countries. All of them had 'tilt' trailers, purpose-built for international transport, whose superstructure consisted of a heavy plastic sheet stretched over a steel frame with wooden side slats to form the shape of a van body, all of which could be wholly or partially dismantled for loading. In most cases, all a driver had to do was to unlace the steel cord holding the bottom edge of the sheet, and hoist the plastic side onto the roof of the tilt, giving full access to the trailer floor. By contrast, I was loading on a traditional British flatbed trailer, and as I sheeted and roped the eight-foot long packs of chipboard, I felt the other drivers eyeing the old-fashioned ritual with some amusement.

Somehow I sorted out the customs clearance, with the help of a local agent, and I was back on the road north through France. I was booked on a ferry from Zeebrugge at mid-morning on the following day, and with no Sunday driving restrictions, it should have been an easy run, even for a novice. Instead, I came to grief on the slopes of the Bonhomme Pass. As I approached the foot of the mountain, I downshifted through the thirteen-speed Fuller gearbox and the ERF growled up the long switchback climb. As always, I scanned the instruments from time to time, and as I neared the summit, I suddenly noticed that the air gauges were falling. Luckily, just ahead I could see a *Routiers* drivers' restaurant, with a large parking area, so I pulled off the road. With the fail-safe air-brake system, once I had stopped there was no way to start without adequate air pressure, and I was stranded. It was a strange preview of what would happen on my first trip to the Middle East, eighteen months later (described in the Prologue).

I poked around as best I could under the non-tilt cab, but could find no obvious sign of an air leak. As I was pondering what to do, another British driver came over to me, and once I'd told him what had happened, suggested I phone Cadwallader's office. I was aghast. Phone all the way to England? I was so naïve that I didn't realise that my new job would, of course, involve phoning and telexing from all over Europe, but right now I wondered whether I'd get into trouble for wasting money. Having given his sensible advice, the other Brit left me alone and I walked over to the restaurant to find a phone. I got through to Mike Goffin back in Oswestry just before the office was due to close for the evening. When I explained the problem, he suggested I talk to Jeff, the workshop foreman, who turned out to have a pretty good idea of what had happened. Jeff explained that the workshop had once inserted a steel baffle along the chassis to protect the plastic air-lines from the heat of the exhaust pipe. "If you look behind the plate, you'll probably find that a joint in the air-line has come adrift. See if you can fix it; if not, give us a call in the morning and we'll sort it out then."

I returned to the ERF and, with Jeff's advice to guide me, soon found that the failure was indeed behind the steel plate. A plastic pipe, part of the air-brake system, had split, but luckily the resulting hole was close to a joint formed with two large steel nuts. I realised that I could cut the pipe just behind the split, and by slightly rerouteing it, bring the new end up to the joint. All I needed were tools but, being new to the game, I didn't have any. I did have a knife, however, and with it I performed the necessary plastic surgery before I went searching for more specialised tools in the shape of two large spanners. It was a warm, dry evening, and there was still just enough light to work by, if I was quick.

At this point, I was given some help for which I still feel grateful. A Swiss driver, seeing I was in trouble, came over and offered to lend me an adjustable spanner to undo the large nut on the air-line. The only problem was that I would need two spanners, one for each side of the joint. "No problem," said the Swiss, in surprisingly good English. "You keep this one, and then you can borrow another." I was amazed at his generosity towards a total stranger, but he insisted I take the spanner and, wishing me luck, went on his way. Now I was almost in business and I approached another driver for the loan of another large spanner that would fit the second nut. Thus armed, I went to work, and in less than half an hour I had repaired the air-line. I fired up the engine and watched with relief as the air gauges climbed to normal operating pressure.

By now it was quite late and, having worked since early in the morning, I should have stopped for the night. I deliberated briefly, but realised that staying the night on the Bonhomme would leave me with no prospect of reaching the ferry on time. Again, my novice status was against me. I didn't have the phone numbers of the ferry companies or the private numbers of either of the transport managers, Mike and Phil, so there was no way of rebooking my passage from Zeebrugge to Dover. Instead, I decided to drive straight through the night, with a couple of short breaks for coffee and food, so that I managed to arrive at Zeebrugge early in the morning, and in good time for the ferry on which I was booked. With my paperwork completed, I pulled into the line of trucks waiting on the docks and went to phone the office. Mike answered my call and there was a brief pause when I announced myself; I could almost hear him thinking, "Oh shit, we've got that new bloke to sort out."

"Where are you?" he asked.

"I'm on the docks at Zeebrugge, waiting for the 10.30am ferry."

"You are? How did you manage that?"

I explained that I'd fixed the air-line, as Jeff had suggested, and driven straight through to Zeebrugge. I could hear the relief in Mike's voice as he congratulated me. Having sorted the truck myself, I was feeling pretty good about the whole affair, and I later realised that I'd passed an unexpected test and proved myself to my new bosses. At any rate, when I returned to the yard, I was given a new Volvo F88-290 while its regular driver took a week's holiday, and the following week I was assigned my own Volvo with a fridge trailer behind it. As a continental driver, I'd arrived.

CHAPTER 7

LIFE ON THE OTHER SIDE

For all my success in fixing the ERF on my first trip, I wasn't rewarded with any time off. Instead, I was sent straight out again in the new Volvo to load chocolate powder from the Mars factory in Slough, west of London, near Heathrow Airport. I'd known this kind of turnround would be the pattern in my new job, but it was still a wrench to be within ninety miles of home and have to head off again immediately in the opposite direction. I phoned home to talk to Jane and the children, and then I was back on the road. I could already see that this was not going to be easy for any of us and in some respects we were back in the same situation that we'd been in when I worked for Abbey Hill in Somerset.

In every other respect, however, my new job was everything I'd hoped for, beginning with the truck itself.

My former vehicles had had their virtues and I'd enjoyed driving all of them, but none of them could compare to the Volvo F88. This was, quite simply, a legendary truck that, with its rivals from the other Swedish manufacturer, Scania, set the standard for drivers in Britain and for much of the Continent. Very few British drivers were lucky enough to drive an F88 and now I was one of them. The Volvo had a compact, all-steel cab, and every driver knew that it had been built to pass the much-vaunted Swedish cab-strength tests and meet the most stringent safety standards in Europe. As with every truck of its day, the engine still intruded into the cab, but the tunnel over the engine sloped down towards the rear, minimising the space it took up. My first regular F88, to which I was assigned in my third week at Cadwallader, was referred to as 'TEW', after its number plate. It had a single bunk, which, although it was narrow by modern standards, felt positively luxurious to me. At any rate, I slept far better on it than I ever had when perched on various Heath Robinson beds across the engine tunnels of my former trucks. Moreover, the cab was well insulated, as you'd expect from Sweden, so it conserved heat well on winter nights. Beneath the bunk, behind the seats and on either side of the engine was a pair of storage lockers, in which I kept food and clothing.

TEW's 9.6-litre engine produced 240hp, which wasn't generous even then, but it was matched to an excellent sixteen-speed synchromesh gearbox. This was a basic eight-speed range-change transmission with a 'splitter' switch – mounted on the engine cover beside the driver – which doubled the number of ratios by giving a high or low option ('splitting') for each of the main eight. The gear-lever itself was light to use and there was a certain satisfaction simply in slipping it through the gate. The Volvo had a commanding presence and its tall doors, with relatively small windows, made it feel larger than it was. With its un-sprung cab, the F88 handled predictably, with very little roll, which was particularly helpful when my trailer was loaded with 'hanging meat', which could move on its hooks and had a high centre of gravity. The steering was much lighter than my Seddon Atki's and the tight turning circle made the Volvo very easy to manoeuvre in confined spaces.

Apart from the new tractor unit, I now had to learn how to operate a refrigerated trailer and know which temperatures were needed for different kinds of load. Even though I'd prided myself on the tidiness of my roping and sheeting, and enjoyed the skill involved in doing it well, I was glad to see the back of it. The fridge trailer consisted of a forty-foot insulated box with a slotted floor and five steel I-beam rails mounted from front to back under the ceiling. From these were suspended hooks, which moved on small steel wheels so that sides of beef, whole lambs or sow sides could be hooked up and slid to the front of the trailer. Most hanging meat was carried without any covering, so the trailer had to be thoroughly steam-cleaned after every load to remove traces of fat, flesh and blood – a job I usually did myself. Refrigeration was provided by a Thermo-King unit mounted on the front of the trailer – and just behind the cab – consisting of a small diesel engine that ran a pump for the refrigerant. The fridge normally remained on at all times when a load was aboard and I soon learned to sleep with the sound of the diesel engine clattering two feet behind me.

I discovered that, at Cadwallader, we drivers had considerable freedom, provided we got the job done. In those happy days, there was no satellite navigation and no electronic surveillance by mission control (as described in the Introduction). There weren't even mobile phones, so the only time Mike or Phil could contact me was when I chose to talk to them by phone or telex. I could leave the yard with a truck worth forty grand, with a load of beef steak worth even more, and be left completely unsupervised until I phoned the office for a backload. It meant that we drivers had to have our wits about us and develop skills that went far beyond just piloting the vehicle.

Simply passing through customs could be a challenge. In those days, every load within the EEC – the European Economic Community, which was not yet a 'Union' – was accompanied by customs paperwork, known as a T-form, plus a CMR (or waybill) that detailed the load. Travelling beyond the EEC required a complex 'carnet' with separate sheets for each country we passed through. Every trip required multiple encounters with customs officials, even if we were travelling to only one country. Driving to Germany, or further afield, involved a customs check at each side of every border. On top of that were permits, which were mandatory for every truck entering France, Germany or Italy. Permits were issued by some department of the Ministry of Transport and they were in limited supply. They consisted of a green front sheet, which included an embossed logo and various official stamps. Stapled to it was a white sheet on which were written the details of the trip, for example, Manchester to Marseille. The theory was that as we entered a country requiring a permit, customs would stamp both sheets and the permit would then be used up, and no longer valid. Cadwallader, in common with most British companies running to the Continent, never had enough permits, particularly since the company's international fleet was constantly growing, as Mike and, especially, Phil brought in new work. The solution to the shortage was simple – bribery.

I learned this in my second week at the firm and my first delivery to France in the new Volvo I was driving as a stand-in. In the company of two colleagues, whom I'll call Paul and Steve, I had picked up the load of chocolate powder from the Mars factory in Slough and was hauling it to the company's plant in the French town of Haguenau, about fifty kilometres from Strasbourg and close to the German border. If I hadn't been alerted by my colleagues, I wouldn't have noticed that they were paying a bribe, so routine was the procedure. We parked our trucks in the row outside the Calais customs office and joined the line of drivers waiting to have their paperwork checked and stamped. I watched as Paul slid his papers under the customs window and the customs officer checked and stamped his T-form. He then raised his stamp above the front sheet of Paul's permit and gave him a questioning look. Paul slid a ten-franc note (about one pound) onto the desk and the officer flipped the permit and stamped the back sheet only, leaving the green sheet unsullied. Trying not to seem too obvious, I took my own ten-franc note from my wallet as Steve repeated the procedure and then, somewhat nervously, stepped up to the window myself. I needn't have worried; the customs officer looked completely bored, and as soon as my money appeared, he slid it into a drawer beneath the desk and passed me my papers without comment. As I turned away, I saw the next driver – from a different company – step forward and go through the same routine.

Back at the trucks, Paul explained that we could now replace the stamped back sheet, on which the journey details were entered, with a blank copy, and the permit would be reusable. Sure enough, in my envelope of paperwork for the trip, I had a couple of blank sheets, ready to staple to the back of the permit when we returned to England. We'd also earned a bonus of £5 – good for a couple of meals in those days – as well as being able to claim our ten francs back as expenses. Steve told me that if we were able to keep a German permit clean we'd get a ten-pound bonus, because it was much harder to do. Since you couldn't bribe the Germans, keeping a German permit clean was, in most cases, impossible. However, I later discovered that there was one small border crossing into Germany from Holland, off the main motorway route to Hamburg,

My first brand-new truck, a Seddon Atkinson 400 in the livery of John Williams of Porthmadog, one of my early employers

Cadwallader gave me my first taste of driving abroad, and a Volvo F88 was my regular truck for the first year of my continental career

Returning from Baghdad in 1979, on my second trip to Iraq for Jack Harrison, based in Brierley Hill in the Midlands

Harrison's Dafs lined up in the Saudi desert, three of the fleet of eleven trucks on regular Middle East work

A rare stretch of dual carriageway on the long haul through the former Yugoslavia, taking us to Greece, and the ferry to Syria

Taking the ferry train across Germany gave foreign hauliers extra transit permits

Ready for drums of orange juice to be unloaded (by hand) in Baghdad

Loading pallets of paper in Essex for delivery to the Iraqi government printing office. The tilt trailer is opened up on both sides

Ferries loading in Volos, Greece, for the two-day crossing to Tartus in Syria. Schedules were unpredictable, and turn-round much slower than on cross-Channel ferries

My home and place of work in the cab of Harrison's Daf 2800 – one of the most spacious cabs back in the 1970s

State-owned Bulgarian trucks lined up on the dockside in Volos. Unlike western Europeans, they had two drivers per truck

Waiting for days for the ferry from Tartus, with communal meals prepared using stoves carried in our trailer boxes. Delays added extra time to every Middle Eastern trip

Trucks aboard the roll on-roll off ferry between Greece and Syria. Crossings weren't always as smooth as in in this picture

Filling up in Saudi Arabia, where £1 bought you 100 litres of diesel. The 3500-mile return trip to Britain cost only £25 for fuel

Trailer boxes under the side of the trailer, and the belly tank behind them, which meant my truck could carry 3000 litres of diesel

What can happen if you fall asleep at the wheel. A European Volvo overturned on the side of the road in western Iraq

Replacing an injector pipe on the Daf's 11.6-litre engine beside the road in Hungary. The turbocharger on the left boosted power to 310bhp

where customs never stamped the permits at all and I could earn an easy tenner by making a minor detour.

Now that I had been given my own truck, I began running regularly to France, with occasional trips to Germany, Belgium and Holland. I loaded in abattoirs anywhere from Inverurie in northern Scotland to Hatherleigh in Devon, and many deliveries to France started with a visit to Rungis, the vast meat and produce market on the southern side of Paris. On a typical trip to France, I arrived in Dover on Saturday evening and collected my customs paperwork from Cadwallader's own agent, CS Clearance – one of dozens of agents dotted around the docks in crowded offices or improvised Portakabins stacked up beneath the legendary 'White Cliffs'. The paperwork was then stamped by customs and I drove round to the dock itself, lining up ready for the Sunday morning ferry to Calais. During the evening and the night, lines of trucks formed up for the six 'link-spans' connecting the docks to the ferries bound for Calais, or Zeebrugge in Belgium. Cadwallader had about seventy trucks on Continental work and there were usually at least a couple of colleagues in the queues with whom to have dinner in the drivers' canteen, or go for a drink in the pub just beyond the dock gates. When the ferry was ready for loading in the morning, I was woken up by a ferry employee banging on the cab. I dressed hurriedly and scrambled into the driver's seat, ready for the line of trucks to move.

In those days, there were two major ferry operators out of Dover. The first was Sealink, owned jointly by the then nationalised British Railways, and their French counterpart, SNCF. The second company was Townsend Thoresen, most of whose ships were named *Free Enterprise I* to *VIII* to underline their rivalry with the nationalised opposition. The names set a buccaneering tone, which, when one of their newer ships, *The Herald of Free Enterprise*, overturned in Zeebrugge a decade later, they may have had cause to regret. The *FE.I*, as it was known, was an inadequate little ship that had only a single door in the stern, so we had to reverse on to it. Townsend's later ships, *Free Enterprise III* and onwards, were proper roll-on-roll-off ferries, with doors at both ends, so that we drove on through the stern door in Dover and out through the bows in Calais. The Channel Tunnel was still a distant dream.

By the time we'd made the ninety-minute crossing to Calais, disembarked and cleared customs, it was around noon when I set off from Calais, taking account of the one-hour time difference. In France, unlike Germany, Italy or Austria, trucks carrying perishable goods were allowed to run on Sunday, perhaps underlining the pre-eminence of food in the French psychology, so although it was Sunday afternoon, we fridge drivers were free to go. In those days, there was a two-hour run on ordinary roads through the Pas-de-Calais before we reached the *autoroute*, and once on the highway, I pulled into the first service station, operated by, and known as, 'Jacques Borel'. Here, I simply killed time, cooking a snack, dozing and reading. There was no hurry, since the customs office in the suburbs of Paris wouldn't open until mid-evening. The Jacques Borel services usually had an array of foreign trucks, either parked until the Sunday ban was over or, like we fridge drivers, waiting to avoid the late afternoon traffic heading back to Paris at the end of the weekend. In a sharp contrast to trucking life in Britain, a solitary prostitute of uncertain age would often stroll up and down looking for business, and presumably find some customers, though none among any drivers I knew.

By late afternoon, I was back on the road again, bowling down the A1 autoroute until I reached the outskirts of Paris, where I parked up at the customs office on the N1 national road, joining a number of English and Irish fridges also bound for Rungis. Here, I cooked dinner in the cab, partly to fill in the waiting time before customs opened and partly to prepare for what was usually a long night's work. It was late evening before we all got our papers back and were free to go. We then all hurried back down the N1 to the *Périphérique* ring road that circles the inner *arrondissements* of Paris. At this time on a Sunday, the *Périphérique* was relatively quiet and we raced around it, despite the occasional tight turns. Each of us was trying to be the first to reach our customers in Rungis, some of whom might have two or three trucks to unload. After a while, I learned where the various deliveries were, but in the early days I might lose precious time finding the name of my importer.

The meat market section of Rungis consisted of several huge buildings, each with an overhanging roof fitted with rails to carry hanging meat. I opened the doors of the trailer and reversed up to the rail. Two or three market workers, clad in bloodstained overalls, and often with a battered Gauloise cigarette hanging from their lips, climbed into the trailer and started rolling the carcasses to the rear. Hoisting each sheep carcass – or beef quarter – up to free it from its hook, they passed it easily down to a colleague on the ground, who in turn lifted it onto the hooks on the market's rails. The heavy joint – a beef hindquarter weighed an average of ninety kilos – was dragged into the cold interior of the market building and my part in its journey was over. Once the long-haul trucks were out of the way, a number of small vans – in those days including the iconic Citroën H-type vans with their distinctive corrugated sides – darted into our place to take the meat to butchers' shops across the city.

As an international driver, I was never required to load or unload, and the time I spent with the doors open at the delivery point was time off. If I could get a clear picture of how long the delivery would take, I might join other drivers at *Le Marmite* (which the drivers always referred to by its English pronunciation), a bar and restaurant that opened late and stayed open until breakfast time. Here, we primed ourselves with a couple of 'café calvas' – black coffee with Calvados – for the next stage of the delivery, which might involve several more hours' driving.

With part of the load dropped at Rungis, I was usually sent onwards to make a further delivery as far away as Angers or Le Mans. This meant that I'd be driving into the early hours and it wasn't always easy to stay awake. On one occasion, it was about two in the morning before I left Rungis, heading for Angers, four hours away. The first hour or so was easy enough, but before long I began to get seriously tired. I stopped for a plastic cup of coffee at a motorway fuel station, but its effect didn't last long, and even though I was practically chain-smoking, I knew I was in danger of nodding off. I opened the window, stuck my head into the cold airstream and started singing at the top of my voice. I even stubbed a cigarette out on the back of my hand. Why I didn't pull over and sleep, I can't recall; I would certainly have had no complaint from the office and I can only think it was plain stubbornness that kept me going. Nevertheless, by the time I joined the two-lane national road off the end of the autoroute, a long traditional French avenue, I was finished. Ahead, I saw a lay-by at the side of the road and a truck with its lights on parked at the further end. I swung my Volvo in behind it, applied the handbrake and slumped over the wheel, not even bothering to switch off the engine or the lights. Sometime later, I woke up suddenly and saw the other truck right in front of me. I was so disorientated that I believed I was still driving and that I was about to collide with the other trailer. It would have been my final thought. It was only when the collision didn't happen in the next split second that I realised I was actually parked. The feeling of relief that flowed through me was strong enough to get me to Angers as planned.

The hinterland of Angers was a favourite place for a reload and I often picked up apples for delivery to markets as far apart as Southampton and Glasgow. It was at an apple-packing plant near the town that I began to realise how different the attitude of management to workers in France was compared with Britain and the antediluvian practices back at Spiller's in North Wales. I was reading a book in the cab one morning, having had a brief chat with the forklift driver who was bringing pallets loaded with cases of apples to be stacked by hand in the trailer behind me. When lunchtime came around, everyone stopped work and headed for cars to go to the local restaurant. To my surprise, the owner of the plant came over and invited me to join them. Together with the forklift driver and a couple of other loaders, I piled into the boss's car and we went off for a convivial lunch together. I couldn't conceive of that happening at home.

On another occasion, I was loading cases of pork back-fat in Nantes on the Atlantic coast in southern Brittany. The meat processing plant was a clean but modest affair, with low buildings at either side of a wide yard. At the end of the yard was the owner's house — a common arrangement in smaller companies in several continental countries. I'd been parked on the premises overnight and as the loading began, the owner of the business, a genial man in his forties, came over to my cab and invited me to breakfast. Once again, I reflected that this would have been unthinkable in England.

It certainly helped that by now I spoke French reasonably well. My lowly O-level French had proved to be a sufficient foundation for me to build a fair degree of fluency, at least when it came to discussing anything to do with the transport business. Now, over excellent coffee and fresh bread and jam, the company boss quizzed me about the pork back-fat I was loading. What on earth was it used for? he wondered. I explained that it was converted into 'pork scratchings', a snack that was particularly popular in northern English pubs. Having already been to a pork scratchings factory – a small and evil-smelling series of sheds near Coventry – I described how the fat was rendered down in vats and the scratchings skimmed off the top as they solidified. Despite being in the meat processing business, my French host was aghast that anyone would eat such a thing. I reflected that it said something about the snack that even an omnivorous Frenchman wouldn't consider it.

As the months went by, I realised that there were two kinds of drivers at Cadwallader; the ones who did the job steadily and those, like me, who liked to go far and fast. There was never any pressure from the company, but some of us simply liked the challenge of covering the ground quickly. Mike and Phil knew their men; they gave short hops to Brussels and Paris to the steady drivers, and the longer hauls to the tearaways. One regular job meant covering the 1200 miles from the Scottish borders to Nice, in the far south-eastern corner of France, in a day and a half. It would have been demanding in a fast car, but in a thirty-two-ton artic it was an interesting challenge that I enjoyed several times, once I was given a fast and reliable truck. I loaded lambs in Dumfries and, having obtained my customs papers at a local office, left mid-morning on a Saturday with the aim of delivering in Nice on Sunday night. Boarding the ferry in Dover, I was leaving the jurisdiction of the British ministry men, and in those days they didn't appear to pay much attention what we did across the water. With the one-hour time difference, it was late evening by the time the ferry docked in Calais and I set off towards Paris, driving down the *autoroute* comfortably over the speed limit, on the assumption – not always justified – that speed cops wouldn't be out at night.

By now, I was into a rhythm and it was easy enough to keep going through the night. With Paris behind me, I aimed for Lyon, 470 kilometres to the south, and only when I'd passed through the city and was clearly in the south of France did I pull over to sleep, in the light of Sunday morning, just past the *péage* – or toll booth – on the A7 autoroute to Marseilles and Nice. I'd definitely broken the back of the job, so I could afford a few hours' sleep and still give myself time to clear customs at Marignane, the airport for Marseilles. With customs clearance, and some sort of dinner, behind me, I quickly covered the 200 kilometres to Nice and finally took to my bed as my trailer was unloaded.

In one particular four-day period a couple of years later, when I had a new Volvo F10, I was feeling so alert that I phoned the office from Nice early on the Monday, instead of sleeping well into the morning. Having been directed to Nîmes to load cabbages for Hull, in the East Riding of Yorkshire – which was effectively coals to Newcastle, given the agriculture in East Yorkshire – I was heading north again by the same evening. It seemed a shame to stop – I was literally on a roll – so I continued up to Calais and shipped across to Dover. I finally reached Hull fruit and vegetable market on Tuesday evening, having even taken time to pick up my six-year-old daughter, Laura, from central London, not to mention spending the usual few hours clearing customs in Dover. In the round trip from Dumfries to Nice, and then from Nîmes to Hull, I'd covered over 2300 miles in three and a half days. On top of that, I'd tipped and reloaded in France and cleared customs three times. In retrospect, it seems a crazy way to have worked, particularly since I was paid by the day and not by the mile. Sometimes, however, I just felt like staying behind the wheel, and being well ahead of schedule had its own weird satisfaction.

The Volvo F10, and longer hauls, lay well into the future, and meanwhile I was running more local jobs to northern Germany and western France. One day, however, when I was chatting in the office with my boss, Gordon Cadwallader, he asked Phil when he was going to send me to Italy. Phil retorted, "As soon as you give him a decent truck." It was probably the realisation that I belonged in the fast group that made Gordon promote me so quickly, but within a week of the conversation, and only a couple of months into the job, I was given a Volvo F88.290. The '290', apart from being less than a year old, had fifty more horsepower to play with than my older F88.

Now that I had a more powerful and reliable truck, Mike and Phil were confident in sending me on longer runs through Germany and France – including the madcap race from Dumfries to Nice – and, more particularly, to Italy. I soon found that Italy had a special appeal as a destination, because driving there was an adventure, particularly in winter, and because the country itself felt so different from northern Europe. And finally, the Italian run led me to a further step in my driving career that I very much wanted, but had no clear idea how to achieve.

CHAPTER 8

ITALY

In those days, driving to Italy was an interesting challenge, and as a destination it was tailor-made for tearaways, since our return loads usually needed delivering as soon as possible. Crossing the border from France through the Mont Blanc Tunnel was like entering a whole new world; edgier, feeling more dangerous than France and, as often as not, with a quite different weather pattern from the one I'd left behind on the other side of the Mont Blanc massif. The tunnel itself burrows 11.6 kilometres through the base of the mountain, at an altitude of 1275 metres (4150ft) on the French side, some 3500 metres below the summit. In winter, I sometimes found that while the Italian side was covered with snow, the steeply zigzagging approach road on the French side might be swept by rain or covered in a sheet of black ice.

Nevertheless, the danger lay not so much in the roads, or even the Italian drivers, but in the possibility of hijacking. Fridge trucks from northern Europe were known to be carrying expensive meat, and the threat of hijacking was real enough that we were not allowed to enter Milan or Turin without an escort to lead the way. Drivers were instructed to wait at the last *péage* before the city for an escort car to guide us to the customer. Apparently, trucks had been hijacked when their drivers had stopped for directions, and although I never met a victim when I was driving, in my later career as a journalist I did hear from others who had come to grief. We drivers suspected that the hijackers got tip-offs from customs officers at Aosta, the clearance point forty or so kilometres down the mountain from the tunnel. It was a reasonable supposition, given our own experience. Whenever I carried lambs into Italy – usually around 1500 small carcasses, because the Italians liked their lamb young – two or three would be kept by customs at Aosta for 'testing'. We were all convinced that the testing was on the customs officers' dinner tables, since the lambs had been signed off as healthy by Euro-certified vets, back at the abattoir where they'd been slaughtered.

Apart from the professional aspects of the Italian run, the country itself felt quite distinct, even from the south of France. The very air was different south of the Alps. In the mountains themselves, it was so clear you could taste it, while down in the Po Valley, the atmosphere could be thick and humid and, in summer, stayed hot throughout the night. The southbound *autostrada* down the Adriatic coast, from Rimini to Brindisi, was a joy to drive, with light traffic, varied terrain and glorious views of the sea, made all the better by the high vantage point of a truck cab. On the other hand, the cross-country route west from Bologna presented a challenging drive through the mountains, on an *autostrada* that seemed to be nothing but tunnels punctuated by bridges that tottered across deep, steep-sided valleys. I have a poor head for heights, and on those long viaducts between the tunnels it didn't help that I was in a right-hand-drive truck, so I was seated near the side of the road, not the middle. This meant that I had a clear view over the guard rail straight to the bottom of the valley. I used to stare resolutely ahead and let the often-dramatic view look after itself.

It was difficult to find a secure place to park overnight. *Autostrada* service stations typically consisted of a few fuel pumps, with the ground around the diesel pumps stained deep brown, and narrow parking areas. In the centre was usually a small bar, serving sandwiches and excellent coffee over high stainless-steel counters. There was scarcely space to park for the night, but, in any case, the service areas didn't feel too safe and I always tried to 'park up' within the confines of our customers' premises.

For several months in 1978, I ran to Italy more than any other country and I got to know the route well. Occasionally I'd enter along the Mediterranean coast, at Ventimiglia, but nearly always I'd take the

Alpine road through the Mont Blanc Tunnel. In those days, there was no motorway east from Mâcon – some seventy kilometres north of Lyon – where we turned off the A6 autoroute and headed towards the Alps and the Mont Blanc Tunnel, 250 kilometres to the east. Instead, we drove along a delightfully varied and demanding national road that led past Bourg-en-Bresse and on through the pretty towns of Nantua and Bellegarde, climbing and dipping on a road that hugged the mountainside, or careered down into deep valleys, and through small towns and villages. The route skirted Geneva, so close to the Swiss border that you could have tossed an apple across it, before turning towards the serious mountains, along a short stretch of autoroute past Bonneville to Cluses. Here began the most exciting part of the drive. The steeply climbing road clung to a cliff face for several kilometres, in places so cramped by overhanging rock that a truck coming down the mountain had to wait as you chugged upwards. This was internationally recognised etiquette; no one wanted to restart a heavy truck on the steep gradient, and any descending truck was easy to stop, since it travelled at little more than a crawl to preserve its brakes.

High up the cliff, the road turned sharply to the right, and headed up a narrow gorge that eventually opened out to become the Chamonix Valley. Behind us as we turned, the steep cliff towered over a steelworks hundreds of feet below. Trucks descending from Mont Blanc had to slow down carefully – particularly on ice – to make the sharp turn onto the cliff road. Failure to do so would result in 'parking in the steelworks', the euphemism for plunging hundreds of feet to one's death. I never heard of it happening, but it was a regular joke among drivers on the route.

I'd usually take a load into Italy, but occasionally I'd tip in France, even as far north as Paris, and then run southwards unladen. Once or twice, Phil even sent me to Italy from the UK with no load at all. The reason was peaches. Cadwallader was getting such a good rate for hauling them back from northern and central Italy that Phil and Mike could justify hundreds of miles of empty running to pick them up. Our main customer was a London fruit importer who demanded that we get the peaches back to Britain as fast as possible, and in practice this meant belting back from northern Italy in a day and a night, with no proper breaks for sleep. I usually delivered to fruit markets at Spitalfields in

London, Southampton or Bristol, but occasionally I'd be sent north as far as Glasgow or Gateshead. It was usually dead of night when I arrived at any market, where I'd park up outside the customer, pull the curtains round the cab and crash out. Occasionally, I'd surface sufficiently to feel the cab rock as the fruit was unloaded, but I could easily ignore it and wake sometime in the morning, aware that everything behind me had gone quiet and the market was now all but deserted. If I was delivering to Glasgow, I usually woke at seven or eight and wandered over to a pub on the outskirts of the market, where the market loaders were finishing their nightshift with a pint or three of 'heavy' – the Scottish equivalent of English bitter. The pub also served a massive breakfast that would set me up for the rest of the day.

One of my favourite Italian jobs was taking beef to US Forces bases in Italy, because I got a taste of American life into the bargain. The first time I was sent to supply the US military, I took a brand-new fridge trailer to the abattoir in Shrewsbury, twenty-odd miles from our base in Oswestry. Here, I was introduced to the American obsession with hygiene. Normal practice was for the abattoir's vet to inspect the trailer for cleanliness, but the US clearly didn't trust a mere Brit to do the job. Instead, I found a finicky American vet who'd driven 150 miles from some US base or other in East Anglia to check that my trailer was pristine. Of course it was, having never carried a load, but I was still told to give the interior a thorough pressure wash with hot water and detergent. I also had to run the fridge for half an hour to bring its temperature down to plus-one degree Celsius – the standard temperature for carrying fresh beef – before the meat could be loaded, and leave it clattering away as the beef was carried aboard. I was irritated, but not as much as the meat porters who had to work inside the trailer while the noisy fridge was running. Normal practice was to start it up only after the load was aboard.

From then on, however, the trip was fun, as I found on my first tour of American bases in Italy. Having cleared customs in Aosta, I headed for my first drop, at the US air-force base at Aviano, near the foothills of the Dolomites, due north of Venice. I arrived in the late afternoon and was told that I'd be unloaded in the morning. In the meantime, once I'd entered the compound and parked up outside the commissary, I was free to use the base's facilities. Now, I was effectively in the USA. I spent US dollars in the bookshop, bought a burger in an American café and topped off the entertainment with an evening at the movies. I even got to salute the US flag or, at least, watch others do so. I was strolling near the centre of the base towards dusk, when a couple of passing cars suddenly stopped in the middle of the road. Their drivers leapt out and stood to attention, their right hands raised in an immaculate salute. Luckily I'd stopped to watch, because I then realised that everyone I could see was also saluting. After a minute, normal life resumed and the cars went on their way. I'd noticed a couple of teenage boys who had also stood to attention, more or less, so I asked them what had happened. "Oh," they told me. "That's the saluting of the flag. It happens every evening when the flag is lowered." Coming from a country of less demonstrative patriotism, I was quietly amazed, but when, years later, I lived in the United States, I realised this was all of a piece with Americans' general reverence for their flag and for their military.

With part of the load removed, I headed south-east to another US base at Livorno, on the coast near Pisa. Again, I reached the base in the late afternoon and was looking forward to another evening in 'America', only to be told by a pair of unsmiling guards at the gate that I'd have to return in the morning. Improvising quickly, I said that would be fine, but I couldn't guarantee the beef would be there in the morning, since my load could easily be hijacked if I had to park up overnight in a Livorno street. One of the guards made a quick phone call and was evidently overruled, because I was allowed to enter the base and spend another evening enjoying American culture. As I was being unloaded the next morning, I noticed that an Austrian truck I'd seen at Aviano was once again delivering milk to the military. We nodded to each other and I realised that, together, its driver and I were playing our small part in the huge and expensive machine that keeps the US military supplied worldwide.

The final drop was at a base near Brindisi, in the southern toe of Italy, a 900-kilometre run from Livorno. This involved running down the west side of the Apennines, around Rome and Naples, before crossing the country to Bari on the Adriatic coast, and making the final 120-kilometre run down the beautiful coastal highway to Brindisi. I hadn't visited the

USA since I was a young child in the 1950s, but I loved the small slice of American life that these runs gave me and I added US dollars to the sheaf of currencies I carried in my accordion-like wallet.

I was often sent to load peaches early on a Monday morning, for delivery in England on Tuesday night, and that meant waiting in Aosta from Saturday to late Sunday evening, ready to run down overnight to load somewhere between Modena and Rimini, and occasionally as far south as Ancona, a distance of 400-600 kilometres. In the summer this was no hardship, and there would often be a group of Brits either waiting for the Sunday driving ban to end at ten in the evening or for customs clearance on Monday morning. One or two of us would drop our trailers in the customs compound, so we could all pile into the freed tractor units and head towards a small lake nearby, stopping on the way to buy some sort of picnic and a few bottles of cheap *frizzante* – sparkling white wine – which we cooled in the lake. It was a relaxing way to prepare for the non-stop run back to England on Monday night or to recover from the previous week's exertions.

One thing it didn't do, of course, was get me home for the weekend, but I had long ago given up trying to get home more than once a month, or even longer. If UK driving had put a stress on my relationship with Jane, continental work eventually took it to breaking point. We might go days at a time without talking to each other; my usual routine was to phone her whenever I returned to Dover or, more rarely, ports further west in Portsmouth or Poole. Returning to England didn't mean I'd be returning home, either, unless I specifically asked for a break. Instead, I would complete my inbound delivery and immediately pick up an export load, as often as not running up and down the M6 motorway on the western side of England without making the extra three-hour run back home. At home, Jane was responsible for every aspect of family life and I was an occasional visitor, whose arrival seemed more disruptive than essential. And while I did miss her and the children, I was part of a different world, one that was sufficiently engaging that I became used to living according to its own logic and its own demands.

Occasionally, I took one of the children with me, though returning them home again after a single trip wasn't always easy. I once had to put my seven-year-old stepson, Jason, on a coach in London to get him back to Caernarfon, some forty miles from home, where Jane went to meet him. I remember dropping the coach driver a couple of quid to make sure that Jason got back on the bus at every stop. Like so many other aspects of our life back then, it's hard to imagine anyone doing the same thing now.

Jane and I got used to being out of contact for days at a time, but I always phoned her as soon as I reached Dover – or early the following morning if I'd arrived too late to call. One evening – which I know was March 9th 1978 – I called home from Dover and was greeted by the gruff Welsh voice of our neighbour, John, "Congratulations, George, you've got a new daughter." Although I had, of course, been expecting the news, I hadn't yet arranged any time off for the imminent birth and found myself caught by surprise by our baby Rowan's arrival. I'd been present in the hospital when our older daughter, Laura, was born – when I was still studying for my MA – but this time I'd been somewhere in central France and was no support at all. And even then it was another twenty-four hours before I could get back to Oswestry and take a few days' break. By the time I reached home, Jane and our baby had already left the hospital in Bangor, and all the help she'd received had come from friends and neighbours.

At a distance of more than forty years, it seems incredible to me that I should have been so wrapped up in driving that I hadn't arranged a break. It somehow never occurred to me to ask for much time off and even the fact that I needed to keep earning money hardly seems to me now to have been any mitigation. It also never seemed to cross my mind that I might be needed at home. I have never had a great opinion of myself and I am still often surprised to find that people need me, or even like me – despite the fact that the children were clearly pleased to see me when I did get home, and Jane would be upset if I was called back to work earlier than expected. By the time I realised all this, it was already too late, but in the early years of my work as a Continental driver, I simply didn't see the danger signs in our relationship.

I had been getting home from time to time, mainly when I was called back to Oswestry every four or five weeks to have the truck serviced.

Often, however, I might call in to the yard for only a few hours, which didn't give me enough time to make the ninety-mile run to our home on the Welsh coast. Whether or not I went home, my truck always needed routine oil changes and other maintenance. This was carried out by a dozen or so mechanics that Cadwallader employed, and the company workshops could accommodate half a dozen tractor units and two or three trailers at a time. On the road, however, I was responsible, like any long-distance driver, for the daily monitoring of oil and water, and the condition of the tyres. Every morning, before I fired up the engine, I'd measure the oil level via a long dipstick reached through a panel in the front of the cab. I'd check the water level in the cooling system and walk round the truck, verifying that all the lights were working and kicking the tyres to ensure they were still hard. And among my growing collection of tools, the first was a 13mm spanner, which I used to adjust the trailer brakes. The '290' Volvo had a reputation for poor brakes, and the first thing Mike told me when I'd been given one temporarily in my second week with the company was to keep the trailer brakes adjusted so as to compensate for the inadequacy of those on the Volvo itself. The routine was simple; I'd crawl under the trailer and tighten the brakes with the spanner until they locked on. Then, I'd slacken the adjusting nut by half a turn so the wheels revolved freely, but leaving the brake shoes only just clear of the drums.

This worked well enough as long as I remembered to do it, and the truck itself usually reminded me if the brake performance deteriorated. Once, however, I was loading in Hastings abattoir and had just decided to make an overdue check on the trailer brakes when it started raining. Not wishing to get wet unnecessarily, I postponed the brake adjustment until I reached Dover, about two hours away. I'd have plenty of time for routine maintenance while I was waiting for the ferry to load. That had to be the day when I was pulled over for a 'ministry' safety check, only the second time it happened in my career as a driver. One overalled Ministry of Transport inspector got his hands dirty, while another, in a ministry-standard donkey jacket, made notes. And, of course, together they quite rightly decided that my trailer brakes were not correctly adjusted. They issued me with a 'GV9', the name for a document that prohibits the truck from moving until the fault has been rectified. The normal procedure is to bring a mechanic out to fix the problem or to have the vehicle towed away. Instead, I offered to do the job myself and the ministry men agreed, but only if I did the adjustment by the book, which involved jacking up each trailer wheel in turn, then verifying that the wheels would spin freely after the brakes had been adjusted. Given that I knew my normal method worked perfectly well, this smacked of officiousness, but I did it anyway and a second notice was issued rescinding the original GV9. These days, the whole process is a great deal more complicated and involves the truck being taken out of service, with an accompanying flurry of paperwork, but in those days it was simpler, and on this occasion I was back on the road with less than an hour's delay. And I caught the ferry I'd booked myself on, in the first stage of another trip to Italy.

Over the summer months, I became quite familiar with Aosta and, when I entered Italy with a load of meat, inured to the vagaries of the Italian customs. The *dogana* were predictably unpredictable and could keep us waiting for most of Monday if they felt like it, or let us go by mid-morning if they happened to be in a cooperative mood. This was all part of the job and although I grumbled with the other drivers, it was just another aspect of the job that needed patience and, sometimes, tact.

It was in Aosta that I found an introduction to the Middle East work I had always wanted. Not that I was looking for it. On the contrary, I was enjoying the work with Cadwallader, earning at least twice as much as I had at Williams, and I wasn't looking for a change. I loved my fast and new-ish '290' Volvo – by some margin, the best truck I'd ever driven – but one afternoon, my smooth weekly routine of peach delivery was seriously disrupted. Aosta was behind and below me as I headed towards the Mont Blanc Tunnel, freighted with peaches. All seemed well as I negotiated the switchback road up the narrowing valley, roaring through various short tunnels en route to the main bore through the mountain. I was used to the noise of the Volvo's engine reverberating from the tunnel walls, but at one point I heard a new and disturbing clatter, apparently coming from the gearbox. I changed down to a low gear, which seemed to reduce the racket, and limped into the next parking place along the road. Whatever had happened to the transmission made it impossible to continue with a load, so after weighing my choices, I decided to leave the trailer where it was and try to get back down to Aosta with the tractor unit alone, so as not to stress the transmission. On the way, I hoped to find a phone to call the yard.

In those days, phoning from Italy was a chore, unless you were in a café with a minute counter that would time your call and allow you to pay in cash. Otherwise, you needed a fistful of *gettones*, or tokens, that clanked through a payphone with remarkable speed when you phoned back to England. I stopped at the first phone I came to and, armed with a pocket-wrenching load of *gettones*, I got through to Mike back at the office. Cadwallader had two strategies for dealing with breakdowns: the first was to have the repair done locally and the second was to send a spare tractor unit from England on the back of a low-loader trailer. The former would probably be even more expensive than the latter, but given my load of time-sensitive peaches, Mike was inclined to save time by having the gearbox repaired. He asked me to phone back in five minutes, after he'd discussed the problem with Gordon and Phil. I jangled my reduced reserve of *gettones* in my hand as the five minutes crawled by. Finally, I phoned back and Mike directed me to the Volvo agent in Aosta.

I continued to nurse the tractor down the mountain and into the town, and found the Volvo workshop without much difficulty. Since it was already late afternoon, I was somewhat surprised, and even more delighted, that the Volvo mechanics got to work immediately. I rejoiced too soon; evidently, the damage was serious and we'd have to wait for a part to be shipped in from somewhere or other. At any rate, I seemed to be stranded for a couple of days and I was now a snail without its shell, since my truck was stuck in the workshop with its cab tilted, so I couldn't sleep in it. Instead, I got a lift to the cheap hotel attached to the customs compound. Once I'd checked in, I went down to the bar-restaurant where I'd spent many an hour waiting for customs in the past and there I found a couple of Middle East drivers waiting for money to be wired from the UK.

This was a surprisingly common affliction for drivers working for less reputable companies, particularly on Middle East runs, and Terry and John had already been waiting for two days when I joined them. The following morning, Terry offered to take his US-built Mack – an exotic truck in Europe – up the mountain to retrieve my trailer. It was my first experience of an American truck and I was as unimpressed with it as Terry was. The cab was horribly noisy, the ride was harsh and the transmission required two gearsticks to complete a range-change shift. Compared with my Volvo, the Mack seemed like a throwback to the 1940s, which, essentially, it was. On the other hand, it was at least a runner. It took us about half an hour to reach my trailer, which was, somewhat to my surprise, just as I'd left it, with the fridge motor still running and the locked and sealed doors intact. Terry reversed his Mack under the trailer, and together we connected the air-lines and wound up the landing legs. With a load on, the Mack was, if anything, even less lovely to ride in, but it did get my trailer parked outside the hotel, where I could keep an eye on it.

I checked in twice a day with the Volvo agent where, after the initial flurry of activity, nothing seemed to be happening. Terry and John made regular visits to the customs agent's office where their money was supposed to appear. We were all equally frustrated, but we gradually got used to hanging around in the restaurant, reading, chatting and, for one long and wine-fuelled evening, reciting and inventing a variety of illogical limericks. Terry seemed to have only one regret: that he had left a perfectly good Middle East transport firm for the empty promise of better pay with the cowboys who now employed him. When he learned that I was interested in Middle East work, Terry urged me to try his old boss, Jack Harrison, known affectionately to his drivers as 'The Pig'. He explained how to find Harrison's office in Brierley Hill in the Black Country, west of Birmingham.

When my gearbox was finally fixed after three days and I returned for the last time to the customs compound to pick up my trailer, Terry's final words to me were to talk to Jack about a job. I left him still waiting for money and I never saw him again, though I presume that he did finally get what he needed. Meanwhile, I headed back to England to deliver the peaches, with a whole new possibility occupying my mind.

CHAPTER 9
EASTWARD HO

I wasted no time in visiting Harrison's office. Although I'd delivered the late peaches to the fruit and vegetable market in Southampton, Mike had called me back to the yard, so Cadwallader's fitters could check the Italian repair. It was only a short detour off the M6 to Brierley Hill so I decided to drop in on Jack Harrison to see if Terry's recommendation carried any weight. I found the office just as he'd described it, opposite the Round Oak steelworks. "You can't miss it," Terry had assured me. "It's right next to a café and there's a sign across the bottom of the window, with Baghdad, Jeddah, Jordan and all Middle East names on it." The office was, in fact, a converted shop, one of a row that included the café, with a Shell petrol station further along the street. The bottom half of the shop windows had been whited out and the names of various Middle Eastern countries were printed across them.

"Jack's always standing in the window with a fag in his mouth," Terry had said, "watching the world go by." But not today. Instead, I found a friendly woman, not unlike Miss John back at Williams, but with a mild Black Country accent instead of a Welsh lilt and a sharper sense of humour. Her name was Jess and she was Harrison's secretary, and transport manager when he was away. The office itself was fairly small, dominated by a wide, modern desk, with a large colour television next to it. The office wall opposite the window was taken up by a board covered with a chart showing the registration numbers of Harrison's trucks, with their destinations written next to them. I glanced down the list and totted up the fleet to total eleven trucks, which, judging by their registrations, were all less than two years old. This was a good sign, though I later discovered that two years is a long time in the life of a truck running exclusively to Tehran. More exciting was the list of destinations. When I'd first entered Cadwallader's office eighteen months earlier, I'd been attracted by a similar, though much larger, chart showing destinations such as Paris, Basel, Munich or Rome. Harrison's list showed several trucks running to Dubai, a couple to Jeddah and a handful to Baghdad. This was the big time, the job I'd hoped for ever since I'd travelled through Turkey at the age of eighteen, when I'd seen those British trucks waiting for a ferry to cross the Bosphorus.

Jess and I were soon chatting like old friends. It seemed that Jack had some vacancies and Jess thought there was a good chance of my being taken on. I explained that I had no Middle East experience, though I had been to the Middle East when I travelled overland to India as a teenager, and as a truck driver I knew my way as far eastwards as Austria. Jess didn't think my lack of experience would be a problem and she encouraged me to phone Jack as soon as possible. After almost an hour, I walked out to the Volvo, imagining myself setting out for Saudi Arabia, or somewhere equally exotic. All the same, I was in two minds as I drove on to Oswestry, less than two hours away. I was well established at Cadwallader and in the fifteen months I'd been at the firm, I'd made some good friends. By comparison with Harrison, Caddy's had a comforting solidity and an easy familiarity. But I decided to pursue the Harrison opportunity; after all, I was in the happy position of looking for a job while still holding one that I enjoyed. What was there to lose?

The next morning, while my truck was being serviced in the workshop, I went up the road to a phone box, where I could phone Harrison without being overheard. I was slightly nervous as I dialled, remembering Terry's account of Jack's fierce manner. Terry had also warned me that Harrison had a disconcerting habit of answering with a false name. Just as well that I was forewarned because a gruff voice answered, "Brown," and paused. I explained who I was and said that Jess had told me to phone him. She'd obviously mentioned me, because Jack seemed to recognise who I was. This encouraging thought didn't last long.

"What Middle East have you done?" Jack asked.

"None," I said. "I told your secretary that I've only done Europe."

"Well…" Jack paused. "You'd better be as good as you cracked yourself up to my girl or I'll wring your bloody neck."

Cracked myself up? I wasn't aware that I'd tried to sell myself at all. On the contrary, I'd gone out of my way to stress my limited experience, because I knew what happened when other drivers did the opposite; nothing made you less popular than pretending to know what you didn't. With a future employer, it was a ludicrous hostage to fortune. I stammered something unremarkable and Jack told me to phone him during the week to try to arrange a meeting when I got back from my next trip. The whole exchange didn't sound particularly auspicious and I said nothing about leaving when I returned to Caddy's yard.

That week, I was due to do a delivery to Bordeaux, a milk run compared with the peaches routine; perhaps my last trip had discouraged Phil and Mike. It was a pleasant excursion out through Poole in the south-west of England, and while western France is lovely country at any time of year, it was improved by the August heat. The backload was seventeen tonnes of red wine, a load to savour, and would take me north through Birmingham again. I called Jack from Cherbourg and arranged to meet him at two o'clock on Sunday.

Promptly at two, I once again parked outside Harrison's office in Brierley Hill. Without the weekday bustle, the area seemed desolate and unfriendly. Round Oak steelworks was quiet, Jack's office was deserted and, of course, the café was closed. I sat in the cab and made myself a cup of tea. By three o'clock, I'd almost persuaded myself I didn't want the bloody job anyway and I was quite happy where I was. That last part, at least, was true. By 3.30pm there was still no sign of anyone and I was just getting ready to leave when a silver Mercedes car pulled up in front of my truck, and a large man in a black overcoat hauled himself out. He wasn't more than six foot, but he held himself very straight. I later discovered that Jack was a former guardsman and he was as impressive as his phone manner was intimidating. As I climbed down from the Volvo, I saw that Jack was looking at it and clocking its new registration letter. Just as my new Seddon Atkinson at Williams had been a reference for Cadwallader, so my new-ish Volvo in Caddy's colours was a recommendation for Jack. He didn't comment, however, but apologised for keeping me waiting; apparently there'd been some unspecified trouble with one of his trucks just down the road. Jack unlocked the office and led the way back into the office where I'd met Jess, past the partition with a window in it through which subcontracting drivers picked up their orders for work out of the steelworks. He sat behind the desk and offered me a low chair in front of it. Whether by accident or design – I suspected the latter – the height difference made me feel further at a disadvantage.

After Jack's threatening manner on the phone, I was expecting detailed questioning about my career to date, but in fact we launched into a long conversation about the transport industry in general and, in particular, how his business had developed since he started it ten years earlier. He had set out hauling steel bar from the Round Oak works opposite and still had contracts for many loads a week, which he almost exclusively subcontracted out, while his own trucks covered the growing Middle East operation. Harrison's outfit might have been a lot smaller than Cadwallader's, but it was evidently prospering since he'd just bought five new Dafs to run a large subcontract to Dubai and Jeddah. The rest of his fleet consisted of a couple of slightly older Dafs and four German-built Magirus-Deutz. Getting ahead of myself, I thought that I'd be happy with a Daf, but I'd always viewed Maggies with suspicion. At one point, Jack admitted that sometimes, when a group of his trucks left together, he'd jump into his car and drive ahead of them to a bridge over the motorway, so he could watch the line of his trucks passing beneath him. I warmed to him straightaway; I'd have wanted to do the same.

After an hour or so, he stood up, walked to the window and, with his back to me, said, "OK, you can have the job, but I'm telling you now that we celebrate Muslim Christmas." Sorry? "That means if a job comes up that needs you to be away over Christmas, you'll have to go." Without even considering what this would mean to Jane and the children, I agreed. After all, Christmas was months away and it would all work out. We shook hands and I told Jack I'd have to give a week's notice at Cadwallader. We agreed I would start a week on Monday, but Jack would have to keep my passport so he could arrange a visa for Saudi

Arabia. Once again I agreed, and it was only when I was back on the M6 motorway that I realised the lack of a passport meant I'd have to work out my notice in the UK.

The following morning I phoned Caddy's office to tell them my news, which caused barely a ripple in the running of the company. However, since I couldn't travel abroad, I would now spend a week on UK work, which meant taking my loading orders from Tony Ellis at the UK traffic desk. Although I'd never worked directly for him, Tony and I had always got on well, and he somehow arranged that my last load would be to ICI's explosives plant at Penrhyndeudraeth, only a few miles across the causeway from my old base in Porthmadog. That meant I'd be able to drop the trailer and take the Volvo home for the night.

It was less than eighteen months since I'd worked at Williams, but my outlook on driving had altered dramatically. I'd travelled to ten different European countries and covered far more of the UK than I had in my previous jobs. Williams seemed a long way behind me, but when I rolled into the ICI plant in the late morning, I was surprised and delighted to run into my old mate Parry, who had also moved on from the Porthmadog haulier. He was now a fitter for ICI and we exchanged news and reminiscences for a few minutes while I waited to tip. With Tony's implicit permission to go home – "Phone me in the morning," he'd said – I headed west to Pwllheli, where I dropped my box trailer on the dockside, as I used to do for Williams. I covered the last few miles as fast as I could and parked the Volvo on the steep hill outside our cottage.

It was a short visit home, as usual, and this time when I left I'd have even less idea of how long I'd be away than I did at Cadwallader. Jane and I both knew that, at best, it would be at least a month, though once the trip was over I would have a clear week at home, which might even be better than the breaks I had at Caddy's. Jane accepted that it had long been my ambition to drive to the Middle East, and even though my new job might make me even more unsatisfactory as a partner, she said nothing against it. With the hindsight of forty years, I'm appalled at my own selfishness. As always, I told myself I was being responsible by earning us all a living, but I was doing it entirely on my terms. The idea that Jane, self-reliant though she was, might actually need me to stick around never entered my head. Or if it did, it was quickly squashed. Money might be tight for a while, too. At Caddy's, a cheque had gone into my account automatically every week; now, I would be paid only at the end of the trip. Harrison paid 'trip money', a set amount for each destination. If each trip went well, I could end up better paid than at Cadwallader, where I was paid by the day. But if there were delays, the job at Harrison would be a financial headache. For once, however, Jane and I had a small cushion and I hoped for the best.

I left as late as I could the following morning and drove back to Oswestry for the last time. I said goodbye to Phil, Mike and Tony, and shook hands with Gordon Cadwallader, who told me I'd always have a job with him if I wanted it. It was a reassuring note on which to launch myself into unknown territory, but I was now in an oddly rootless condition. I no longer had a truck to call home and I had none of my in-cab equipment – sleeping bag, stove, cooking gear and tools – which I had stashed with my brother, Ben, in London a few days before. And I still had a night to kill before I could present myself at Brierley Hill. Not wanting to waste any money, I decided to spend the night in the less-than-salubrious digs above the Hollies transport café, close to where the A5 trunk road met the M6 motorway. One of my Cadwallader colleagues gave me a lift to the café, before he headed on south to Dover. I wished I were running with him and I felt very alone without the protective shell of my truck. I had an enormous supper, for which the always-open Hollies was justly famous, and tried in vain to listen to the TV above the hubbub of chatter. Finally, I gave up the struggle and passed a miserable night between the Hollies' yellow brushed-nylon sheets. It was a depressing beginning to my Middle East career and, if I'd only known it, a harbinger of crises to come.

CHAPTER 10
THE MIDDLE EAST – FIRST STEPS

The next morning, I had no trouble in finding a lift from the Hollies with a southbound driver, who dropped me at the nearest motorway junction to Brierley Hill. When I arrived at Harrison's offices on the morning of Monday September 25th 1978, I had only a vague idea of what I would be doing, and no clue what my first destination would be, but I immediately faced the first of a series of setbacks, in the shape of the Saudis.

As soon as I met him, Jack told me that the Saudi Embassy had refused to give me a visa, and for the stupidest of oversights on my part. In those days, British passports showed the bearer's occupation and I had never bothered to change mine from 'student' to 'truck driver'. As long as my travels had been confined to Europe, this hadn't mattered, but the Saudis were more particular. In any case, my passport photo, taken when I was two months shy of eighteen, showed a beardless youth who couldn't possibly have masqueraded as a long-haul driver. In the week that Jack had had my passport, another of his drivers had taken it, along with his own, to the Saudi Embassy in London. When it had been rejected, the driver, Brian 'Whispering' Smith, had returned to London to take my passport to the central London passport office in Petty France, where the job description had been amended. This had taken so long that there had been no time left for the Embassy to issue a visa before I departed. Jack told me I'd have to pick up a Saudi visa in Jordan, en route. "I ought to charge you £50 for the cost of sending Brian down to London twice," he added, darkly. At that early stage, I hadn't learnt to read his moods and it was a poor beginning to our relationship. I didn't yet know, as I would later learn, that Jack's bark was considerably worse than his bite, and in the year I worked for him, he never followed up on his blustering threats. In fact, his only concern was to make sure his drivers didn't cheat him. As long as we were straight with him, Jack would forgive almost anything else, as I soon discovered, since the visa debacle was only the start.

At least I had almost learned my destination. I was due to leave later in the week either for Jeddah on the Red Sea, or Dubai, clear across Saudi Arabia at the far end of the Persian Gulf. If I'd thought Basel was a glamorous destination when I left Williams to work for Cadwallader, Jeddah and Dubai were a whole new world. Meanwhile, wrong-footed from the moment of my arrival, I spent an uncomfortable couple of hours cooped up in Jack's office, while I waited for the arrival of Hippy John, an experienced Middle East hand whom Jack had hired to cover the rush of work to Dubai. We were to go together that afternoon to Evesham, an hour and a half to the south, to load a trailer in the yard belonging to Spiers & Hartwell, a haulage company that had grown up carrying farm produce from the Vale of Evesham, but now combined this with traffic to the Middle East. Spiers were the main contractor to Weir Westgarth, a Glasgow-based company that was then building huge desalination plants in Dubai and Jeddah. With the help of several smaller subcontractors, including Harrison, Spiers & Hartwell were shipping up to fifty trailer-loads a month of assorted pipework and pumping equipment. These were trunked down by Hartwell's own vehicles from Glasgow to Evesham, where they were sorted into loads for the international trucks to pick up. Jack had decided that I should spend a couple of days loading trailers in Evesham for other drivers, before leaving myself on Wednesday evening.

Hippy John arrived mid-morning and the reason for his nickname became clear. His shoulder-length hair, prematurely grey, was held back by a decorated headband, and if he wasn't a hippy in the San Francisco sense, he certainly looked unusual for a British driver. I was intimidated by the vast array of tools and equipment he had brought in his van, as well as a large quantity of tinned food and general supplies. Jack had allocated him to one of the Magirus-Deutz 310s, whose V10 engine was rated at 310bhp, a high output in those days. John spent the best part of an hour loading tools and spares into the cab and securing a large wooden chest to the chassis behind it, before we set off together in the solo tractor unit to load the trailer he would be leaving with that night.

John spent much of the drive down to Evesham complaining that "it wasn't our bloody job to load", but as a driver on my first day in a new job, I was inclined to be cooperative. When we arrived at Hartwell's yard, half a dozen trailers stood in various stages of loading and ours was halfway ready. I climbed onto the bed of the trailer and helped guide the crates and pipes into position. John complained loudly on the sidelines, but finally joined in, all the while making it clear that he was doing everyone a favour. Since I'd been driving a refrigerated truck for the past year, it was hard work to scramble all over the trailer, sorting out where each item should go, but I quietly enjoyed it. Besides, if I were to be responsible for hauling a trailer over 4000 miles of sometimes bad or non-existent roads, I wanted to be sure the goods were on properly.

When John's load was complete and secured, he and I reassembled the 'tilt'. This consisted of a series of steel posts and crosspieces down each side of the trailer, between which were slotted wooden slats to maintain the van-like shape of the tilt and hold the load in place. Over the whole construction came a heavy plastic fitted sheet, with eyelets every few inches along its bottom edge that fitted over steel loops along the trailer's folding sideboards. Through these loops, securing the tilt sheet in place, we threaded a plastic-sheathed steel cable whose ends met at the rear of the trailer. Loops in each end of the tilt cord would be fastened with a customs seal in Dover, which would, in theory, go unbroken all the way to the trailer's final destination, under the international *Transports Internationaux Routiers*, or TIR, agreement.

With the trailer finally ready for the road, John and I headed back to Brierley Hill, where Jack was busy organising the paperwork for the load we'd brought back, so that John could leave that evening. Two other trucks would be travelling with him and, although I didn't realise it at the time, the other two drivers were greenhorns like me. Hippy John would be shepherding them both to Dubai. I wasn't sorry to see him go; his constant grumbling about the unavoidable – and, in my view, necessary – chore of loading had been dispiriting and had added to my sense of dislocation.

Once John and his newbies had left, Jack took me in his Mercedes to pick up the truck I would be driving. Jack didn't have a yard of his own and, with his trucks returning home so rarely, he didn't really need one. Instead, his tractor units and trailers were parked all over Brierley Hill in the yards of various friends and rivals in the transport business. Five minutes from the office, we drove through a wide, open gateway in a remote part of the steelworks and into a hard-dirt compound filled with flatbed steel trailers and assorted tractor units belonging to other firms. Jack's Merc purred to a halt in front of another Magirus. Even discounting the distorting effect of sodium street lighting, my new motor was not a prepossessing sight. It was painted in a busy colour scheme of yellow and bilious green, the livery of Davies Turner, a London freight forwarder who had made a speciality of Middle East work. The paintwork alone proved that Harrison was one of Davies Turner's regular subcontractors. Although it was less than two years old, judging by its registration plate, the Maggie had obviously had a hard life. I later discovered that its previous driver tended to hit things, which accounted for the fact that the cab leaned slightly to the left. At some stage in its short career, the front left cab mounting had been broken and hadn't been properly repaired. Inside, I was dismayed to find that instead of a radio-cassette player, there was an eight-track tape player, which even in 1978 was obsolete. I realised that my extensive collection of cassette tapes would do me no good, and that once the radio went out of range of the BBC or Radio Luxembourg, I'd be without any entertainment at all. The rest of the cab was equally unappealing, but I decided to defer a spring clean until the following day. We returned to Jack's office, where he surprised me by striding to the Shell station nearby and buying me a blanket, having learned that all my gear was stashed in London. Once he'd left, I found a phone box to call Jane, which did little to dispel my loneliness, and then took the Maggie to the nearest cinema for an exciting night out in downtown Dudley.

The next day, I was sent to pick up a trailer from the Gilflex rental company in Birmingham, which I then took down to Spiers & Hartwell's yard at Evesham. It was another fine September day and my spirits rose when I met one of Hartwell's own drivers, Tony – a cheerful chap about my own age, and known as 'Spud' to distinguish him from the two other Tonys in the firm. Together we loaded my trailer, guiding the assorted pipes and crates into place, and unslinging them from the crane hook. Spud was quite particular about the process and I realised I had been right the previous day to take an interest in the distribution of the load. With the trailer loaded and the tilt secured, I decided to clean out the interior of the cab and wash the outside, while I waited for my paperwork. Might as well start straight, and there are few things more discouraging than having an untidy truck to work in.

I cleared out the assortment of bottles and newspapers that littered the floor and, to my amusement, found some souvenirs jammed behind the end of the bunk that spoke volumes about the previous tenant. No fewer than four pairs of discarded women's knickers suggested the previous driver was as enthusiastic as he was untidy. When I later described my find to a long-time Harrison hand, he wasn't in the least surprised. I never dared mention it to the driver himself, though he and I later shared various adventures that, sadly, had nothing to do with women. By the time I'd cleaned the cab, my papers were ready and I returned to Brierley Hill, where I dropped the loaded trailer in a yard belonging to another of Jack's accommodating friends and picked up another Gilflex rental trailer.

Now that I had a cab in which to stow things, I decided to stock up with food for the journey, which I now knew would be to Dubai. I figured on being away for five weeks and whereas there had been cheap places to eat across Western Europe, if I were to wait for a restaurant to appear in the deserts of Saudi Arabia, I'd be getting very hungry. Self-sufficiency had felt good in Europe, but it was a necessity further east. Taking a leaf from Hippy John's book, I bought £50 worth of canned food, long-life milk, and crackers as a substitute for bread. With these provisions stowed on the bottom bunk, I headed back with the empty trailer to spend the night in Evesham and avoid an early start from Brierley Hill. At the back of my mind was Jack's warning to keep checking the wheel nuts of the Magirus, since Maggies had a tendency to lose their wheels. I resolved to check them first thing in the morning in Hartwell's yard. In any case, I didn't believe that they could have loosened in the few miles I'd driven the truck; as often as I had been used to checking the wheel nuts of my Volvo, they had never been slack. What I didn't reckon with was that the Maggie's wheel nuts might not have been tightened for some time before I took over.

Meanwhile, I had to contend with the truck's uncooperative ZF gearbox, which made me miss my previous truck more than anything. In place of the slick sixteen-speed Volvo transmission with its smooth synchromesh, the Maggie had an eight-speed range-change constant-mesh box with an extra low crawler ratio. This meant a return to double declutching on each gear change, but the ZF box was much more finicky than the Fuller box I'd been used to in all my trucks at Williams, and I had to get the revs exactly right to make the shift go through. Too many times on that first run to Evesham, I was greeted with a graunching noise that meant restarting the whole gearshift. I'd figured out the Maggie's gearbox by the time I reached Hartwell's yard, but I never learned to like it.

Meanwhile, loading was fun, freed from the drag of Hippy John's complaints. Several of Hartwell's own trailers were parked outside the large, modern warehouse in the middle of the yard. The Weir Westgarth equipment was stacked inside and out, some crates up to eight-foot high, but most of them half that size. I now felt quite at home in Hartwell's yard and Spud greeted me as an old friend, as we loaded side by side. I envied him his trailer. I was stuck with a basic UK rental trailer but his was properly equipped for Middle East work. It had a 2500-litre 'belly tank' bolted fore and aft between the main chassis beams, and extending below them, which would allow him to fill up with dirt-cheap diesel from the countries where it was extracted. On the right side of the trailer, which would be the nearside on foreign roads, were two large steel boxes for stowing food, cooking equipment, tools, spares and water. From two hefty steel hooks hung a set of snow chains. Having none of these refinements on my own trailer, I felt somewhat ill prepared. However, I assumed the weather would be fine in central Europe this early in the year so that I wouldn't need chains, and as for the convenience of trailer boxes, I had already reconciled myself to using my cab for stowage.

Probably because this was the day I would be leaving for Dover and Dubai, this was the afternoon when the papers took forever, and it wasn't until teatime that I was ready to roll. I phoned Jack to let him know I was on my way and he told me I'd be leaving that evening, with a new companion. He'd already informed me I'd be running with another driver, though I had yet to meet him. He was yet another newcomer at Harrison's, but Jack told me he had Middle East experience. I had mixed feelings about this. On the one hand, it would be useful to be with someone who knew the Middle East, but on the other it would mean living in each other's pockets for up to five weeks, so a lot depended on whether we suited each other. At Cadwallader's we'd chosen our own companions, drivers with a style similar to our own, and the nature of the job had meant I'd usually run alone. I hoped for the best, but feared the worst.

If the Saudi visa fiasco had been the first unwelcome portent of things to come, the second came even before I set out on the journey proper. All seemed well as I rolled northwards from Evesham to join the motorway, but I stopped just before the motorway to check my lights and when I tried to restart, the parking brake wouldn't come off. I checked the three air pressure gauges and all seemed normal. I tried pumping the footbrake, which sometimes releases the handbrake. Nothing. I climbed up behind the cab and disconnected the air-lines from the trailer and discovered that the fault seemed to lie with the rental trailer itself. Eventually, after an hour of fiddling about, I decided to phone Jack and tell him I'd be delayed, but I felt decidedly stupid. If I was unable to fix what must be a minor fault in Worcestershire, how would I fare in the desert?

Using my tachograph card to flag down a passing truck, I hitched a ride to a phone box and explained the situation to Jack. He told me the truck had just returned from being serviced by the Magirus dealer and it was up to them to sort it out. I didn't fancy being on the other end of the line when Jack called the dealer, but whatever he said, it still took the mechanic two hours to arrive. I didn't ask him why it had taken so long to drive the fifteen miles from the city and I just hoped he wouldn't discover that I'd overlooked something obvious. While I held a torch in the gathering dark, the fitter worked under the trailer, checking all the potential weak spots, as I had done. I was relieved that he was having trouble, because it made me look less foolish. Finally, after another hour, the fitter managed to release the brakes, though he wasn't confident that the problem wouldn't reoccur. I didn't really care, as long as I was on my way.

It was nine o'clock by the time I reached the office, and the parade of shops was depressingly dark, apart from the light spilling out of Jack's office window front. Jack was still there, waiting to see me off. Now I knew why the television was part of the office equipment. Sitting in the low chair in which I had been interviewed was the other driver, whom Jack introduced as Maurice. He was about forty, with a lopsided and diffident grin, but he seemed friendly enough and he promised Jack he'd look after me. While Jack checked our papers and counted out our running money, Maurice and I went out to inspect the trucks. He was also driving a Magirus, so at least neither of us was likely to outpace the other. However, my confidence in him was slightly diminished when he suggested we check the water level in the radiators, since the Magirus was famously air-cooled and didn't need any coolant. However, I didn't think too badly of him; after all, I hadn't driven one myself until Monday, though I had long known about the Maggie's cooling system. Somewhere in the back of my mind lurked the wheel nuts. Oh well, I'd check them in Dover.

Since I had to stop in west London to pick up all my gear from my brother, Ben, I left before Maurice, agreeing to meet him early the following morning at a Little Chef café on the A2 between London and Dover. Jack went through my papers with me and made me count the stack of 6000 Deutsche Marks – about £1500 in those days – that I'd need for fuel and expenses. When all was ready, Jack and I shook hands in a rather formal way and I was off, expecting to be gone for five weeks. As I drove through the orange-lit streets of Dudley, watching people strolling along the pavements, and going in and out of friendly-looking pubs, I felt an unusual sense of unreality. Here were folk going about their homely business and I was setting off into the night on a 4000-mile run that would take me away for at least a month, mostly through countries I'd never yet visited.

By the time I'd picked up all my travel gear from my brother's flat in Chiswick and reached the café on the A2, it was two o'clock in the morning. Maurice had already arrived and his cab was dark, so I parked beside him and crawled onto the top bunk. One of the deficiencies of the Magirus's cab was a lack of curtains, apart from a short one in front of the bunk, so it was impossible to blot out the lights of the car park – gloomy though they were – let alone get undressed in private. I was too tired to care and I wasn't planning on more than three or four hours of sleep if we were to reach Köln that afternoon. But for my brake delay, we'd already have been on the ferry.

I woke at first light and dressed hurriedly. I banged on Maurice's cab until I got an incoherent shout of acknowledgement and went into the café for some tea. 'Little Chefs' were never my idea of a proper place to eat, and their soulless uniformity seemed all the worse because so many of them stood on the site of former traditional transport cafes that once sold decent breakfasts and properly resolute tea. Today, however, the plastic blandness of the café matched my mood, and however uninspiring the tea was, I was into my second cup before Maurice staggered in, looking quite as bad as I felt, but still managing to grin feebly. We drank our teas in near silence, having decided to make straight for Dover and eat breakfast on the ferry.

An hour later, we rolled down the familiar Jubilee Way viaduct that sweeps in a wide curve over and down to Dover's Eastern Docks – with the famous white cliffs away on our left – and parked in the customs shed. Early on a Thursday morning there was no queue and we huddled in the small, glassed-in room outside the customs window to have our TIR 'carnet' stamped. I had used carnets before, having once travelled beyond the EEC to Hungary for Cadwallader, but this one was much longer. The yellow booklet consisted of twenty foolscap sheets, with counterfoils, on which were printed the details of the load, its weight and value, and the route we would follow from Dover to Dubai, specifying not only the countries we would transit but each border crossing we would use. At the entry and exit point of each country, a page and its counterfoil would be stamped, so that each transit country required two sheets. The list of ten countries for this trip looked routine or intimidating, depending on whether you were the bored-looking customs officer stamping the carnet or the excited new boy who'd be doing the driving: Belgium, Germany, Austria, Yugoslavia (as it then was), Greece, Syria, Jordan, Saudi Arabia, Qatar and the United Arab Emirates. While we checked that each page had indeed been stamped, to avoid problems later, a customs officer emerged from the office to seal our trailers, threading a woven steel wire through the loops at each end of the tilt cord and then through a lead disc, which he clamped to the wires. It would be impossible to unthread the cords and open the tilt without breaking the seal, so, in theory at least, an unbroken seal meant that nothing could have been smuggled in or out of a transit country. Under the international TIR agreement, transit countries were supposed to respect the seal of the country of origin, but the further east we went, I found out, the less this was true.

With the TIR customs rigmarole completed, I was back on familiar turf as Maurice and I drove round to join the lines of trucks at the dockside. We were booked on a Townsend ferry to Zeebrugge, and as I waited for the usual loading routine, I decided, at last, to check the Maggie's wheels. The wheel-brace consisted of a socket at one end of a steel bar, which had a hole across the other end, through which I inserted a plain four-foot bar. Slotting the socket onto each wheel's ten nuts in turn, I stepped onto the cross bar and gave it all my weight. There was, as I expected, a little slack in all the nuts, but on one of the rear wheels, as hard as I turned the wheel-brace, the nuts refused to tighten. My heart sank. Clearly, the nuts had become so loose that the twin wheels had worn the studs and damaged the threads. At the very least, the studs would have to be replaced, and possibly the wheels.

Maurice and I considered the problem, but there was not much we could do on this side of the water, since we were already lined up to load. Instead, we decided to cross over to Belgium, as scheduled, and try to fix the studs there. I felt sick and, frankly, fearful of Jack's reaction when I phoned him, as I would have to. With five weeks of driving, and ten countries in front of me, I hadn't even managed to leave England without jeopardising two wheels, and I would probably lose them within a matter of miles if I attempted to continue. I wondered whether Jack might even send another driver to replace me since we were still so close to home, though I persuaded myself this was unlikely, given that we were already slightly behind our tight schedule. Weir Westgarth required that their equipment spent only two weeks in transit, so we had only fourteen days to reach Dubai. With my experience of the peach run, I supposed Jack would face some kind of financial penalty if we were late, which was likely to make his reaction all the worse.

Maurice was very kind about it, as we discussed the problem over breakfast in the ferry's driver canteen, and resisted what must have been considerable temptation to make fun of my predicament; perhaps he was simply relieved that it hadn't happened to him. "We'll have to phone Jack," Maurice said, but I wanted to try to arrange a repair first.

"Let's see if there's a Maggie dealer in Zeebrugge," I suggested. "At least we'll be able to find out what the damage is. And at any rate, we've had it, as far as reaching Cologne tonight goes." The two-week deadline was looking delicate and we still hadn't reached Belgium. Maurice said he would phone Jack and I sheepishly agreed to let him take the heat.

By the time we'd finished breakfast, the ferry had already left the harbour. We bought two cartons of cigarettes each, for ourselves and to use as tips where necessary, and returned to our cabin in the bowels of the ship, hoping for four hours' sleep before we docked. Through the curving steel wall of the cabin, I could hear the sound of the sea swishing against the hull, and the cabin throbbed quietly with the vibrations of the engine. In spite of my worries, I fell asleep, and in no time the door of the cabin was thrown open and the steward snapped on the light. "Come on, gents," he shouted. "We'll be in in fifteen minutes." I know this wasn't true, and that he only wanted us out of the way so that he could clean the cabins in good time for the return crossing. Feeling the worse for wear and in no mood for work, or talking to Jack, I went to find a cup of tea in the steward's tiny galley. Maurice and I leaned against the counter and exchanged desultory conversation with the few other drivers on board. We returned to our trucks as the ferry nosed up to the link-span, with the bow door hoisted high on hydraulic rams.

The tide was low, so the link-span from ship to shore was fairly steep and the harsh sound of the air-cooled V10 reverberated against the steel sides of the ramp as the Magirus grumbled up the slope. It was a typical

Zeebrugge afternoon, overcast and blustery. Puddles of water showed that it had been raining earlier, while patches of sand across the tarmac had been blown from the nearby beach. The ferry terminal stood apart from the main dock area and the tall grey buildings looked cheerless along the seafront. Maurice and I parked to one side and joined the other drivers in the short queue for customs. Most of the other drivers needed only a single stamp on their T-forms, but a TIR carnet needed annotating and the process took longer. The drivers behind us muttered about being held up.

With the customs out of the way, we found a phone and called Jack. Maurice did the talking and my imagination supplied the other side of the conversation. "Hello, Jack? This is Maurice. We've got a bit of a problem." I cringed as Maurice looked at me. "The wheel nuts are loose on one of the rear wheels of George's unit; looks like it'll need new studs." Maurice listened and looked at me again. "Well, I don't think he's too happy," he said. He listened a little longer and hung up.

"There's a Maggie dealer in Bruges, Jack says."

"OK," I said. "I'll drop the trailer and take the unit in. It's only about twenty k's and it should be all right if I take it steady." We agreed that Maurice might as well stay in Zeebrugge while I drove to the Magirus workshop and have them assess the damage. The middle of Bruges is a beautiful medieval town with narrow streets surrounding a magnificent market square and, to my amazement, the Magirus dealer was near the town centre, not in the more industrial outskirts. It was just as well that I didn't have the trailer with me, because it would never have been able to negotiate the tight corners. It was by now nearly one o'clock in the afternoon and I worried that it would be too late to repair the truck that day, but I was told to bring the unit straight in; truck dealers generally have a different understanding of urgency than their car counterparts. I reversed from the street into a long garage with an arched roof. The building seemed incongruously old for a modern truck workshop and had probably been a warehouse for centuries before garages were necessary.

While I watched, a fitter removed the offending wheels and the foreman examined them. People in the Flemish part of Belgium rarely admit to knowing French, but they will make an exception for a foreigner, so I was able to understand the foreman's explanation, though the damage was painfully obvious when I looked at it. The two wheels had worn around the studs, so that the holes were elongated, rendering the wheels unusable. It would be necessary to replace not only the ten studs, but also to fit two new wheels. The cost would be about 14,000 Belgian francs or £200. I was aghast; at this rate, I would have spent my running money before I even left Europe. Trying not to think of the impending conversation with Jack, I told them to go ahead. In any case, there was no alternative, and while the work went ahead I found a bank and changed sufficient Deutsche Marks to cover the bill. I did my best to enjoy the medieval town square but I was too preoccupied with the truck to relax, and soon returned to the garage, where the repairs were completed in less than two hours. I opened my expenses account with the entry: 'wheel repairs – £200'. A great start.

The garage threw in the cost of a call to Jack and I found him surprisingly calm, even when I told him the cost. "I don't mind this time," he said, "but you'd better not do it again." Which is what I thought. "I think we'll have to nickname you 'wheel nut'," he continued, "unless I can think of anything worse."

"We won't make the train tonight," I told him, "but we'll be there in plenty of time for tomorrow's train."

"Right," he said. "Phone me from Spielfeld (at least two days away on the Austria-Yugoslav border) to let me know how you're getting on, and this time, *check those bloody wheel nuts.*" This last instruction was quite unnecessary. For the rest of the trip, I became a wheel nut fanatic. If it was a failing of Maggies that their wheels came loose, it wasn't going to happen to me again. From Bruges to Dubai and back to Birmingham, I checked the wheels two or three times a day, to the great amusement of my fellow drivers, particularly when I explained the reason.

It was dusk by the time I returned to Zeebrugge, where Maurice and I hitched up my trailer and cooked ourselves a snack. Even though we'd scarcely left home, we were already in self-sufficiency mode, which seemed more pronounced now that I was, in theory at least, a Middle East driver. It never occurred to us to go to a restaurant, and after my recent expenses I was inclined to be frugal. Köln was only four hours away and since the train didn't leave until early evening, we could reach it comfortably the next day, without any need for an early start. Now, finally, I hoped we could be on our way.

CHAPTER 11

THROUGH EASTERN EUROPE

The next morning, we set off through the flat, damp countryside of northern Belgium, heading towards Gent and Antwerp. On either side of the motorway the land was divided into small fields separated by water-filled ditches, like *Alice Through the Looking Glass*. Here and there a farmer ploughed with horses, an incongruous picture beside a motorway filled with speeding cars and trucks. With only a short break for breakfast in a parking area on the outskirts of Antwerp, we reached the Aachen *Süd* crossing into Germany by lunchtime.

All German borders were a complex affair in those days, with several forms to be filled in and stamped, and now the whole process was made more time-consuming by our TIR carnets. To my surprise, Maurice seemed to have no idea what to do, which I found vaguely disquieting; wasn't he supposed to be showing me the way? Having crossed into Germany enough times for Caddy's that I had learned the German customs rigmarole, I could at least begin to balance the books on the wheel nut fiasco. Maurice followed me from one customs window to another, as we gathered the necessary stamps on the *laufzettel* paper, proving we'd covered all the customs requirements. Without it, we'd be unable to pass through the barrier at the compound's exit and enter the country.

If Köln sounds romantic, with its medieval cathedral that miraculously survived Allied attempts to destroy it during the war, where we were heading was anything but. Skirting the city altogether, we left the *autobahn* to enter a vast railway goods yard, where we would be putting our trucks onto a train. With transit permits in short supply, particularly for smaller outfits such as Harrison's, some bright spark at the German transport ministry had come up with an idea to make a little extra money for the *Deutsche Bahn* national railway. Foreign hauliers could have as many transit permits as they wanted, provided that they took the ferry train from Köln to Munich, for which they'd be charged a tidy sum. Since Germany lay astride the route to the Middle East, there was no avoiding it, and when Maurice and I trundled into the yard, several other Middle East trucks were already waiting to board. Check-in was in a small hut manned by a bored, middle-aged railway man who scarcely looked at us. We were, after all, just another piece of freight.

I followed Maurice's trailer as we lurched across the uneven ground to join the short line of waiting trucks. Two of them belonged to Hicks of Rhiwderin, in South Wales, and were driven by a pair of brothers. The older, Alan Hobbs, was of medium height, with a large bushy beard in the style of an American mountain man. His younger brother, Rob, was tall with matinee idol looks that suited the image of a long-haul adventurer. Alan was having trouble starting his Mercedes, but my offers of help with a tow were unnecessary, for Rob simply reversed his own truck – a towering Ford Transcontinental – against the rear of his brother's trailer and shunted it until it started. I was impressed by the cavalier simplicity of the solution.

Alan and Rob were both headed for Qatar, along the same route that Maurice and I would travel to the United Arab Emirates and Dubai. Maurice suggested to me that we should hitch up with them and seemed relieved to be with some more experienced drivers. My doubts about him grew stronger; I knew from experience in Europe that two drivers were slower than one, even if they were perfectly in tune with each other's style, and four could be quite unwieldy. To prove the point, this trip ended up taking seventeen days altogether; on my next trip to Dubai, two months later and travelling alone, I made it in eleven. Meanwhile, Rob and Alan were congenial company, and whatever they thought about having two novices with them, they were kind enough not to say. For

Maurice was, indeed, a novice in trans-European travel, as I'd suspected at the German border. It turned out that his experience of Saudi Arabia was limited to two years of 'internals' – driving within the country for foreign-based contractors. That meant he might know his way around the desert kingdom – no great challenge, given how few roads it had – but he had no more experience of crossing a Middle Eastern border than I did. When it came to Western Europe, he had considerably less. If Rob and Alan would put up with us, I was going to learn a lot more from them than I would from my company colleague.

The gloom of the afternoon was deepening to dusk by the time the train was shunted to its loading position. It consisted of a series of low flat cars, each connected by steel plates to form a continuous deck. At the far end was a single passenger carriage. One by one we drove onto the tail-end wagon, the Brits led by a couple of drawbar trucks belonging to the German post office, and lurched our way along the train to the end, parking one behind the other. Alan showed me how to chock the wheels of my truck with steel wedges that had to be fixed in position with wing-headed bolts. He told me to bring whatever I needed for the night, for there were no facilities on the train, apart from a cramped railway toilet. One of us took a stove, another a kettle, we all brought food, and each of us carried our own mug and sleeping bag. As we trudged the length of the train to the carriage, we looked like a huddle of wartime refugees, draped with all our worldly possessions.

Once in the carriage, we each found a compartment to sleep in before gathering in groups of four or five to make tea and prepare supper. There was no heating, and the cold compartments wouldn't begin to warm up until the locomotive was coupled to the front of the train. As we cooked and ate our meal, we were shunted around the goods yard for some time while the rest of our train was assembled. Rob told me that we were low priority and likely to be sidelined from time to time en route, to make way for faster traffic. The train finally finished its lurching shunts by about nine in the evening and we were on our way. We separated into our various compartments and prepared for sleep, stretched out on the fold-down couchettes.

No city presents its best face to its railway lines and Munich, on the grey last day of September, was no exception. The train rattled and grumbled its way through acres of goods yards and finally came to rest in a siding between lines of container trains. We gathered our possessions and jumped down onto the gravel between the lines. The morning was cold and damp and my hands resented having to fiddle with the chocks against the wheels of my truck. At the head of the line of trucks, the two post office wagons rumbled down the shallow unloading ramp, but once again, Alan's Mercedes wouldn't start, and it blocked the way for all of us. Rob and I removed the heavy batteries from his Ford and lugged them along the train to Alan's truck. Together, we hoisted them onto the railway wagon and connected them to the flat batteries with jump leads. With the extra power, the Merc started immediately and we carried Rob's batteries back. The whole operation took about twenty minutes, but at last we were able to disembark.

At some point the previous evening, Rob had persuaded Alan that it wasn't worth going any further that day since we wouldn't be able to get all the way across Austria before the ban on trucks came into force that afternoon – it being a Saturday. Austria goes one better than the many European countries that ban trucks on Sundays, by prohibiting them from 3pm on Saturday until 10pm on Sunday. I would have preferred to get as far as we could; even if we didn't make it across Austria – and there was still a chance of that – we would at least have made some progress. Maurice, in what I was beginning to recognise as his depressingly cautious style, thought we had better stick with Rob and Alan, and I didn't push the point. After all, he was supposed to be taking the lead. Besides, all the other eastbound drivers had already left and it might be better to carry on with someone who knew the way. Nevertheless, I spent the weekend in a vaguely depressed state; I knew that – not for the first time, nor the last – I had gone against my own better judgement and had lost at least two days.

After giving our trucks a general check-up and, in my case, checking all the wheels, we spent the day in the centre of the city. I made a nostalgic visit to the main Munich Railway Station where, ten years earlier, I had caught a train for Istanbul at the start of my five-month trip to the Middle East and India. Nothing seemed to have changed and the Istanbul train was waiting for its afternoon departure, just as it had when I had boarded it. In the evening, all four of us went to the cinema opposite the station to see Clint Eastwood displaying an excellent command of German.

Sunday was a waste. It was far too early in the trip to have a whole day off, but rules are rules, especially in Germany, and we weren't allowed to move until ten that evening. I tried not to speculate that I could already have been in Yugoslavia if I'd had the courage of my convictions. One consolation was 'Siggy's', the downmarket restaurant across the road from the goods yard that had become a hangout for Middle East drivers waiting for the train back to Köln. Siggy, the eponymous owner, was a camp, erratic man, who, as I got to know him later, was never actually sober and sometimes falling-down drunk. His main redeeming feature was that he cooked vast meals at prices that varied with his moods. He was also known to give free meals to drivers when they returned destitute from a particularly disastrous trip. But despite the friendly warmth of Siggy's, it was hard, as always, to relax completely when we knew we had to start work late in the evening. By nine o'clock, we were all anxious to leave. We finally decided to risk a nine-thirty departure, gambling that we wouldn't meet a cop who was a stickler for the ten o'clock threshold.

We set off into the night, with Rob in the lead, in a convoy of five trucks, having been joined by another Brit over the weekend. There must be some law of physics that dictates that each succeeding truck in a convoy has to go five miles an hour faster than the one in front and, as tail-end Charlie, I was giving a fair impression of Stirling Moss. Even so, almost every traffic light was red by the time I reached it, but I barrelled through on the tail of the truck in front, for fear of being left behind. In the past year, I'd become familiar with a number of German cities, but Munich wasn't one of them and I couldn't afford to lose sight of the others. I managed to jump a dozen lights undetected before we finally reached the A8 *autobahn* and settled down for the two-hour run to the border at Freilassing, near Salzburg.

Here, the German and Austrian customs offices were in the same building on opposite sides of a large hallway. As a portent of the new world ahead of us, I almost tripped over a Turkish woman squatting outside the building with her skirts spread, peeing copiously into the gutter. Even though I'd been through this border twice before, the procedure seemed to have changed, and even Rob and Alan seemed confused; it wasn't until one in the morning that we were allowed through the barrier and on into Austria. By now we had all lost steam, and within half an hour we were parked up in a lay-by for what was left of the night.

In those days, it took five or six hours to cross Austria – I could have made it on Saturday, damn it – and having cooked breakfast and shared the contents of a teapot, we hoped to be in Yugoslavia by early afternoon. About thirty kilometres south of Salzburg, we turned eastwards off the *autobahn* and climbed a road through a long narrow valley known to British drivers as the 'Ho Chi Minh Trail'. We met a succession of low bridges that Maurice and I only just cleared, because our wretched Maggies had an extra plate between the chassis and the fifth wheel, raising our trailers slightly above the four-metre clearance that was the international standard. On the return journey, this extra height would be the undoing of Maurice, but we didn't know that yet.

At the top of the trail, the valley opened out and the road followed the line of the River Inn between two ranges of mountains rising to 2500 metres. Although the day remained overcast and threatened rain, the view was still beautiful and I enjoyed the drive. At intervals we met trucks returning from the Middle East, covered with a month's worth of mud and dust. We flashed headlights in an exchange of greetings with each of them, for there were few foreigners on this road who weren't heading beyond Europe. We detoured through Bruck to avoid paying the toll on the Tauern Tunnel – our running money had to last us a long time – and by midday we were passing through Graz towards the Yugoslav border.

As we reached the border crossing at Spielfeld, we came to the end of a line of trucks waiting to leave Austria. In those days, Spielfeld was not simply the border between two countries, but the dividing line between Western Europe and everything that lay to the east. Partly because I had never driven further east before, I had a strong sense that everything would be different on the other side, and whenever I crossed the border subsequently, I felt the same mixture of anticipation and apprehension. None of us voiced such thoughts, but I sensed that even the old hands,

Rob and Alan, felt that we were about to leave civilisation behind. We ate lunch at 'Mama's', another traditional resting place for Middle East hands, where news was swapped and rumours inflamed. A favourite pastime for drivers on the way home was to exaggerate the difficulties ahead and they found it particularly irresistible if they met a novice. Luckily for my peace of mind, there were no other Brits in the restaurant.

Outside, the chaotic press of trucks approaching the barrier was the first sign that the gentlemanly queuing at western borders was behind us. Alan gloomily predicted that it would take us two hours to pass. On this border, the Austrians seemed straightforward and it was the Yugoslavs who were upping the ante. First, we had to present our passports and TIR carnets, before joining a second queue to pay our transit taxes for Yugoslavia. In Austria, the transit tax was a flat rate per mile; in Yugoslavia, they also took into account the weight of the load. I changed 600 marks into dinars to cover the road tax and the cost of fuel en route; I'd been holding off refuelling until we'd left Austria, since diesel was half the price across the border.

Completing the paperwork was less than half the battle. Now we had to wait until the Yugoslavs saw fit to raise the barrier, which they did only once an hour, and then only to allow three or four trucks to pass. The 'queue' consisted of four lanes of trucks trying to squeeze through a gateway wide enough for one, and since most of the other trucks were Greek, Turkish or Yugoslav, there wasn't much chance of cooperation. It was simply a question of being alert for the times when the traffic moved and making sure I pushed into any available space before anyone else. On a later trip, when I found myself with three other Brits waiting half the night, we lined our trucks together across all four lanes and only moved forwards when we were sure all of us were awake, so that nobody could pass us as we napped between moves.

It was already dusk by the time Rob reached the barrier, while the rest of us were stuck in the morass of trucks behind him.

"Is this normal?" I asked him as I stood beside his cab.

"You can never tell with these bastards," he answered in his South Welsh accent. "If they want to, they'll keep you here for hours for no reason."

As we waited, a hitchhiker approached us and asked Rob for a lift. He seemed likeable enough and he spoke English with what I took to be an Australian accent – it turned out he was from New Zealand.

"I'm sorry," Rob told him. "The last bloke I gave a ride to nicked some money, so I don't give lifts anymore."

"How far are you going?" I asked the crestfallen hitcher.

"Athens." I looked him over again, but I'd already made up my mind. I knew from my experience of hitchhiking home from Turkey ten years earlier how hard it was to get lifts in Eastern Europe.

"I'll give you a lift as far as Greece," I told him, "but you'll have to excuse the truck; it's not as good as his." I gestured at Rob's new Transcontinental towering above us; my Magirus looked decidedly road-weary by comparison. The hitcher's name was Peter and he'd been in Europe for several months. I was glad to have an English speaker with me because I'd been unable to get a squeak out of the radio and the eight-track was useless. We stowed Peter's rucksack on the bottom bunk, next to my food and cooking gear, which we'd have to move every night to make room for him to sleep.

"This is the first time I've had a lift in an English truck," Peter told me.

"I'm not surprised," I said. "Most drivers are only interested in picking up girls, and there are precious few of them."

As we were talking, the barrier swung upwards and Rob and several others were allowed through, but just as I reached the bar, the soldier manning the exit slammed it down in front of us. A Yugoslav customs officer came to the door and asked whether I had anything to declare. I said no, but he stepped up into the cab and glared round, before stepping down without a word and disappearing into the customs building. Meanwhile, Rob had parked a little way up the road to wait for the rest of us. To my surprise, it took only another half an hour for all of us to pass through the barrier, but it had still been six hours since we'd arrived at the Austrian side of the border.

Now we took up the formation that would continue as long as we ran together. Rob led the way and I followed; Maurice came third and Alan brought up the rear. It was unfortunate for him to be at the back since his Mercedes was less powerful than the Ford or the two Maggies, but he and Alan thought it better to have an experienced man in the rear, in case Maurice or I were left behind. We set off for Maribor, about thirty-five kilometres away, and I kept as close behind Rob as I could. Whenever he passed a slower-moving vehicle, usually local, I'd do my best to squeeze through as soon as possible after him. Within five miles, I could no longer see Maurice in my mirrors.

Rob and I pulled into the car park of the big motel at Maribor that we'd designated for our rendezvous and waited for the other two to arrive. The parking area was clogged with trucks from many different countries, including a couple from Iran. By that time, Iran was already in the political uproar that would end with the Ayatollah Khomeini taking control the following year, and Harrison's had stopped running there, so I was interested to see Iranian trucks so far west. After more than half an hour, Rob and I were just beginning to get worried when Alan and Maurice pulled up beside our trucks. Apparently, Maurice had had a puncture, which had held them both up. I felt vaguely guilty that I hadn't been the one to help my fellow Harrison driver, but Alan seemed unfazed. None of us knew this was a portent of disasters to come.

While the Hobbs brothers cooked a meal in Rob's Ford, Maurice, Peter and I squeezed into my cab for 'camion stew', a concoction made of canned contributions of meat and vegetables from as many drivers who were sharing it. After supper, we all took advantage of the relatively clean washing facilities in the restaurant, since they would henceforth be few and far between. In the bar, we discussed how far we'd travel the following day. It was now Monday evening and we'd all be taking a ferry from the Greek Port of Volos to Tartus in Syria. The ferry service had recently been set up to allow trucks to avoid Turkey, where the political and economic situation had already deteriorated into the chaos that would lead to martial law in eighteen months' time. Many exporters, including Weir Westgarth, were insisting that their loads be routed around Turkey, whether we liked it or not.

Neither Maurice nor I had a ferry schedule, which was, in any case, somewhat erratic, but Rob thought there was a sailing on Thursday morning. We decided to push on the following day and reach Volos on

Wednesday afternoon, in good time to book on to a ship for the following morning. The distance was about 1300 kilometres, so we couldn't afford to waste any time, particularly since the Yugoslav speed limit for trucks was a mere 70kph – not that we paid much attention to it. As we headed south-east the next morning, through Zagreb and on towards Belgrade, the weather improved considerably. By mid-morning, I was driving with the window wide open, browning my right arm in the sunshine. Once again, Rob set a fast pace, but I wasn't sorry that he ignored the slow speed limit; our driving styles were well matched.

For most of the way across Yugoslavia, the land was flat and featureless, with endless, black-earth fields running into one another to the horizon. Usually, they were planted with corn, which, in this late season, had browned and bent in untidy rows and was in the process of being gathered. Alongside the main road, there was a secondary track, along which oxen trudged, trailing dilapidated wagons. Occasionally, we'd see a light horse-drawn cart, or a tractor, often carrying several people perched behind the driver. From time to time, the monotony was broken as the road ran through stretches of planted woodland. The country seemed poor but not destitute.

The main road itself was a nightmare, even in the good weather. The two-lane *autoput*, as it was known in Yugoslavia, was nicknamed *autokaput* by British drivers, and with good reason. As the main route linking East and West, it was used by a bewildering variety of vehicles, and international trucks from all over Europe and the Middle East funnelled along this single road. Yugoslav traffic moved fairly slowly, while the international trucks and coaches weaved their way through it. Local lorries, overburdened with tottering trailers, trundled along the flat road, while buses would career past them, only to stop suddenly to set down passengers, holding up the very lorries they had just risked everything to overtake. Private cars, driven with a recklessness matched only by their drivers' lack of skill, added to the hazards, particularly when they were passing oncoming traffic. Several times I was forced to brake sharply to avoid smashing into some over-ambitious driver in an underpowered car. Perhaps the worst were Turkish *gastarbeiter* – guest workers – returning from Germany to their homeland, cars packed with passengers and roof racks groaning with German-bought possessions. On my next trip I came across one of these Turkish cars on its roof at the side of the road, with a crowd gathered round, and the bodies of the driver and a passenger spilling out of the doors. Just to make things worse, Yugoslavs had the practice – then still rare in Western Europe – of setting up wreaths at the roadside to commemorate the fallen. These appeared at appallingly frequent intervals, and often the twisted and burnt-out wrecks of past accidents would be left disintegrating at the side of the road where they'd come to grief.

None of this seemed to deter Rob, who picked his way past the slower traffic with familiar ease. Once again, I was determined not to be left behind, and I had the advantage of a slightly more powerful engine, which helped me keep up. One of the biggest problems of the *autoput*, somehow worse here than elsewhere in Europe, was driving a right-hand drive vehicle on a road where everyone drives on the right. Passing cars was easy, because I could see over the top of them; overtaking trucks was a different matter. As long as I was far enough back, I could see round a truck reasonably well, but if I let myself get too close, I had to pull right across the road before I could see whether it was safe to have done so. Often, I found myself swinging the wheel violently back to the right to tuck my truck safely behind some ponderous Yugoslav lorry. It was an advantage to have a hitchhiker in such circumstances, sitting on the side of the cab nearest the middle of the road, and I used Peter as an early warning system.

By the time we'd been driving for half an hour, Maurice and Alan had once again disappeared from the view in my mirrors. Assuming that they could look after each other, or at any rate that Alan could take care of Maurice, I concentrated on keeping up with Rob. After three hours, he pulled off the road into the car park of another large roadside hotel and I parked in line behind him. I jumped down from the cab and joined Rob at the side of the road.

"Where are the others?" he asked.

"I don't know," I said. "I haven't seen them for a while, but they should be all right." Rob didn't seem unduly worried either and I offered to make tea.

"You should get your hitchhiker to do that," he said, but I preferred to do it myself and returned to the Maggie to put on the kettle. Maurice and Alan didn't arrive until we were already into our second mug. Maurice swung his truck across the road and parked next to mine, while Alan lined up next to his brother. Strict etiquette was observed; Harrisons parked together and the Hicks trucks paired off separately. Maurice didn't seem to register the fact that we'd been there at least twenty minutes before him, but while he busied himself in his cab, Alan was full of complaints.

"He just won't pass anything," he said. "I pull out to show him it's all-clear but he just stays put." As I had suspected, Maurice wasn't an easy man to run with, but he was such an amiable guy that it was hard to be cross with him for long. All the same, I was glad I was paired with Rob and I felt guilty that Alan was stuck with Maurice.

The pattern remained the same for the rest of the day. Rob and I would storm ahead, and Maurice and Alan would roll up at each rendezvous twenty minutes behind us. Even with these delays, however, by early evening, we were well south of Belgrade and approaching Niš, where we would turn due south towards Skopje, the capital of what is now Northern Macedonia, and the Greek border. Now, however, we had further hold-up, as Maurice had picked up another puncture and I discovered that he didn't have a jack; for his last puncture, he'd used Alan's. I was shocked that anyone could set off on an 8000 mile round trip without any way to change a wheel, and I could see that Rob and Alan were surprised, though none of us voiced our thoughts. Instead, we all worked together to change his wheel and this time Peter did make tea for the rest of us. I could tell that the Hobbs brothers regretted having hooked up with Maurice and me, but they never voiced their frustration, at least not to us, and Maurice seemed happily oblivious. No more than two hours later, he blew a third tyre and used up his last spare. It made no sense that four of us travelled the same road but only one of us picked up punctures, but equally it seemed unreasonable to blame Maurice for his misfortunes. He just seemed to have become the Jonah of our little expedition.

Making up for the delay, we pushed on through Tuesday night, with only a short break to wait, inevitably, for Maurice and Alan near Skopje.

It was a full moon and the moonlit scenery looked magical as we passed through the steep, wooded valleys of Macedonia. Shortly after dawn we stopped for breakfast, and managed to reach the Greek border by mid-morning on Wednesday. I was pleased because this was my first new country of the trip, but even so it had an odd familiarity, as if something of Greece had rubbed off on me from some deeply buried cultural trace. Or perhaps it was simply that we had left the regimented atmosphere of Yugoslavia, which, though it was Communist-lite compared with most Eastern Bloc countries, was still a totalitarian regime.

There was hardly any traffic at the border and all four of us were through in less than an hour, and rolling south to the port of Volos. I dropped Peter on the main road to Athens as our small convoy turned off towards the coast. I was going to miss his company, for I still had nearly 3000 kilometres to go to reach Dubai, with no radio or music to break the monotony. And then there was the return trip to face without entertainment, though that turned out to be anything but dull.

Volos was as unlike Dover as a town could be, while still remaining a ferry port. Horse-drawn carriages plied their way along the sea front, wooden fishing boats lined the quay, and the ferry terminal was a vast dusty arena with lines of trucks – mostly Bulgarian – around its perimeter. There was nothing that looked like the link-spans of northern European ferry terminals and no sign of a ship. We parked up four abreast next to the small cabin that served as a booking office and added ourselves to the list for the following day's sailing to Syria. There was nothing to do now but wait.

And wait. For when the ferry did arrive in the middle of the following morning, the turnround proceeded at a snail's pace. The ship itself, named the *Falster*, was a large, orange-coloured vessel that seemed well cared for, as I expected of a company based in Sweden. I was yet to meet the *Falster's* sister ship, the *Scandinavia*, which turned out to be as unkempt as it was unreliable. In the time it took to load the *Falster*, a Dover ferry could have completed an entire round trip to Calais and back, but finally the ship departed, with fifty-odd trucks and drivers aboard. After our high-speed run through Yugoslavia, the ferry was a strangely passive experience. For two and a half days, we had nothing to do but eat, sleep, gossip and watch a succession of movies shown on the ship's 16mm projector. Compulsory viewing was the recently released *Smokey and the Bandit*, in which an American truck driver outwits traffic cops and battles bikers to enthusiastic cheers from the ship's all-trucker audience. By the time I stopped doing Middle East work, I must have seen the film a dozen times on various crossings, but we never seemed to tire of it. In the evening, the movie menu switched to some mildly erotic romps shown by the sole female crew-member, who was in charge of the projector. She might charitably have been described as late-thirtyish, but still became strangely more attractive as the evening wore on.

CHAPTER 12

SYRIA AND BEYOND

O n the morning of our third day at sea, we reached the Syrian port of Tartus. To my mind, this was the start of the Middle East run in earnest. If I'd thought Volos a little lacking in organisation, the chaos on the Tartus quayside was mesmerising. I leaned against the ship's rail and watched as Syrian trucks, some of them wartime relics dating back to the 1940s, lumbered along the quay, ludicrously overloaded with timber and looking as if they could capsize at any moment. Other trucks hauled containers, chained down on trailers that were too short for them, while small pick-up trucks wove their way between the colourful artics. In a few minutes, I'd be pitched in among them and it looked a daunting prospect.

When it was our turn to disembark, I rolled off the ferry ramp and stuck manically to the rear of Alan's truck as we threaded our way through the lines of local lorries heading in and out of the docks. The ground itself was treacherous; potholed and uneven, with occasional pieces of rusting steel poking out of the ground at random, ready to snag our tyres. We pulled over onto a haphazard parking area before the dock gate and I breathed a sigh of relief. I'd covered only about a quarter of a mile and I was already wired. Our Syrian customs agent sought us out and led a group of drivers to his office nearby. Alan had warned me we'd be here for hours while our paperwork was translated into Arabic, but we passed the time changing money. Several shabbily dressed men had already accosted us to offer their money-changing services, but Alan and Rob recommended 'Four Eyes', also known as 'The Bandit', both for obvious reasons. We'd need Syrian pounds, Jordanian dinars and Saudi riyals, and The Bandit rattled off rates for all three. Then, the bargaining began. I had no idea what the proper rates should be and nobody even mentioned a bank. Instead, Rob and Alan started arguing the rates to our advantage and succeeded in wheedling a little more from Four Eyes than he'd offered. It was all friendly enough and we parted with honour satisfied on both sides. Maurice and I now had all the currencies we would need to pay for fuel, road tax and customs agents' fees across the Middle East.

By early afternoon, all our paperwork had been rendered into Arabic and we were ready to leave. The four of us formed up in the same order we'd adopted before and set off. I rolled up to the dock gate, where my pass was inspected and the single steel pole raised to allow me through into Syria. The early part of the route was straightforward, as we trundled along well-paved roads to the outskirts of the town, and southwards along the coast road towards Tripoli. After about twenty kilometres, we turned eastwards in the direction of Homs, then the third largest city in Syria, but now obliterated by the endless Syrian civil war. The road began to deteriorate as we climbed steadily from the coast to the mountainous spine that runs north to south through the western part of the country. The road zigzagged up the mountain, and where it had decayed to dirt it remained as black as asphalt, dyed by spilled oil and clouds of exhaust fumes from badly tuned diesels. Suddenly, we found ourselves running through lines of open-fronted shanty shops on either side of the road, lit, even in the daytime, by garish neon lights. This was a duty-free zone that lasted about a mile, where one could buy anything from truck tyres to cigarettes, and maybe a great deal that was less respectable. It transpired that the road here skirted the Lebanese border – on which side I was never entirely sure – and the variety of shops would have shamed a western mall.

We reached the outskirts of Homs by mid-afternoon, skirting the city itself and heading south towards Damascus. Homs is 2500 feet above sea level and the atmosphere was quite different from the oppressive humidity of Tartus. Gone was the greenery of the coastal strip; we were now in high rocky country, through which a rough two-lane tarmac road continued for 150 kilometres to the capital.

Over tea, we discussed our plans for the rest of the day. As the clear novice, I was ready to take any sensible advice, and we agreed to continue round Damascus and aim for Daraa, on the border with Jordan, ready to do battle with Syrian customs the following day. The Hobbs brothers warned us about 'Damascus Hill', the 50-kilometre descent from the highlands to Damascus. For good measure, they threw in warnings about driving at night in Syria, where trucks are just as likely to have white lights at the rear and red lights, or no lights, at the front, as the conventional arrangement. This turned out to be true, but, as I later discovered, no real impediment to night driving if you were in a hurry. We set off again and I discovered that Damascus Hill was spectacular, but not unduly dangerous if you took care. The worst obstacles were slow-moving local trucks, most of which crawled down the long hill in sensible deference to their grossly overloaded condition.

Damascus itself was a puzzle. Once again, we were taking what passed for a ring road, but the few road signs we saw were, naturally, in Arabic and of little help to a European. As usual, I was following Rob, as we passed sprawling bus terminals, workshops, garages, shops and poverty-stricken housing. In spite of the fact that I was only a follower, on my next trip I discovered to my satisfaction that I had indeed learned how to circumnavigate the city, which turned out to be easier than it looked. In many ways, the outskirts of Damascus reminded me of provincial Turkish cities, as I had experienced them ten years earlier when I travelled through Turkey in the months before I went to university. The prevailing conditions were heat, dust and noise. The Magirus had no air conditioning, but even if it had, I preferred to drive with the window down because it gave me a better connection with the city around me. Even when I later drove a truck that did have air con, I almost never used it.

We parked up for the night on the outskirts of Daraa, ready to tackle the Syrian border next morning. We were up at first light and tagged on to the customary long line of trucks. I brewed myself some tea in the cab, holding the kettle in place on the stove as I moved forward, one or two truck lengths at a time; it took us a couple of hours to reach the border itself. Here, we presented our papers at a low desk in an open-fronted office. As I stood in the group of drivers, peering over their shoulders, I was reminded that one of Harrison's drivers had earned the nickname 'Ratchet Neck' for the same behaviour. By midday, we'd passed out of Syria and entered the Jordanian border point at Ramtha. There, to my surprise, I found Hippy John, who had been held up by the lack of a Saudi visa, but was now ready to continue to Jeddah. I didn't feel so bad about the wheel nut affair, since, even with the weekend's delay it had cost us, Maurice and I had caught up with the old Middle East hand.

Meanwhile, Maurice and I had our own Saudi visas to sort out, and we were introduced to a go-between who was well known to Middle East drivers. This was a deaf-mute boy still in his mid-teens who took charge of our paperwork and arranged for a taxi – one of his own small fleet, I discovered – to take Maurice and me, plus a couple of Austrian drivers, to the Saudi embassy in the Jordanian capital, Amman, the following morning. This would give more than enough time for our customs papers to be completed, but just to be sure, I spent a little time hanging around in the agent's office. On the wall was a large map of the Middle East that had something odd about it that I couldn't put my finger on. Eventually, I realised that Israel wasn't marked on the map at all. Instead, without borders, was an area marked 'Palestine' in English and Arabic. Making sure I couldn't be overheard, I imprudently joked to Maurice that it was no wonder Arab countries could never defeat the Israelis; they couldn't find them on the map.

Despite the TIR agreement and the British customs seal, the agent told us that our papers couldn't be completed without customs looking at the load, and the otherwise friendly Jordanian customs officers insisted on opening our trailers and peering inside – at least they stopped short of emptying the trailers for inspection. Once they had given the contents a cursory glance, our tilt cords were again sealed together. We then finally parted company with Rob and Alan, who already had Saudi visas and had no reason to remain in Ramtha. Maurice and I were on our own together, for the first time in over a week, and early the next day we set off in the taxi for the two-hour drive to Amman and the Saudi embassy.

The embassy itself was unfriendly to the point of hostility and we had to line up across a harsh, white courtyard in which there was no shade. There were three windows: one for non-Arabs, another for regular Arab visitors and a third for *hadjis* – pilgrims to the holy city of Mecca. We sweated in line for well over an hour before we could present our passports and visa fees, only to be told that the visas wouldn't be ready until the following day. This turned out to be normal, but one of the Austrians unwisely offered a bribe to speed things up, and the official's response was to slam down the window in disgust. After another prolonged delay, we learned that the Austrians would have to present their passports the next day, because the Saudis were too offended to deal with them, but at least Maurice and I had our applications in already. We speculated whether the Saudi officer was offended by the very idea of a bribe or was upset because it was too small.

Back at Ramtha that afternoon, our deaf-mute friend told us the taxi would return our passports the following day; there was no need for us to go back to Amman. We celebrated with a beer in a nearby café, but when we emerged into the sunlight, the effects of just one drink seemed compounded by the heat and I felt too lightheaded for comfort. It occurred to me that the prophet Mohammed knew what he was doing when he forbade his followers to take alcohol, given the conditions they lived in.

After two nights at Ramtha, we were more than ready to leave, and as soon as our passports were returned, shortly after lunch, Maurice and I set off for the Saudi border at Haditha. We had no intention of crossing that day; better to deal with a border early in the morning than risk being up all night or being stuck in no-man's land. We parked up on some hard sand a little way off the tarmac road, just short of the Jordanian side of the border, and pitched in together to make tea and supper. Both of us lacked the sort of equipment that was standard for Middle East drivers, including a picnic chair each, so we sat in my cab with the doors wide open, hoping in vain for some cooling breeze.

Early the following morning, we approached the Jordanian border post, which consisted of a series of open-fronted tents at the side of the road. Each had a large steel desk across the front and a simple wooden bed at the rear. A generator chattered behind the tents, providing power for a fan. The genial Jordanian customs and passport officers greeted us in English and we were through into no-man's land surprisingly quickly. The Saudi side was slower and it took us over an hour to advance up the queue to the barrier. Here, we were questioned about whisky and 'sex books', neither of which we had, and the border guard rummaged through our belongings in the cab. I wondered whether some tins of ham would be considered contraband, but he didn't notice, and perhaps couldn't read, the contents. We pulled into the truck compound and took our paperwork and passports into the customs office.

It was already so hot that I found myself walking along three sides of a courtyard, because they were shaded, rather than face the sun on the fourth side. We were glad of the ceiling fan whirring above us as we added our papers to a line of carnets along the counter. Since we were in transit, our trailers weren't turned out, though like the Jordanians at Ramtha, the Saudi customs officers once again broke our seals. The whole process took until late afternoon – I later discovered this was lightning speed for Saudi Arabia – and towards evening we were through the last barrier, with over 2000 kilometres of desert ahead of us.

For the first several hundred kilometres, we'd be running beside the H4 'Tapline', an oil pipeline that ran from near Dhahran on the Persian Gulf to Jordan. Construction of the pipeline began in 1947 and it was, at one time, the largest oil pipeline in the world. It was originally intended to go to Haifa, but when the state of Israel was established, the pipe was routed instead to the eastern Mediterranean port of Sidon, in Lebanon. Following the 1967 war, and constant arguments over transit fees between Saudi Arabia, Syria and Lebanon, the line now terminated in Jordan. Later, after the first Iraq war in 1990, when Jordan sided with its Iraqi neighbour against the US-led coalition that included Saudi Arabia, the Saudis cut off the oil supply to Jordan and the pipeline is now derelict.

We reckoned on knocking off a couple of hundred kilometres before stopping for the night, but after only an hour we came across a handful of British trucks parked off the road on the other side from the Tapline, all belonging to Harrison. We pulled off the road and drew up next to them. After a rapid round of introductions, our newly discovered colleagues got back to the matter they'd been dealing with all day.

All five of them were returning from Dubai, three of them in Jack's new Dafs and two driving the same model of Magirus as we were. One of the Maggies had suffered some driveline problem that couldn't be fixed in the desert, so the drivers had decided to recover the stricken truck themselves. That meant loading it onto another truck without, of course, a crane. Instead, the drivers had spent all day excavating a ramp that would allow them to reverse a truck down so that its trailer bed was level with the ground. Then, they'd pulled the dead Maggie onto one trailer and loaded its own trailer onto another. Finally, as Maurice and I arrived, they were jacking up the tractor unit and removing its wheels, before lowering it back to the trailer deck, to bring its overall running height below the level of any bridges they were likely to meet back in Europe. I was impressed by their combined ingenuity and a little envious of their easy camaraderie, which Maurice and I hadn't managed to achieve in ten days together.

The two of us pitched in to help with the endgame and to make tea. It was already nearly dark by the time the whole operation was finished, so we cooked a communal meal and ate together. The Harrison veterans filled us in on what to expect on the rest of the run to Dubai and, better still, replaced Maurice's three blown tyres with the now redundant wheels and tyres of the broken-down truck. We parted at first light the next morning, Maurice and I heading south, and the rest of the Harrison crew aiming for Tartus and a ferry back to Europe the following day. Less than an hour later, Maurice blew his fourth tyre (triggering the series of events described in the Prologue), leaving me alone in the desert, with my own truck disabled for lack of air.

CHAPTER 13
ALONE AGAIN

As I drank my second mug of tea, I got up and wandered to the front of the truck. It looked a sorry sight, with its tilted cab leaning drunkenly to the right, but at least I could now get at the engine. I peered at the compressor, which looked like a miniature single-cylinder engine bolted to the side of the big V10. Frankly, I hadn't much of a clue about what to do with it. With no air pressure in the system, I couldn't check for leaks, but after pondering the problem for a while, I decided to try running the engine to see if there was any life in the compressor after all. If Maurice was right, I was wasting my time, but it was better than sitting for a week doing nothing. Besides, I had only one book left unfinished, which was, ironically, *Zen and the Art of Motorcycle Maintenance*, in which the irritating protagonist grapples with his continually defective motorbike. There were certain parallels between my situation and his, but not enough to make me like either the book or its narrator.

I stepped up on the driver's side of the cab, reaching in through the open door to start the engine. With one hand on the loud pedal, I revved the engine to about 1000rpm, watching the air pressure gauges. They remained stubbornly at zero and I was about to give up when one of the needles flickered. I boosted the revs and the needle climbed a little more. I laughed out loud; whatever else might be wrong, it couldn't be the compressor, for the gauges couldn't rise without it. Leaving the engine at idle, I peered at every visible part of the air system and put my ear to various joints, but couldn't detect a leak. I checked the gauges again and, to my amazement, they were continuing to climb. I had been at the roadside for two or three hours, but now I was back in business. I had no idea why the air system had suddenly decided to behave, or why it had failed in the first place, but at least I could now travel a little further. It was enough to make me euphoric, even if I still had the cab to contend with.

I switched the engine off and set about the tricky task of lowering the destabilised cab back to its driving position. I turned the valve on the cab tilt pump to the lowering position and starting pumping carefully, watching the narrow hydraulic ram that did the work. The cab was so far askew that I worried the ram could be distorted or even ripped off, leaving me unable to lower the cab at all. I stopped pumping and considered the problem. Luckily, I had a chain, the one I'd used to pull Maurice out of the sand, and a 'dog', or ratcheted lever, that hooked into the chain to tighten it. I fastened the chain between the chassis and the rear corner of the cab behind the broken mounting, and tightened it until it began to pull the cab back into line. Then, I worked the tilt pump again. By alternately tightening the chain and working the pump for a few strokes, I managed to steer the cab down safely, but the process took me nearly an hour. I started the engine, checked that the air gauges were still behaving, and restowed my gear where it belonged. Finally, five or six hours after I'd first been forced to stop, I was ready for the road. I had no idea how long the air system would hold up, nor did I have any confidence that it would keep working as it should, but at least I was on the move again. I felt almost affectionate towards my unlovely Maggie as I put it into first gear and let in the clutch.

It was by now mid-afternoon and Maurice should be hundreds of kilometres ahead of me. I didn't need a thermometer to tell me that it was hotter than hell and I'd been warned that tyres on a loaded truck could easily blow at speeds above 50mph. Besides, I couldn't take any kind of risk, despite having two spares, because Maurice had my jack. At only 40mph, it's a very long way across Saudi Arabia, but that's the speed I set myself. The local traffic was sporadic, but notable at one point when I was passed by a Toyota pick-up with a camel sitting in the back. Big Jordanian

Mercs roared past me from time to time, but I kept doggedly to my limit, for hour after hour until the sun began to set. I kept a watchful eye on the air gauges but they continued to show all was well, and I finally began to relax. The road was monotonous, but I was enjoying the alien landscape and the feeling of space and emptiness in all directions. The desert was featureless and mostly flat, and even when there were small settlements around a fuel stop, there was no vegetation. The sand, when I pulled over for a tea or pee break, varied from a heavy grain that packed down hard enough to drive on, to a consistency more like talcum powder, overlaying the harder stuff. The powdery sand swirled around my sandals when I stepped in it and blew up behind the truck when I pulled off the road.

With no belly tank beneath the trailer, I had to stop once or twice at rudimentary filling stations, where a couple of dusty pumps stood by themselves in blackened, diesel-soaked sand, while their minder took shelter from the sun in a dilapidated shed. The first time I filled up, I could scarcely believe that the price was only seven riyals – one English pound – for one hundred litres. On my next trip, when I did have a belly tank, it meant I could take on 2500 litres, enough to get me all the way home from Saudi Arabia and then some, for only £25. The economics of Middle East transport were beginning to make sense.

At dusk I stopped for a quick meal and, before continuing, laid out a packet of crackers and tubes of processed cheese on the engine cover, where I could reach them from the driver's seat. Now the temperature was beginning to drop, relatively, I figured I could pick up speed, at least as far as the Maggie would let me. The truck had a low-geared drive axle, presumably for the eastern Turkish mountains on the run to Tehran, and its top speed was frustratingly just short of 60mph, but I kept my foot flat to the floor in an effort to make up time. I knew that the real secret to fast long-haul driving is not speed but persistence, and I ended up driving almost through the night, with a brief two-hour kip before dawn to take advantage of the relative cool. The darkness added to the feeling of disconnectedness that came with driving through the desert and I might as well have been on the moon. Only the steady rumble of the Maggie's V10 kept my mind on Earth. I calculated and recalculated the distance I had come, and how far I still had to go, but the truth is that I had little idea of the distance to Dubai and I had no map. This may sound absurd, but there were so few routes through Saudi Arabia that there was no need for one, and in my year of driving to the Middle East, I never did bother to get a map covering anything east of Greece.

The following day I was back to my tyre-protecting crawl, but even though I had kept driving almost continuously for a day and a half, by dusk I'd still seen no sign of Maurice. He might be way ahead of me, but that seemed unlikely, given his customary caution. I began to wonder whether I had missed some turn, but there had been only two changes of direction since I'd entered the country, so I wasn't unduly worried. Then, sometime after midnight on the second night, I came across a huddle of trucks parked next to a garishly lit restaurant. In among them was the dull red of Maurice's dusty Gilflex trailer. I slowed to a crawl and considered what to do. Etiquette demanded that I should park up with him and that we should carry on together, but I'd been enjoying my solitary run, and the fact that I had made up several hours on Maurice, despite my restricted speed during the day, simply underlined the difference in our driving styles. I knew I shouldn't leave a colleague stranded in the desert, but wasn't that just what Maurice had done, however justified his reasons? I let the truck drift to a stop and argued with myself. He wasn't in trouble, but I had been and I'd sorted it myself, with no help from Maurice. On the other hand, we might need each other later on. What would happen if my air failed again? He'd just leave me again, wouldn't he? After a couple of minutes of dithering, I decided that I simply hadn't seen him and it would indeed have been easy to pass him without noticing. I put the Maggie back in gear and set off again, feeling only vaguely guilty and a lot happier to remain on my own.

A little further on, I noticed a glow on the horizon ahead. For some reason I noted the mileage on my odometer, so when I finally reached the source of the light, which had been growing steadily brighter, I knew that it had been visible for nearly one hundred miles. Off on the left side of the road was a vast field of towers, flaring gas into the night, with plumes of fire and smoke blasting upwards. Even though the fires were probably a mile away from the road, the heat was so intense that I had to shut my window. It was a hellish sight, made worse by the roar of combustion, and even in a country as oil-rich as Saudi Arabia, the waste of energy seemed insane. I continued past the fires and took a short break. By now I had been driving for two days and nights with only a couple of short sleep breaks, but I was on a roll. I passed out of Saudi Arabia and into Qatar, which seemed altogether more friendly than its giant neighbour, and in the evening I finally reached the United Arab Emirates. Here I completed the final customs clearance in less than an hour – the Emiratis seemed a good deal less paranoid than the Saudis – and late in the evening I reached the Wier Westgarth site, about thirty kilometres south of the town – not yet a great city – of Dubai. The site itself would become the vast Jebel Ali desalination plant that allowed Dubai to grow to its current eminence, a growth in which I and my fellow drivers played an unremarked but not insignificant part.

I was expecting to spend the night in the truck as usual, but once through the gate, I was directed to a parking place and, even though it was past midnight, a smiling Indian led me to a barracks block where I was given a single, air-conditioned room and access to a shower. Better still, he offered to take care of my laundry. This was five-star treatment after the past few days, and the first shower – or proper wash – I'd had since leaving the ferry at Tartus.

I woke early and was directed towards a large open-sided marquee, where I found breakfast and half a dozen British drivers, all of whom were working for other small companies on subcontract to Spiers & Hartwell. A couple of them were already unloaded and were taking a day's civilised break at the Weir Westgarth compound before heading homeward across the desert. The rest of us joined forces to strip down our tilt trailers to allow cranes and forklift trucks access to the loads. It was hard, dirty work in the hot sun, but we enjoyed an easy camaraderie that came from working together and being able to share a joke after days of solitary driving. Unloading took most of the day, with a break for lunch back at the marquee. Here, I noticed the Westgarth workers scarfing up handfuls of what appeared to be white mints, from bowls distributed down the long tables. These turned out to be salt tablets and I grabbed a handful myself.

By late afternoon, we'd unloaded all our trailers and rebuilt the tilts, leaving an opening at the back for customs officers at successive borders to check that the trailers were empty. I felt obscurely proud as I surveyed my truck, unloaded after a two-week journey and ready to return to Europe. There was only one job left to do and that was to contact Jack. Joe Berrington, a driver for a Bristol-based company called Oasis, and fast becoming a friend, had discovered an unattended phone that would dial through to England. We were, oddly, three and a half hours ahead of UK time, which meant Jack would still be in the office.

It was the first time I'd talked to him since leaving Austria, apart from a telex from the Jordanian border at Ramtha. He was pleased to hear that I'd arrived and tipped, but less happy to hear that I'd parted from Maurice. I explained what had happened, omitting only that I had seen Maurice, and passed him, two nights earlier. Instead, I maintained that I must somehow have missed him. It was hard to read Jack's answering grunts, but inwardly I felt quite at peace with my decision; after all, Maurice had done two years of internals in Saudi and must have known his way around. If I could find my way here in one piece, so could he. Jack seemed to accept my story and told me to call him again when I got back into Austria, which seemed a world away from where I was. It takes a certain fatalism to run a company in which you're out of touch with your drivers, and your expensive machinery, for weeks at a time, but it clearly felt quite mundane to Jack.

It's hard to imagine, at a distance of over forty years, how much I valued that phone. Calling from the Middle East was close to impossible, or at least too difficult to bother with except in an emergency, and when we did communicate it was by an impersonal telex. Now I had my hands on a phone, and a free one at that. I picked up the receiver again and called home. The ringing tone went on and on, and I finally realised that Jane was out. There was no reason why she shouldn't be, of course, but I felt an unreasoning resentment that she wasn't there to talk to. It had been almost two weeks since we'd spoken to each other – all the way back in Munich – and of course there were no answering machines in those days, so I couldn't even leave a message to show I'd been thinking of her and the children.

I pulled my mind back from North Wales and emerged from the air-conditioned office into the forty-plus heat of Dubai. Now the trucks were unloaded, there was time for a little relaxation, and we all took ourselves off to the site swimming pool before dinner. The expatriate engineers were here for months, maybe years, at a time and the company was apparently looking after them. Use of all the site facilities was extended to the drivers who brought the components for the huge desalination plant taking shape along the sea shore. When I returned to my room, after a few beers in the bar, I found my laundry, neatly folded, on the bed. I could get used to this.

Joe and I, with several others, decided to take it easy the following day, when all we had to do was take our paperwork into town for the customs clearance that would allow us to leave. I haven't visited Dubai since it developed into an upmarket combination of Marbella and Miami, but in those days it was a far smaller town, with some streets still surfaced with sand, and a relaxed, provincial atmosphere. A driver named Kermit and I offered the use of our tractor units to make the twenty-mile drive into the town centre, and Joe and another driver joined me in my cab. We parked in a shady square near the centre and I was about to lock the Maggie when Kermit told me there was no reason to.

"This place is so safe," he said, "that I could leave my wallet on the fuel tank and it'd still be here when I get back." I looked sceptical so he proceeded to do just that. I may have been impressed but I wasn't persuaded, and I locked my cab as carefully as I had all along the road. Paperwork consisted only in showing a customs officer the signatures that proved we'd delivered the goods, which earned us the exit stamp we needed. We strolled back to the trucks and, to my amazement, Kermit's wallet was just where he'd left it an hour ago. It's a stunt I wouldn't have tried in London or Brierley Hill, let alone nearly 4000 miles from home, but the others didn't turn a hair. It wasn't the only sign of safety in Dubai. People we'd met in the street had been friendly, and many of the women were out in public and unveiled. Back at the Westgarth site, most of the labourers and ancillary staff were Indian and I noticed a number of their countrymen on the street. Underlining the fact that they represented a significant slice of the population, we'd passed a number of Indian restaurants and ended up eating an excellent curry in one of them. I was in a relaxed and satisfied mood as I trundled the Maggie back to the

Weir Westgarth site, but that changed rapidly when I saw Maurice's truck drawn up at the gate. He was surprised, and none too pleased, to see me.

"Where have you been?" he demanded. "I went back to find you." I didn't believe that for a moment; he'd been hundreds of kilometres down the road when I passed him, but I apologised profusely and suggested I must have passed him unnoticed in the night. The other drivers, sensing a scandal, asked what had happened and I told them my edited story, which they seemed to accept. I certainly didn't want to be known as someone who left a colleague in the desert, and even though I felt quite justified in what I'd done, I didn't risk finding out whether they agreed. Now, however, I was in another dilemma. Should I stay another day or two to help Maurice, or should I leave, as planned, with the others early the next morning? To my relief, a couple more Brits had arrived that evening, so Maurice would be able to unload and run home with them. I decided to stick to my plan and Maurice himself could see the sense in it. However, I had enough residual feelings of guilt not to suggest that Maurice return my jack. Even though he hadn't mentioned any more tyre trouble since we'd parted, it seemed likely that his need on the return journey would be greater than mine.

CHAPTER 14

BATTLING BREAKDOWNS

Shortly after dawn on the morning of Tuesday 17th October, the six of us who were returning to Europe had a final breakfast, pocketed a handful of salt tablets and set off. We were all hoping to reach Tartus in time to catch the ferry that we believed was scheduled for the coming Friday. It was a tall order, but we were well rested, and with empty trucks there was no need to worry about blowing tyres by speeding in the heat. Six was an unwieldy number of trucks to run together, so without much discussion we divided into threes, Joe Berrington, Kermit and I making up one of the trios. I was quite jealous of Joe's motor, a towering Ford Transcontinental that seemed to dwarf my Magirus, while Kermit had a Volvo F88, the excellent truck I had given up for the dubious pleasures of the Maggie. We decided that the two groups would meet for the night at 'The Mirrors', a roadside restaurant well into Saudi Arabia. The other group set off ahead of us and we three were content to go a little slower at first, to allow a separation between our two groups. Apart from anything else, it made no sense to arrive in a crowd at each border, since we would only waste time waiting for each other.

By late morning, we'd left the United Arab Emirates and transited the southern edge of Qatar back into Saudi Arabia. With empty trucks, border formalities were considerably quicker, and inspections simply required the customs officer to step up onto the trailer's rear under-run bar and peer through the triangular hole where we'd folded back the rear sheet of the tilt. At this rate, we'd have an easy run back to Tartus. I shouldn't even have entertained the thought.

At first, we had a merry time in Saudi, sometimes driving three abreast on wider stretches of road and tossing snacks between our trucks, more for the fun of it than from any necessity. At one wide piece of road, we caught up a slow-moving local wagon and divided around him to overtake, still side by side, enjoying the driver's startled expression. At our next stop, however, Joe noticed a problem with his trailer. Instead of the usual single cylindrical belly tank, Joe's firm had fitted his trailer with four standard 450-litre truck tanks, strapped to the chassis and linked with a series of pipes. From one of these, diesel was trickling into the sand. Since the whole economy of the trip depended on running all the way home on dirt-cheap Saudi diesel, the leak had to be fixed. We peered under the trailer and discovered that there wasn't one leak, but two. The needlessly complex network of pipes must have vibrated loose, and in the hour or so it took us to isolate one tank, all three of us ended up with our arms covered in diesel. We couldn't afford to spend too much of our water on washing, so we'd have to live with the smell.

We'd scarcely got going again before my Magirus at last decided to play its air games again. As the air gauges dropped, I pulled off the road onto some hard sand and the others drew up alongside. Having two more drivers to address the problem was certainly good for morale, but we didn't manage to identify the cause until, after half an hour of apparently fruitless fiddling, the air pressure started building again. We set off again, only for Kermit to notice a little further on that diesel was once again dripping from Joe's extra tanks. Once again we crawled under his trailer to try to fix the problem, but without plumbing tape, it was hard to get the pipe joints as tight as we wanted.

We finally reached our rendezvous just as the others were going to bed, having had a relaxing evening in the Mirrors restaurant, named unsurprisingly for the mirrors that lined its back wall. They made good-natured fun of us for taking so long, but the three of us were now linked by the bond of hardship and we shrugged it off. We were too tired to eat and simply collapsed into our bunks, resolving to start very early the next morning to make up time.

We were an hour further up the road, just after dawn, when my air failed again, but at last I found out what was wrong with it. I'd pulled over with enough air still in the system that we managed to identify a leak coming from the 'blow-off' valve. This is designed to prevent undue pressure building up in the system if the driver doesn't use the brakes for a while. In some old trucks, particularly Fiats and the older French Berliets still favoured by the Bulgarian national transport company, the valve would operate so regularly that the truck would sound like a wheezing asthmatic trying to catch every breath, but mine was evidently open all the time.

We tried to unstick the valve by belting it with a hammer, and finally I decided simply to jam it closed. I sawed the end off a small electrical screwdriver and hammered its plastic handle into the outflow tube of the valve. To prevent the pressure from building too far, I then slackened off a connection to the air-horn, just enough to allow excess air to escape. This mad solution actually worked, all the way back to the north of England, where I delivered my return load from Austria. There, on a roundabout in Oldham, the screwdriver fell out, having survived for over 3000 miles. By now, of course, I knew the ropes; I sacrificed another small screwdriver, hammered it home and made it back to base in Brierley Hill.

Meanwhile Joe, Kermit and I still had to reach Tartus in time for the ferry, with little more than a day to manage it. Once again, the other three, with their trouble-free trucks, caught us up as we were grappling with the repairs. They stopped just long enough to commiserate – and in truth there was little they could contribute – and carried on. The rest of the day was spent in a hare and tortoise relay, with we three playing the tortoise. Joe's tanks continued to cause problems and at one point his exhaust brake jammed closed. This was an auxiliary braking device that blocked off the exhaust gases and created a back pressure on the pistons, thereby slowing them down.

In those days, an exhaust brake was a fairly primitive affair, and in the Ford's Cummins engine, it consisted of a steel slide that closed off the exhaust at the manifold. With the slide jammed closed, the engine produced no power. We worked out that the slide could be held open if we closed off the cylinder it moved in with an empty baked bean can that

I supplied. I hastily wolfed down the beans, being reluctant simply to empty them on the ground, but the other two thought cold beans were too unpalatable to join me.

The effect of our serial breakdowns was that we never took any proper breaks. All our stops were devoted to repairs, instead of decent meals and sleep. For the rest of the time we kept driving, still hoping to make the boat. We were rewarded by slipping into Syria from Jordan just before the border closed on the Thursday evening. That left us a straight run to Tartus, only 350 kilometres away, but still a tricky journey over the mountains in the dark. Now we were within striking distance, we could afford to stop to cook a reasonable meal, though what we really needed was a wash. We had, in the end, managed to stop the leak from Joe's tanks, enabling him to fill his tanks in Saudi Arabia, but the struggle had left us filthy and reeking of diesel.

We reached Homs, high on Syria's central mountain spine, sometime after midnight, where we found the other three parked up for the night, with their cab curtains drawn. With an unspoken agreement between us, we drove on a little further and stopped for a brief consultation; we wouldn't wait for them and we wouldn't stop. It would be sweet triumph to arrive ahead of them in the queue for the ferry. We still had to negotiate the tricky, dirt road descent to the coast, but finally, at six in the morning, we reached Tartus and joined the haphazard line of trucks waiting for the boat. The others rolled in behind us an hour or two later. By late afternoon, we were all safely aboard the *Falster* and taking our overdue showers. The following morning, more to pass the time than in the hope of achieving anything, Joe and I removed the blow-off valve from my truck and took it down to the ship's engine room, where we were allowed the run of the well-equipped workshop. We dismantled the valve but couldn't find any obvious fault, so we reassembled it, complete with the doctored screwdriver.

The remainder of the return trip seemed anti-climactic. It was almost as if the Middle East had sensed the arrival of a novice and thrown non-stop dramas in my way. At any rate, I was returning with a good deal more knowledge and experience than I'd expected, and the confidence that came with having overcome a variety of problems. It was a strange echo of my first trip for Cadwallader, eighteen months earlier, when I'd broken down on the return from Basel and established myself in the company in one go, by sorting myself out unaided.

Two days after docking in Volos, Joe and I crossed the Austrian border at Spielfeld, where we ate the traditional returning driver's breakfast of *spiegeleier mit schinken*, or fried eggs and ham. We called our respective bosses for loading instructions and found ourselves sent to the same chipboard manufacturer at Pitten, near Vienna. It was now mid-morning on Tuesday, but we managed to get loaded, clear customs and make it as far as Linz, en route to Munich, for the night. The following evening we were back on the train, and by Thursday lunchtime we were in the line of trucks on the Zeebrugge docks, waiting for the ferry to Dover. This was thoroughly familiar from previous trips to Germany and the Benelux countries, but now I had my first Middle East trip behind me and I felt a new sense of satisfaction.

While we waited, I was astonished that Joe started cleaning his truck thoroughly, laboriously using a bucket and cloth to wash away all the grime from his cab. By the time he'd finished, it looked as if he'd been no further than Brussels.

"Why are you bothering?" I asked him. "You'll be back in your yard tomorrow night and you can steam-clean the whole truck."

"That's just it," he said. "All that stuff we've been through, that's for us. When you get back with a truck covered with mud and dust, it gives them a thrill as if they'd done the trip themselves, but it's us that did the work. They don't deserve to share it." Joe's attitude had an almost samurai quality and made an obscure sort of sense. Although I never followed his example, this was the final lesson I learned from Joe, who had become an unofficial but far more effective mentor than Maurice had been. When we parted that evening at Dover, Joe heading west and I aiming for delivery near Oldham the following morning, it was like leaving a long-established friend. It was hard to believe we'd met less than two weeks ago, but our shared misadventures had created an unmistakable bond.

I was tipped by the following afternoon and heading back to the motorway, when the relief valve played its final card, as I've described, but by late Friday afternoon I was heading south on the M6. I'd already arranged with Jane to pick me up on the Saturday morning from Brierley Hill, which meant a five-hour drive in our old car, and I'd settle up with Jack in the morning. Meanwhile, I had one last night on the road, so, as I approached Keele, where I'd spent five years as a student, I phoned Dick Maidment, an old university friend who'd been my American politics teacher, and arranged to have dinner with him and his wife, Susan. By chance, other old Keele friends – all lecturers at the university – were due for dinner with the Maidments, so I shifted abruptly from one world to another. The assembled academics were mildly interested in my adventures and I gave them a brief summary, before we moved on to politics and other matters of mutual interest.

At one point in my description, I looked at Dick – a good friend, an inspirational teacher and one of the smartest men I've ever met – and I wondered whether, for all that, he would have been able to take a troublesome truck from England to Dubai and back as I had. It was an unsettling thought and I realised that I'd become part of a world that was so far from the academic life I'd once shared with these friends that no description could really bridge the gap.

The next morning, I was back in the trucking world as I rolled down the M6 towards Birmingham and Brierley Hill. I pulled up outside Jack's office and, by chance, he was walking back from the nearby Shell station. I climbed down from the cab and strode confidently to meet him, feeling so different from our first encounter. As he shook my hand, Jack said, "Good, you're smiling after your first trip. That's always a sign that you're suited to it." He made no mention of my early troubles, and the fact that I'd got back in one piece seemed to have wiped the slate clean. We checked my surviving paperwork and my expenses, and Jack gave me a cheque for £850, the 'trip money' for a run to Dubai. It had taken me five weeks, which worked out about the same as I would have earned at Cadwallader in the same amount of time. My own expenses had to come out of that; the £1500-worth of D-Marks were all for the truck, but even with the extra cost of the new wheels, I still had some of them left.

We'd just finished our business when Jane arrived at the wheel of our old Vauxhall. I saw a new, courtly side of Jack when he met her, and later when I did indeed celebrate 'Muslim Christmas' on my third trip, he tried hard to send her flowers in my absence, but was defeated by Interflora's inability to locate our remote cottage on their map. Meanwhile, I had a week's break in front of me before the next trip, and by evening I was back at home at the end of the Llyn Peninsula, in another world as far removed as one could imagine from the deserts of Arabia. It turned out that I would actually have more time at home, a whole week after five weeks away, than I had managed when I worked for Cadwallader. There was room to relax, spend time with the children and go out with Jane for what had become our traditional welcome home dinner in the local pub. I was even able to do a few jobs around the house. It looked as if Middle East work was going to be better for all of us.

CHAPTER 15
SAUDI ARABIA

have described my first excursion to the Middle East in some detail, partly because the first time one does anything it tends to stick particularly in the memory, and partly because it was full of incident, though in one way or another, that could be said of every trip I made to the Middle East. At any rate, after a week at home, I headed back to the West Midlands, and a couple of surprises.

Jack had two pieces of news when I returned to Brierley Hill for my second outing. One was that he had upgraded me from the old Maggie to one of his almost new Daf 2800s, and the other was that he and Maurice had parted company. I was very pleased about the Daf, but scarcely surprised about Maurice, who had seemed ill-suited to the work. Apparently, the last straw – apart from the numerous tyre blow-outs – had been when he'd managed to tear down some overhead power lines on the Munich tram system, by driving under a bridge that was a little too low. He hadn't even noticed, but had been seen and identified. The Munich police had asked their British colleagues to investigate and two coppers turned up at the office a couple of days later. Presumably, it had cost Jack, or his insurance company, rather more than the cost of my two wheels to put things right.

Jack shrugged off the incident and briefed me on my next trip. I'd be going to another Weir Westgarth desalination site, this time in Jeddah, on the Red Sea coast of Saudi Arabia. I'd be loading that afternoon and would then head straight for Dover. With a successful first run behind me, I was a good deal happier as I set off for Evesham to load another trailer with desalination components, and the Daf was an amazing improvement over the Magirus I'd suffered on my first trip.

I had admired Daf's 2800 flagship since it was first launched some four years earlier, and its tall, square cab had a purposeful air quite lacking in the Magirus. Gone with the Maggie were the garish colours of Davies Turner; instead, my new truck was painted in Harrison's bright yellow livery, with his name in black and red on the sides and the words '*GREAT BRITAIN – MIDDLE EAST*' stretching boldly across the cab above the grille. Above the windscreen was a factory-spec sun visor, whose lines blended in neatly with the cab roof. The cab height gave excellent visibility and the pleasure of looking down on almost every other road user, except drivers of Ford Transcontinentals. The engine was advanced, too, with both turbocharging and intercooling to give a power output of 307bhp and torque of 855lb-ft, both considerable figures for the time.

Best of all, the gearbox – a vital part of the driver's experience of any truck – was an Eaton-Fuller thirteen-speed non-synchromesh transmission. I was familiar with the basic nine-speed version, which had featured in all the trucks I'd driven for Williams Transport, and the ERF I'd driven for my first week at Caddy's had had the thirteen speed, but it was still a while since I'd driven one. Jack tactfully suggested that I wait until he left before setting off, so he wouldn't hear any gear crunching as I relearned my way around the Fuller box: "If I'm not there, you won't have any trouble," he added. He was right; the gearshift seemed comfortably familiar, with the added advantage of a splitter on the upper range of gears, giving twelve normal ratios in all, plus a deep crawler ratio, which I never had to use. The tall gearstick stuck straight up from the cab floor and looked unwieldy at first, but turned out to be so light and easy to use that I often dispensed with the clutch pedal altogether. The trick – easier with a slow-revving truck engine than in a car – was to match the revs and road speed so accurately that the shift slid through without having to separate the engine from the gearbox by means of the clutch. It's a technique that most American drivers use all the time, once the truck is moving.

The interior of the cab was a revelation, with two wide bunks behind the seats, a very low engine tunnel and all manner of places to stow bottles and small odds and ends. Full curtains that pulled across the doors and the windscreen meant that I'd have the privacy at night that the unlamented Maggie had sorely lacked. The Daf even had two cigarette lighters, one for each seat, perhaps reflecting the smoking habits of its Dutch designers. When I became a truck journalist some years later, I discovered that Daf had a reputation for understanding drivers' needs, and the cab interior reflected that. The bunks themselves were particularly well thought out because the top berth could be raised full height or lowered halfway down to form an excellent sofa, while still leaving stowage room beneath it. The big 2800 was the best truck I'd ever lived in and I couldn't have been happier.

Almost as welcome as the tractor unit itself was the trailer it pulled. Instead of the bare-bones rental unit I'd had before, I now had a fully equipped Middle East trailer, with a huge 2500-litre 'belly' tank slung between the chassis rails, and two large steel boxes bolted on one side beneath the trailer floor, in which I could store all my food and equipment. I no longer had to share the cab with a stove, two five-gallon water bottles, five weeks' supply of food and sundry tools. For the outward trip, the belly tank was filled with the low-tax red diesel sold to farmers and operators of site machinery. I wasn't allowed to use this in Britain or Western Europe, so I'd effectively be exporting the fuel outside the EEC. The tank had to be customs sealed in Dover, and covered by the EEC's customs T-forms as far as Spielfeld on the Austrian-Yugoslav border, but once I'd crossed into Yugoslavia, I'd be running on cheap fuel all the way to Saudi Arabia, where I'd now be able to refill the belly tank even more cheaply.

The second trip was uneventful as far as Austria, where I began to hear some unwelcome clatter from the engine. I was less nervous than I'd been with the wheel incident when I reported this to Jack, and he seemed quite sanguine, since the Daf was still under warranty. He directed me to the Daf dealer in Graz, where the engine was diagnosed to have some problems with its camshaft and the tappets that controlled the inlet and exhaust valves. It was now mid-morning on Saturday and parts would not be available until Monday morning, so I was effectively 'weekended' again. I slept in the truck parked in the workshop yard and the efficient dealer had me back on the road by lunchtime on Monday. The delay turned out to my advantage because when I reached the Yugoslav border at Spielfeld, I was delighted to hook up with Joe Berrington again, who was on his way to the same Weir Westgarth site in Jeddah as I was. We had already proved to be very compatible running mates and we remained together for the whole round trip.

Joe had already proved a generous teacher and once we were through the Yugoslav border, he showed me how to transfer fuel from the trailer's belly tank into the tractor unit's road tank. A broad hose ran from the belly tank to the front of the trailer, where it was hooked up against the headboard. We unhooked it and put the end into the Daf's road tank and then disconnected the red air-line, one of three lines controlling the trailer brakes. The red line is under constant pressure – once its tap has been opened – to keep the fail-safe brakes off, so we connected it to a socket in the trailer headboard, which was attached to another pipe leading into the tank. When I turned on the red line's tap again, it rapidly built up air pressure in the belly tank, forcing the diesel through the fuel pipe to the road tank. It was a remarkably simple system and avoided the need for an extra pump, which would have been less reliable and much slower. Now, with enough fuel to get the truck to Saudi Arabia, and enough food for myself, I felt very satisfyingly self-sufficient. While we were stopped in a parking area, I opened up my trailer box and we set out our picnic chairs and cooked ourselves a meal. We may have been sitting in a scruffy car park, but it felt a whole lot more civilised, and less cooped up, than cooking in the cab.

With no Maurice or tyre blow-outs to slow us down, it took less than three days to reach Volos, where we discovered that the ferry schedules had become more erratic and unpredictable, and we waited two further days for the arrival of the *Scandinavia*, sister ship to the *Falster* I'd travelled on before. The Swedish company that had begun operating between Greece and Syria was essentially camping out in Volos. There was no land-based infrastructure; instead of a link-span on the dock to load the ferries – as there was in every northern European ferry port – each ship merely lowered a loading ramp onto the dockside. The ferry office was a temporary cabin plonked down in the acres of unpaved parking area, where we cooked, ate, slept and relieved ourselves, since the toilet facilities were rudimentary – to put it politely.

Few of the waiting drivers were inclined to spend much money on drinking or eating out, but on various crossings the long delays made us desperate for any diversion. One afternoon, a British driver insisted that a group of us accompany him to a nearby brothel where, he boasted, he would get a free ride. With little else to do, we went with him, while he explained that he'd been sampling the brothel's delights the previous day, but had been hurried out before he had finished. He was a big man and the manager, or pimp, had obviously decided that a freebie was the best way to deal with his vociferous complaints. We duly trooped upstairs and sat in the most depressing waiting room I've ever seen. The only thing sadder than the world-weary prostitute herself were the men waiting to buy her services, and when our new friend duly claimed what he'd come for, I reflected that I'd have paid good money to avoid being there at all.

On another occasion, a few of us were sitting in a café where a group of US sailors were occupying a neighbouring table. We fell into conversation with them and discovered that they were from the USS *South Carolina*, a 10,000-ton nuclear-powered cruiser anchored in the bay. The ship was on a goodwill mission, they told us, and their job was to find local people to visit the ship. We pointed out that we were no more local than they were, but they shrugged this off, and we soon found ourselves speeding over the harbour in a powerful motorboat, whose V8 Detroit Diesel truck engine was of particular interest to us drivers. I'd never been on a warship before and I was fascinated by the whole visit, which took nearly two hours including refreshments. Since my only experience of ships was ferries, with their large open public areas, it was something of a shock to see how little space was wasted in a warship and to realise how closely all its crew had to work together.

When the *Scandinavia* finally arrived, it was clearly a poor relation compared with the *Falster*. Several of the cabins were simply containers bolted to the deck, and lacked ventilation or washing and toilet facilities, which were housed in a separate container nearby. It didn't help that the weather was bad and, being a poor sailor, I spent most of the miserable crossing in my bunk. The *Scandinavia* was also a less reliable ship than the *Falster*. On a later trip, we limped most of the way back from Syria on one engine and, at one point, lay becalmed for several hours, like *Compass Rose* in *The Cruel Sea*, as the ship's mechanics carried out some repair on the remaining engine.

Tartus, this second time, lifted my spirits and now that I knew the routine, I enjoyed arguing with Four Eyes, the money-changer. I was also prepared for the leisurely pace at which our paperwork would be processed, though, in fact, it was no worse than in Italy. And in Italy, they didn't have the excuse that everything had to be transliterated into Arabic. We made a relatively rapid transit through Syria and into Jordan, and on this trip I didn't need to visit the Saudis in Amman, since I had acquired a multiple entry visa from their embassy in London. At that time, truck drivers were the only category of visitors that were allowed multiple entry visas, which was a measure of how important international truck traffic was to the Saudis. All the same, we didn't want to tackle their border late in the day, particularly since this was a different crossing than the one we'd used en route to Dubai. So, once we'd passed Amman, Joe and I parked up at the side of the road for a brew and some supper. Across the road was some sort of military installation and after a while, the Jordanian corporal on guard duty wandered across the road to talk to us. He spoke good English and seemed friendly enough, so I invited him to join us in the cab for a mug of tea. We then proceeded to have a lively discussion about Middle Eastern politics, something I would generally have avoided, in which he told us that there were only two good governments in the Middle East: the Jordanian and the Israeli. I couldn't have been more surprised.

The next morning, we set off again for the Jordanian border at Halat Ammar. The Jordanian border office may have been in a different location from the one I'd used on the trip to Dubai, but it was once again a row of tents along the roadside, where we were processed by an affable officer wearing an Arafat-style *keffiyeh* headscarf. Behind him, on a low divan, sat his colleague, elbow on one knee, with the inevitable cigarette staining his fingers. By Middle Eastern standards, the process was positively slick, and within twenty minutes we were free to roll a couple of kilometres through the brief no-man's land and join the long line of trucks waiting to enter the Saudi customs area.

Ahead was a column of Jordanian artics; big, imposing bonneted Mercs standing high on twenty-four inch wheels and sand tyres. Jordanians were the Middle Eastern equivalent of the Dutch – competent international truckers who went everywhere, in numbers disproportionate to the small size of their country. I once even saw one of their desert Mercs in Dover. Jordanian trucks generally seemed well cared for, though their orange paintwork was always a sun-faded matt, with the original gloss long since burned away. Interspersed among them in the line ahead of us was a motley collection of shabbier Syrian trucks, including large American bonneted vehicles dating from the '40s, laden with ungainly towers of timber, like the trucks I had seen on the docks at Tartus in my first glimpse of Syria.

Each truck was held at the barrier – a counter-weighted pole across the road – while its driver was interrogated. When I finally reached the head of the line, I was asked what soon became a familiar mantram of questions: "Whisky? Sex books? Pistol?" No, naturally, in every case. The penalty for whisky smuggling was severe, with rumours of drivers doing six months' jail time for trying to take through only a couple of bottles. With spirits fetching a price of £50 a litre on the Saudi black market, I could see the temptation, but never understood why anyone would give in to it. 'Sex books' even included the English newspaper *The Sun*, with its 'Page 3' photo of a topless girl, because I did once see a driver have his *Sun* confiscated, though with nothing more than a reprimand.

Once through the line, Joe and I headed through the gates of a vast walled compound, lined with dozens of trucks reversed in neat rows against the walls. We took our papers to the office of our customs agent and settled in for a long wait that made the Italians in Aosta seem lightning slick. Nothing happened for the rest of that day, and the following morning we were instructed to take our trucks and park them against an unloading dock in a vast open-sided shed. Here, a group of Indians – temporary workers imported to do grunt work for the Saudis – proceeded to unload our miscellaneous crates, some of which were given a desultory examination by a pair of uniformed customs officers.

I soon learned not to be fooled by their languid air, because I was told to dismount my spare tyres so they could be deflated and examined for contraband, creating the problem for me of reinflating them using one of the truck's air-lines. The whole rigmarole took several hours, and it wasn't until the evening of the second day that Joe and I made our escape. Once again, we lined up before a pole across the road for a final check of our paperwork, before being released onto the road for Medina and Jeddah.

A sign in Arabic and Roman numerals announced that Jeddah was 1200 kilometres ahead and I soon discovered that the distance was marked ten kilometres at a time for several hundred kilometres before the signs stopped, perhaps because the gang setting them up found the countdown as discouraging as I did. Saudi Arabia is vast, and at 830,000 square miles, almost twice the size of Britain, France and Germany combined, with a population in those days of less than ten million. When I later consulted a map, I discovered that a third of the country was actually south of the Tropic of Cancer, with the south-eastern tip of the country a mere fifteen degrees from the Equator. Jeddah was itself in the tropics and I was looking forward to seeing my first Saudi city; on my earlier excursion, I hadn't gone anywhere near a centre of population, and had seen only one or two villages in my whole tramp down the north-eastern side of the country.

We decided to push on for a few hours into the night. There were two advantages of night driving in Saudi Arabia. The first is that it was cooler, so we could travel faster, and the second was that the BBC World Service came through much more clearly on the radio. Every British Middle East driver I knew was a World Service listener, but it could sometimes feel a little bizarre to be hearing British and world news while hurtling through the empty desert in the dark. On a later trip, I was tuned in to a programme about US politics at about two in the morning, when I heard the voice of my former American history professor, David Adams, commenting on some new development in the United States. I wanted to shout out to him: "Hey, David; I'm here, out in the desert, listening to you." I think I did actually shout out – you do a lot of talking to yourself behind the wheel of a long-haul truck.

The disadvantage of night driving on that particular road was the danger. The road itself was two-lane blacktop, which, for long stretches at a time, was only just wide enough for two trucks to pass each other. Cruising at about 60mph, I often had to swing the truck slightly to the right as an oncoming truck passed me, as he did the same, so that we almost danced past each other, with our outer wheels right on the edge of the road surface. The danger lay in the road itself, which was often built up six inches to a foot above the surface of the sand itself, so a misjudgement would probably mean rolling the truck onto its side. At high speed, and with me sitting on the side of the truck nearest to the edge of the road, that would not have been pretty.

Day or night, international drivers had a standard procedure for overtaking in pairs. The first one of us past a slower vehicle would remain on the wrong side of the road, with the offside indicator on, to show the following driver that the coast remained clear. This reduced his risk and meant that, as a pair, we were able to travel faster than we would if the first truck had constantly to wait for the second. It was also, bizarrely enough, rather entertaining.

The next day we reached the outskirts of Medina, a holy city that, like Mecca, is open only to Muslims. Ahead was a police checkpoint and a huge sign in a dozen languages, including Japanese and Korean, announcing that all non-Muslims should divert around the city on what we western drivers called the 'Christian bypass'. We were flagged down by the Saudi police and it was the only time I have ever had a traffic cop ask me my religion. On later trips, I wasn't stopped, but merely waved onto the bypass; presumably with a British truck, the chances were strong that I was an infidel.

Now that we were on the road between Medina and Mecca, a new hazard appeared – busloads of white-clad pilgrims careering along as if the driver no longer cared whether he and his exalted passengers lived or died. At any rate, they seemed blind to any rules of sensible overtaking, and several times I had to brake for a bus driver who'd tried to squeeze past an oncoming vehicle when he shouldn't. Close to Jeddah, we passed the road to Mecca on our left, with another hoarding forbidding access to non-believers, and after that we were relieved of the dubious entertainment of pilgrim transport.

Just short of Jeddah on the evening of our second day in Saudi, Joe pulled over with the sensible suggestion that we shouldn't tackle an unknown city on an empty stomach – another lesson in patience that I filed away as future practice. We cooked ourselves a meal in the cooling evening air – the temperature was down to about thirty degrees Celsius – washed down as always with hot tea, and continued on. Jeddah itself was a large sprawling mess of a city, which seemed largely under construction. Huge wooden packing cases littered the landscape and there were several diversions round emerging new pieces of road. We had no idea where Weir Westgarth's desalination site might be, but we did know that it would be large and on the shore of the Red Sea. With this intelligence, we actually found it quite quickly, but were disappointed not to receive the same welcome as we'd had at the site in Dubai. We were, however, given the offer of an empty air-conditioned office to sleep in, and I removed the two mattresses from my Daf – Joe's, as in most trucks, were fixed – and we moved into the welcome cool of the Portakabin. We'd have to wait a full day to unload, since we'd managed to arrive on the site's day off, but we took the opportunity to do some washing, hanging our clothes to dry on lines slung between our two trailers.

Early the following morning, before the day heated up, we began unloading and discovered something about our countrymen that filled both of us with shame. It was our job to dismantle our tilts, and Joe and I stripped down each trailer in turn to allow access for a crane to hoist off the crates. Just as the Dubai site had imported Indians to do the donkey work, so the Jeddah site employed men from various African nations – Somalis prominent among them. The crane driver and four labourers were Somalis – four very friendly and helpful guys who spoke enough English that we could share jokes and laughter as we worked together in the fierce sun. The whole operation was overseen by a pair of Brits who were as boorish as the Somalis were graceful. They were blatantly rude and racist towards the Africans, calling them idiots when they didn't do something quickly enough and generally treating them like inferior beings. The Somalis shrugged this off – a measure of how routine this attitude was. When it came to lunchtime, the two Brits suggested we have lunch in their air-conditioned canteen, but with only a look between us, Joe and I opted for the more congenial company of the labourers, who invited us to join them in what turned out to be a large open-sided marquee. One of our lunch companions actually confessed to being from Israel and to be working under false papers. In those days (and, for all I know, even today), Arab countries forbade imports from any company that had associations with Israel, and direct contact between Israel and Saudi Arabia was forbidden. All Middle East drivers had to carry, and produce when required, a letter known to us drivers as the 'blacklist', which declared that neither the company nor the shipper had any Israeli or Jewish connections. It was a distastefully anti-Semitic document, but without it a truck and its contents might be refused entry to any Arab state. How our friend had managed to find entry as a labourer, I didn't ask, but I was conscious that he had paid us a compliment by trusting us with such dangerous information.

CHAPTER 16
AN INTERLUDE ON SMUGGLING

The return trip was incident-free, and Joe and I ran homewards together, parting only to reload in Austria, before we met up again in Munich to take the train. Christmas was approaching and Joe wanted to take in a little more seasonal cheer than British customs allowed at the time, so he bought several bottles of spirits, hoping to hide them in one of his spare tyres. The only snag was that his wheels were difficult to dismantle, while my trailer wheels still had the old system of a sprung steel ring holding the tyre in place around the rim, which made the process easier. We duly stripped down my spare tyre, hid the bottles inside it and partially reinflated it, using a connection to the trailer brake lines. Joe loaded the spare onto his own trailer and I took one of his on mine.

It was dark by the time we reached Dover the following evening and presented ourselves one after the other at the water-guard where we did our personal customs clearance. Now that I was driving a truck that was not only visibly equipped for ultra-long-distance runs, but also carried the legend '*GREAT BRITAIN – MIDDLE EAST*' across the front, I was questioned in more detail than I had been when I was returning from anywhere in Europe, but Joe's bottles remained undiscovered, as we knew they would. We parked side by side in the vast parking area, where hundreds of trucks were lined up while their loads were cleared through customs.

We'd known that Joe would have to take the booze back since it was hidden in my spare, but we hadn't planned where to make the exchange.

Now that we had a few hours on our hands while our paperwork was being processed, we decided to do the job there and then in the docks. Joe proposed to hide the bottles in his cab, since the water-guard check was completed and his cab wouldn't be examined again. It was still a risky idea, but somehow Dover seemed tame compared with Middle-Eastern customs compounds, and we were both slightly high after completing another successful trip, so we scarcely thought about the risk. Under the glare of the orange sodium lights, and with the aid of a torch, we unbolted the spare tyre from my trailer and wound it down to the ground, using the small hand-powered winch installed above the spare itself. We again stripped the tyre down and, while I kept watch, Joe retrieved the bottles and hid them under his bunk. We were just reassembling the wheel when two of the dock police appeared on their regular patrol. They were quite solicitous and when we explained that we were just replacing a flat tyre, they stayed to help us, holding the torch as we remounted the spare under the trailer. Joe and I could hardly keep from laughing, and laugh we did once they'd left, but mainly from relief that they hadn't appeared five minutes earlier. It was my only foray into smuggling, even though I had been only an accessory. Once was quite enough.

The penalties for smuggling into the UK may have been less harsh than they were in Saudi Arabia, but they could still bring a jail sentence and, at the very least, put an end to my international driving career. Even if I had been tempted, which I never was, the rewards appeared to be paltry, particularly compared with the risk. I learned this one day the following year, when I was parked up in a rest area off a Dutch motorway. I was making myself some lunch in the cab when a car pulled up beside me and the driver gestured that he wanted to speak to me. I wound down the window, but wasn't inclined to come down from the cab; there was something slightly off about the stranger and I opted to keep the advantage of looking down on him. He asked me where I was loading and, without going into details, I said I'd be picking up a load nearby. He then asked whether I would be prepared to take an extra pallet into the UK for him. I wouldn't have said yes under any circumstances, but I was interested in the details. It was quite simple, he said. Once I'd loaded, he'd meet my truck wherever it would be convenient for me and put the extra pallet aboard. Once I'd passed through customs in Dover, he would arrange to have the pallet taken off my hands in England – again, wherever it suited me. I asked what would be on the pallet.

"Books," he said, vaguely, for which I read 'pornography'. And how much would I be paid?

"£200," he answered, clearly expecting me to be impressed. In fact, I was as shocked as I was insulted. He wanted me to risk my job (and freedom) for what amounted to little more than a week's wages? Even at a year's wages, I wouldn't have done it, so, none too politely, I turned him down. He maintained that other drivers did it for the same money, but I was not persuaded. The would-be smuggler got back into his car and took off with an angry squeal of tyres. As I continued my lunch, I reflected that the low price, and his obvious assumption that I would be interested, showed there were some mugs out there who were prepared to take the bait. Apart from the dubious honour of smuggling pornography that was presumably so nasty that it couldn't be imported legally, the risk was literally incalculable. What if, for example, he had chosen to tip off Dover customs for his own reasons? This wasn't as far-fetched as it sounds, in the light of an earlier incident that had occurred in the eighteen months I'd been driving for Caddy's before joining Jack Harrison.

Unusually, I had swapped my fridge trailer for a tilt to make a delivery to France and had reloaded twenty tonnes of untreated 'green' sheepskins from Belleville, between Mâcon and Lyon in central France. The fact that the load was bound for Dolgellau, in the sheep-rearing heart of Wales, was odd in itself, but I'd become used to carrying coals to Newcastle on a number of occasions and I didn't pay much attention to the anomaly. Since the load wasn't subject to any customs duties, and was only going from France to the UK, there was no customs seal on the trailer, so I was very surprised to find myself singled out as soon as I rolled up to the water-guard in Dover. I had no sooner engaged the handbrake than two officers slapped a seal on the rear of the trailer and sent me directly to one of the inspection bays, where trailers could be examined in detail and unloaded for inspection if necessary.

This was highly unusual. Physical customs inspections were rare, and happened only once the paperwork had been presented to customs by whichever agent we were using. Now, however, I'd been summoned immediately. Moreover, I was brusquely questioned by two more officers, who wanted to know whether I had helped load the sheepskins. No I hadn't, thank goodness, since they were still 'green' and even bloody, and smelled less than salubrious. All I had done, I explained, was to roll back the tilt for loading before spending an hour in the cab while the sheepskins were piled into the trailer. They seemed satisfied that whatever might be in the trailer, I wasn't responsible and they let me go. The truck, however, was stuck, as I explained to an exasperated Phil Spittle, our transport manager, on the phone.

Customs now wanted the whole trailer to be unloaded for examination, but the men who would have to do the work flatly refused to handle the bloody skins. What's more, the manager of the inspection bay wouldn't allow them to be stacked on his pristine concrete loading dock. Hours passed while both sides tried to negotiate a way round this impasse; finally, I got permission to drop the trailer where it was and move my Volvo tractor unit to somewhere quieter for the night. The next morning, the situation still wasn't resolved and I was becoming something of a celebrity among the agents who scurried around the customs area, carrying papers and arranging clearance. I got used to comments such as "still here, then?" and, finally, just "baa, baa", accompanied by a grin.

In the end, the unloaders agreed to do the job, provided they were given special protective gear and a bonus of £30 – more than a day's pay in those days – but the manager still refused to allow the skins to sully his dock. Instead, Cadwallader had to send a second tilt trailer down to Dover so the skins could be transferred from one trailer to the other, while customs examined each one. This took me into my second full day in the docks. By now, the officers themselves had realised that I had nothing to do with whatever crime was being committed. When I asked one of them whether there had been a tip-off, he told me he wasn't at liberty to say, while making it clear with a nod and wink that, yes, there had been a call that my trailer was carrying drugs. In any event, nothing was found and I wondered whether the warning had been designed to make my truck the focus of attention, while the contraband was actually on another vehicle off the same ferry. I was finally allowed to leave and never heard anything more about it officially, but for months afterwards I was greeted by sheep noises whenever I presented myself at the customs agents' window.

Although I was never tempted to smuggle anything through any border, when I spent a couple of days with Joe Berrington on the Saudi border at Halat Ammar, we whiled away the time by working out a foolproof way of smuggling a whole trailer-load of whisky into the country. At the price of contraband liquor at the time, it would have been worth half a million US dollars, but we had no intention of putting our idea into practice.

CHAPTER 17
MUSLIM CHRISTMAS

I returned to Jeddah twice more, and Dubai once, in the year I worked for Harrison, and made three trips to Iraq, at about the time when Saddam Hussein formally assumed the presidency. I became familiar with the routines, comfortable with Arabic customs and Customs, and I loved journeying through the desert. In those days, it was still possible to drive off the road in the evening, park on some patch of hard sand and find oneself completely alone. Once the truck itself had stopped ticking as it cooled down, a deep silence would descend, broken only occasionally by a passing vehicle back on the road. The heat became comfortable as the sun set – and in winter, the desert could actually drop to freezing, according to the weather reports I could pick up on Israeli radio when I was in Jordan. I was doing a job I'd wanted for more than a decade and it was only the fact that it didn't pay well enough that eventually made me give it up.

My third trip, to Dubai, had me leaving only a few days before Christmas, because, according to Jack, the load had to be delivered on January 1st. Neither Jane nor I were amused, but celebrating 'Muslim Christmas' was a condition for taking the job and there was no going back. I did the whole trip alone and I must have been the only driver on Weir Westgarth work over Christmas, out of the fifty-odd loads a month that the company normally dispatched with various transport companies. As I result, I made it to Dubai in only eleven days, even with a full day's wait in Volos. I arrived at the Greek port late on Christmas Eve and was told that the *Falster* would be in early the following morning. *Good*, I thought, *I'll have some sort of Christmas dinner on the boat.* There were no other Brits on the quayside, which heightened my loneliness, but I expected to see the ship moored by breakfast time. Naturally, I was disappointed, but, still hoping for a decent lunch on board, I made myself a large bowl of porridge and settled down to wait for the ferry to berth. At lunchtime there was still no sign of it, but I found a phone to call Jane back home, which was helpful, at least until I put the phone down again, feeling both lonely and guilty that I wasn't at home with my family. I wandered along the dockside, but most of the cafes were closed and I didn't feel like nursing a lonely beer. Instead, I sat in the cab, legs stretched out across the engine cover, and read for most of the day. In the end, the ferry didn't arrive until after I'd gone back to bed for the night, and we didn't leave until Boxing Day; that bowl of porridge was all I ate that day and was certainly the poorest Christmas dinner I've ever enjoyed.

Once in Syria, I hardly stopped, and it wasn't until early on New Year's Eve that I came across another Brit, a few hours short of the Qatar border. We shared a meal and set off again. As midnight approached, we were cruising along the empty desert road at a steady 60mph and on the stroke of New Year, we exchanged greetings by flashing our lights at each other. A few minutes later, we reached the nearly empty border at Qatar, where we shook hands and welcomed in 1979 with a chorus of *Auld Lang Syne*, to the bemusement of the few sleepy customs officers. When I reached the Weir Westgarth site right on schedule, around dawn on New Year's Day, I was met with incredulity. Unload? Today? This was a *Scottish* company, I remembered, and the whole site was enjoying a day off for Hogmanay. I cursed Jack for making me miss Christmas for no good reason.

My next visit to Jeddah was unusual. I was back home when I received a call from Jack, who wanted to verify that I had a multiple entry visa for Saudi Arabia. I did. Apparently two of our drivers were stuck in the Jordanian customs compound at Ramtha because the Saudis had suddenly stopped issuing visas to non-Jordanians at their Amman embassy. It seemed a typically arbitrary move from what I had come to view as a quite arrogant nation, but Jack was stuck with the consequences. To solve the impasse, he proposed to fly me to Amman and have me take one of the trucks into Saudi Arabia. I would tip it in Jeddah, bring it back into Jordan and then take the second truck to Jeddah. Meanwhile, the two drivers, 'Bubbles' and Brian 'Whispering' Smith, would return to the UK together in the first truck. From my point of view, the only snag was that I'd have none of my own gear, since I would be travelling by air.

On the other hand, I got a flight to Jordan on what I later discovered was one of the last services run by British Airways using a Vickers VC10. In those days, I hardly ever flew and the trip was a welcome novelty. It was quite bizarre to be wafted from London to Amman in five hours, instead of driving the distance in a week to ten days. I arrived in Amman late in the evening, and by the time I'd found a taxi to take me the hundred-odd kilometres to Ramtha, it was well after midnight before I was stumbling around the truck compound, searching for the two Harrison Dafs. When I finally found them, I roused 'Bubbles' – whose proper name I have, unfortunately, forgotten – and slept on his second bunk for what remained of the night.

The next morning we set off for the border, which we all called by its Saudi name, Halat Ammar, some 450 kilometres south. It was a hairy drive. The change of routine had put all three of us in a holiday mood, and with Brian taking the lead and me riding shotgun with Bubbles, we took some unreasonable risks. Several times, Brian would pass a truck and then call Bubbles on his CB radio to give him the all-clear to overtake, even though he was unsighted. Bubbles would pull out on a bend made blind by the rocky cliff beside us and pass a slower Jordanian truck. We had only Brian's word for it that we wouldn't meet another vehicle head-on. Sitting on the passenger side, and therefore where the driver should be in a left-hand-drive truck, I was at least able to act as some kind of lookout.

The last straw, and the nearest I have come to dying in a truck, was when Bubbles pulled out from behind a local lumberer and I just had time to scream, "No!" as a huge Jordanian Mercedes barrelled down on us. Luckily, Bubbles reacted instantly and swung the wheel back, saving both our lives, but the oncoming truck still scraped the side of the Daf, ripping off its mirror arm and shaving the protruding door hinges so that the door would no longer open or close. As both of us began to realise how close we'd come to being wiped out, we all calmed down and made it to the border in one piece. When it came to choosing which Daf to take through to Jeddah, I insisted on taking the undamaged cab, with the excuse that the other two would be returning to the UK several days ahead of me and would have to deal with it for a much shorter time than I would.

The arrangement worked as planned and within five days, I was back at the border with the first empty trailer. Although I'd had to do the work, I didn't envy the other two having to sit around for nearly a week with nothing to amuse them and no facilities beyond their own supplies. We swapped the trailers and shared a quick meal before the other two headed for home, and I returned to do battle with the Saudi border. This time I had a 'flying load' consisting of three large-diameter sections of pipe that together weighed only seven tonnes – so light that I (and the tyres) would hardly notice it. Between them, the pipes took up the whole length of the trailer, and the tilt was unsealed because one section was slightly too wide to fit between the sideboards.

Even though a glance through each pipe made it immediately obvious that I couldn't be smuggling anything in the load, I was still held up for more than a day in the Saudi customs compound, but, as it happened, I didn't mind at all.

Once again, I was the only Brit in the compound, so I wandered along the line of trucks and came across a group of Iranians sitting comfortably on a large carpet spread out in the shade between two of their vehicles. They were absorbed in a game of backgammon, a very popular pastime across Eastern Europe and the Middle East, and I stayed to watch. All long-haul drivers know at least a few words of German and between us we had enough vocabulary, and a wealth of shared experience, to establish a good contact. After a while, I was invited to play and all the hours I'd spent at university playing *tavli*, as my Greek and Turkish friends called it, paid off. I was proud to be able to give these Iranians a good game and I spent a happy couple of hours playing and watching games with them, and accepting their offers of tea.

It wasn't the only time my backgammon experience helped me socialise with foreign drivers. A couple of years later, I found myself 'weekended' in a rural service area by the side of an Austrian *autobahn*. I was parked next to a pair of Romanian fridge trucks, each of which had two drivers, as usual. We Brits believed that the Romanian government wouldn't allow a driver to venture abroad alone for fear he might defect. The Romanians were also known for moving slowly, perhaps because they were in no hurry to return to what was then a rather depressing country, under Ceaușescu's communist dictatorship. I carried very little fresh food, but these guys had a compartment in their fridge trailers for their own provisions, and one of them was in the process of making a chicken and vegetable stew. The other three were playing backgammon.

Once again, I began to watch, and once again I was invited to join in. After an hour or so, the Romanians pressed me to join them for dinner, which was a good deal more palatable than my own canned camion stew, and in return I replenished their beer supplies from the service station shop. We had a highly convivial evening, once again sharing enough German to be able to establish our mutual distaste for customs officers in general, and Austrian ones in particular, as well as swapping opinions on various trucks. The following morning, as I was enjoying a Sunday lie-in, I was roused by one of the drivers banging on my cab, shouting, "Colleaguer, colleaguer." I peered round the curtain to see one of my new friends holding up the backgammon board in one hand and two bottles of beer in the other.

Meanwhile, back in Saudi Arabia, I parted from my Iranian friends and set off south for Jeddah for the second time in a week. I was on the home stretch late the following afternoon and was planning to have dinner at the Weir Westgarth site; now that I knew where it was, there was no reason to fuel myself before reaching the city. As I cruised along at about 55mph in the late afternoon sunshine, I idly registered a pick-up truck coming towards me on the other side of the two-lane blacktop. I then watched the mirror in horror as the pick-up veered towards my trailer, hit the front axle and cannoned off across the road, where it came to rest down a small bank on its roof. I didn't have to brake much since the offside tyres on the front of the two trailer axles seemed to have been smashed against the rear wheels, so that they juddered to a halt.

I climbed down from the cab and nervously approached the other vehicle, half expecting to find, if not dead bodies, then at least some serious injuries. At the back of my mind was the fact that I was the foreigner, and although the accident was in no way my fault, I thought I'd be held to blame. When I'd first driven to the Middle East, I'd been bombarded with advice and information, including the fact that if I were involved in an accident in Saudi Arabia, I would always be considered at fault. Apparently, the law would say that if I, as a foreigner, hadn't been in the country, the accident couldn't have happened, so if it *did* happen, I had to be the cause. I had hoped never to find out if this unassailable, if loopy, logic held true, but now I might have to.

As I approached the pick-up, its two occupants were already crawling from the wreckage, apparently unscathed. Within moments, we'd attracted a crowd. It's a feature of Middle Eastern countries that although the landscape may appear completely deserted, as soon as there's an incident, people pop up out of the sand to voice their opinions. Sure enough, we were rapidly surrounded by a score of gesticulating locals, who, miraculously, seemed to be on my side. One man, with a little English, said he'd seen the incident and it was entirely the fault of the pick-up driver. This was certainly helpful, but I wasn't completely reassured until I discovered that the driver was from Yemen. We were both foreigners and I almost laughed with relief. In a remarkably short time, two cops appeared and the friendly crowd seemed to be telling them my side of the story. Nevertheless, the officers insisted on taking the three of us to the nearest police station. I locked my truck and got into the back of their Chevrolet Caprice, a softly sprung monstrosity that the driver proceeded to hurl down the road with no regard for its appalling road-holding. Within an hour, we were at the police station, a little way up the road to Mecca and past the large, multilingual sign barring it to non-Muslims.

Having survived the ride in the Chevy, and knowing that the other driver was Yemeni, I was surprised to find myself quite relaxed. The senior officer at the station asked for our stories and, having no Arabic to speak of, I drew a sketch showing the progress of the pick-up, its collision with my trailer and the subsequent damage to my axle. The Yemenis said nothing,

Back at Cadwallader for my second stint, loading hanging beef in Oldham for delivery to Romania, for two years one of my regular jobs

The same truck, six days later in Romania. Eastern Bloc roads were dusty in summer and muddy (or icy) in winter

Self-sufficiency on the road; cooking breakfast on the battery box of my Volvo F10.
The trailer's fridge unit is behind me

Beef hindquarters hanging from
the trailer rails, ready for unloading
in Bucharest

Cadwallader trucks make up part of a long queue at an Eastern Bloc border, which could take many hours to cross

Parked up unladen beside the road in Hungary, before heading for a short-cut back to southern Germany through Austria

My Volvo F10 cab with my six-year-old daughter Laura in Romania. Cadwallader's were happy to let drivers take our children with us

Drivers (including me) blockade the ferries in Dover, in protest at a customs go-slow. I got involved in all-night negotiations to break the deadlock

My then brand-new F10 coming down from the Alps on its first run to Italy, to deliver beef to various US military bases across the country

At the Italian entrance to the 8.5-mile tunnel under Mont Blanc. In winter, the weather could be wildly different on each side of the mountain

Although I often ran alone, it was a pleasure to link up with a colleague for some or all of a trip through eastern Europe

Taking a break on the way to Romania, one of my favourite destinations, years before the break-up of the Eastern Bloc

A Mercedes Actros from the late 1990s. Cab comfort and vehicle performance were a huge improvement compared with the trucks I used to drive

Road testing a Mercedes Actros in my later career as a journalist, when my experience as a professional driver was a major asset

OCTOBER 1990 £1·20

TRUCK

INCORPORATING **TRUCK&DRIVER**

IVECO

480 /// *TurboStar*

IVECO

G154
MMA

TO THE WALL

We haul to East Germany and try to make it pay

CHAMPAGNE COMPETITION

DRIVE THE MAGNUM WITH US IN FRANCE

Following my career behind the wheel, I shifted to journalism, becoming a part-owner of Village Publishing publisher of *TRUCK Magazine*. The October 1990 edition of the magazine was our first as the new owners but when shown the drawings, they nodded in agreement. With the facts settled, the officer asked how much I wanted in compensation. Slightly surprised by this summary justice, I did a quick estimate that remounting the axle would cost £1000, so I asked for 7000 Saudi riyals. I reckoned to get the job done in Tartus, while I waited for the homebound ferry. The Yemeni driver just laughed, with a universally recognisable gesture meaning 'broke'. I tried to insist, but after a few minutes of argument the officer simply waved us out of the door, clearly indifferent to the fate of two foreigners.

The three of us walked back half a mile across the sand to the main road, where one of my truck's assailants flagged down a minibus in the gathering dusk. I was glad he did, because I was unable to recognise that the bus was for hire. I was less amused to find that he wouldn't even pay my fare, but on the whole I reckoned I'd been lucky to escape without any legal or bureaucratic entanglements. The minibus dropped me off at my truck and, in what was now the early evening, I made myself a cup of tea before investigating the damage to the trailer. I was much calmer than I'd been six months earlier when my unlamented Magirus had lost its air. Mug in hand, I squatted down to examine the trailer axles.

It wasn't pretty. The front axle's mounting bracket had been smashed free of the chassis rail, shifting the axle back until its two offside tyres had been jammed against the wheels behind them. This was what was called a 'spread-axle' trailer, with a couple of feet between each set of wheels, so the force applied must have been considerable – at least I'd learned that Toyota pick-ups were well built. As I considered the problem, I soon realised that with the light load I could safely run the trailer on only one axle and, besides, I had only fifty-odd kilometres left before I could unload.

Luckily, the large pipe sections were secured by several chains and tensioners, which, even if this had been my own truck, would not have been part of my regular equipment. I figured out which ones I could do without for the last few miles and used two chains to suspend the broken axle from the chassis rails, pulling them tight with the tensioners so that they wouldn't sag when I removed the wheels. It was heavy work. Each of the wheels weighed seventy-odd kilos and the trailer floor was about at the level of my shoulder, but I managed to manhandle them aboard. After an hour's hard work, I was ready to roll. I washed off the worst of the dirt and sweat I'd accumulated, had another cup of tea and continued to the Weir Westgarth site.

A few days later, back in Tartus, I found a welding shop that agreed to restore the axle mounting for the equivalent of £500. It's a measure of my independence as a Middle East driver that I didn't look for a telex to consult Jack. When I got home, he did query the decision to spend so much on the repair, but I pointed out that without it I wouldn't have been able to carry a backload from Austria, which would have lost him more money than I'd spent. He grunted his agreement.

I had completed my third visit to Jeddah and had crossed Saudi Arabia enough times to consider myself a competent Middle East driver. I had learned to negotiate a variety of different borders; I had figured out how to deal with cultures quite different from anything I'd met in Europe; and I had solved a number of technical breakdowns unaided. In doing so, I had developed enough confidence to overcome my habitual tendency to assume that others knew more about the job than I did, and at last I felt that I was on top of my game.

I came back to Brierley Hill to find my truck number matched on the planning board with Lahore in Pakistan. Jack told me he planned to send me and Brian 'Whispering' Smith on this unusually long-distance run, but, because it was as new to him as it was to Brian and me, he would pay us by the week rather than the trip and trust us not to cheat him. I felt that the fact that Jack had chosen me, alongside the much more experienced Brian, for this pioneering journey was an encouraging endorsement. The contract hadn't yet been finalised, so in the interim I was loaned out for three weeks to another Middle East veteran, John Yorkston Paxton, to drive his second truck, an older Daf 2600, on short trips to France.

The 2600 had been launched way back in 1962, and as a full double-sleeper tractor unit designed around the driver, it was way ahead of its time and set a new standard for driver comfort. In contrast, Leyland didn't launch the 'Ergomatic' cab I'd had on my AEC at Abbey Hill until two years later and even then it couldn't hold a candle to the Daf. Nor, despite this ground-breaking history, could the 2600 itself compare with its successor, the 2800 that I normally drove. But for the lure of Lahore, I would have been decidedly unhappy, particularly since on one rainy morning outside Paris, I woke up in the old Daf to discover through the BBC that Margaret Thatcher was our new prime minister.

To my lasting regret, the trip to Lahore fell through and never resurfaced. Instead, I found myself making three runs in succession to Iraq, which taught me enough about that country that I took an almost personal interest in the three wars that benighted country endured in the following decades, first with Iran and then twice with the USA and its assorted allies.

CHAPTER 18

IRAQ

Apart from the dictates of common humanity, my sympathy with Iraq grew from the fact that in 1979 it was a surprisingly welcome place to visit, and I came to regard the country with some affection. Baghdad was, under the dust, still a beautiful city, and the people seemed quite relaxed, notwithstanding the authoritarian government led, still unofficially, by Saddam Hussein. Women were allowed to appear unveiled and there was something disarming about the way young soldiers (male) would patrol the streets hand-in-hand.

My first visit to Iraq was a curiosity. I hadn't thought much about the 'blacklist' document dissociating Harrison and its customers from Israel, until I was sent into a factory in Essex to pick up my first load to Baghdad. The plant made concentrated orange juice, which was loaded straight to the trailer floor in five-gallon plastic containers. While the trailer was being loaded, I wandered around the yard and found a large stack of empty wooden crates marked 'Jaffa', an Israeli trademark. "Oh yes," the yard foreman told me, "the oranges came from Israel" – but that's not what it said on the paperwork, which made no mention of Jaffa or Israel. The 'country of origin' box was marked UK, as if the oranges came from the extensive groves of sunny Essex. As I set off, loaded with twenty tons of Israeli juice, and armed with the obligatory 'blacklist' paperwork claiming that neither Harrison nor the exporter had anything to do with Israel, I could only hope that Iraqi customs officers had a very limited knowledge of geography.

I needn't have worried; by the time I'd reached the Iraqi side of its border with Syria, I'd been through several sets of Arab customs without any query. The Iraqi border post was some 200 kilometres – nearly three hours – from the Syrian side. As I rolled up to the barrier to leave the Syrian side, I was approached by a customs officer who wanted a lift through to Iraq. I wasn't particularly keen since we'd have no way of communicating, but I wasn't going to refuse someone who might be in a position to help or hinder me in the future. He climbed into the cab and after we'd exhausted our few words in common, I tried to entertain him with some music. He wasn't impressed by my collection of western rock music, but then I remembered that I had a live recording of the legendary Arabic singer Oum Kalthoum, considered to be the greatest of all Arabic singers, and famous all across North Africa and the Middle East. My new friend was wreathed in smiles when he heard the tape, and together we listened to it twice as we crossed the lengthy no-man's land to Iraq.

The Iraqi border itself was as slow as the Saudi's, even though I never had to have my truck unloaded for inspection. At any one time, there might be at least a hundred waiting trucks from all over Eastern and Western Europe, with Bulgarians by far the largest national group. From another driver, I discovered that the procedure was to put my passport and TIR carnet together and add them to a line of similar paperwork all across a long counter in the customs office. My heart sank as I estimated that there were around a hundred sets of papers in front of mine, and I noticed that other drivers simply returned to their trucks to wait, so at first I did the same. However, after half an hour or so, and prompted by the example of Joe Berrington on previous trips, I went back to the office and hung around, offering a cigarette to one of the customs officers as he came to pick up another carnet. After an hour or so, I gave him another and he asked me with a gesture where my papers were. I pointed to my passport, still way back down the order, and he plucked it out of the line and processed it in five minutes. Joe was right; treat customs officers as human, don't disparage them to other drivers in the mistaken belief that they didn't understand English, and the whole job would go better. A couple of cigarettes and a little civility had saved me hours.

Now I had to retrieve my passport, which had apparently been sent to another office in a small separate building. Here, there was no semblance of order. A scrum of dozens of drivers from a wide range of Eastern and Western European countries, with Bulgarians and Hungarians in the majority, were crowded round a single window where we were to pick up our passports after they'd been inspected. This was slow-going because every detail had to be copied into a large ledger: name, nationality, passport number, 'passport city' (where it was issued), type of truck, registration, etc. Delaying the process even more was that most passports were from Europe and the details had to be transliterated into Arabic. I fell in with a couple of Brits at the back of the crowd and we prepared ourselves for a long delay.

Suddenly, the office door opened and an Iraqi customs officer called out to us, "British?" With no idea what he wanted, and therefore slightly nervous, we admitted we were and he beckoned us into the office, parting the crowd of drivers to let us through. Once inside, he waved to a tall pile of passports and explained, mainly by gesture, that he wanted one of us to record their details for him. I volunteered, but explained that I couldn't write in Arabic. No problem, apparently. As long as the details were recorded, it didn't matter whether they were in Arabic or European script, and I'd be saving him the trouble of having to decipher western writing. I sat down and started copying down the details. Naturally, I fished out our easily recognisable British passports from somewhere down the pile and began with them. We spent an affable hour with the Iraqis, swapping cigarettes while I filled a couple of pages of the dusty ledger. When I felt I'd done enough, I gestured questioningly to the completed pages and the Iraqi officers beamed with pleasure. We shook hands all round and made our escape; once again, I'd avoided several hours of waiting.

I might have considered this pro-British bias to be just a freak, but two trips later the same thing happened again. This time it was in the large compound some twenty kilometres west of Baghdad, where drivers had to wait for their exit papers to be stamped after delivering their loads. This could take a couple of days and we drivers had to sweat it out in the desert. Trucks parked haphazardly on the sand, usually grouped by nationality, and the whole area was decorated with little piles of desiccated turds, a testament to the total lack of facilities, apart from the portable offices used by customs themselves.

Here, the usual deal was to leave our papers in a briefcase outside the office in the evening, thus establishing the order of processing the following day. On this occasion, however, the system broke down when some impatient Turks simply grabbed their papers and crowded round the door, again leaving a few of us Brits relegated to the back. To my amazement, the door once again opened with the shout of "British?" from a customs man, who beckoned us through the crowd. The Turks were far from happy, but the official made it clear he would shut up shop if they didn't let us pass. This time we didn't have to do any work, merely swap handshakes and cigarettes before being given our exit papers, duly stamped. One of the Brits, a former Rhodesian also called George, almost wept with relief since he'd been waiting for almost a week. Once again, an Iraqi's pro-British sentiment had saved us hours, possibly days. That was over four decades and two wars ago, and sadly I doubt whether you'd find any Iraqi customs officer ready to help a British driver now, even if it were possible to drive to Iraq in the first place.

Meanwhile, the friendliness of its officials had given me a good feeling about the whole country, and when I arrived in Baghdad, and managed to find the destination for my load of orange juice, I found an equally welcoming gang ready to unload. To cap it all, I then went off to the British Club, encouraged by some old hands I'd met at the border, where I had a couple of cool beers in air-conditioned luxury and fell into conversation with Leyland's representative in Iraq, whose job was to take care of the extensive Leyland bus fleet that served the capital. It seemed odd that Iraqis should feel so friendly towards citizens of the country that had once been the country's quasi-colonial ruler, but perhaps it was our familiarity that made us welcome.

I returned to Tartus in the company of Rhodesian George, who drove for another company. I am forever grateful to him because he asked, somewhat sheepishly, if we could stop by the roadside and take a picture of him and his truck next to a road sign. I was happy to oblige because he then took a picture of me and my Daf, next to a sign saying, *Baghdad 130 kilometres*. I still have a framed copy on my mantelpiece. A little further on we pulled off the road to cook supper, but when we tried to start up again, my unladen truck simply spun its wheels. George's Scania, with the benefit of a differential lock to prevent one driving wheel spinning against the other, was back on the paved road in no time, but I had no such lock and, to my chagrin, had to be towed off the sand, using two long chains tied together to link the back of George's trailer with my tractor unit. A couple of years later, I met George again in Dover and he burst out laughing. "I remember you," he said, "jumping out of your Daf and yelling, 'Two fucking cigarette lighters, and no diff-lock.'."

I returned from my first foray into Iraq ready to put into effect the plan I'd agreed with Jane before I left. We were then somewhat short of money, so we had decided that I would turn straight round and go back to the Middle East without taking any time off. It seemed like a sensible idea at the time, and Jack was only too happy to oblige, but both Jane and I came to regret it, because in the end I was away from home for over two months.

It was weird to get as close to North Wales as Brierley Hill, only five hours from home, and spend no more than an hour or so at the office, sorting paperwork and swapping to another trailer already loaded with pallets of paper destined for the Iraqi government printing office in Baghdad. Jack had arranged for my truck to be serviced by the Daf dealer in Dover on my way out of the country. While the truck was in the workshop, I went to a supermarket to stock up with food, and after less than thirty-six hours in England, I was on my way eastwards again.

This trip went without incident until it came time to clear customs after I'd delivered the paper in Baghdad. Once again, I was stuck out in the desert waiting for my exit paperwork to be stamped when news came through that Egypt and Israel had signed a peace treaty, which marks the date as 26th March 1979. The reaction of Iraqis was to down tools and take to the streets, whether spontaneously or with 'encouragement' from the government, we couldn't tell. The customs officers simply failed to appear that morning and we heard rumours that vast crowds were demonstrating across the country. A handful of drivers decided to see for themselves, so one of them dropped his trailer and the rest crowded into his cab and headed towards Baghdad. The rest of us thought they were crazy and, within a couple of hours, we were vindicated. The drivers returned much chastened and showed us the handprints on the side of the cab where the crowds had tried to turn the truck over. A Volvo F10 is a big machine, but apparently so many people had tried to push it on its side that they might have succeeded if its driver hadn't managed to force a way out.

With no likelihood that we'd be seeing any customs action for a while, one driver, whose fridge trailer was standing empty, invited some of us to camp out in the back, where he could cool the trailer down from time to time. We moved mattresses, sleeping bags and cooking equipment into the fridge and lived there for two days and three nights. The next morning, we were alarmed to see a huge convoy of loaded tank transporters heading past us along the road towards Jordan and, therefore, Israel. I lost count at sixty and they kept coming. In the early afternoon, the convoy returned empty – a line of modern transporters made by the German heavy truck company, Faun – only to return with a second batch of tanks a few hours later. We began to be seriously worried that a war was brewing, which, apart from the wider tragedy, would almost certainly close the borders by which we were expecting to leave, thus stranding us in Iraq. I was not the only driver who tried desperately to tune in to the BBC World Service to find out what was happening, but we seemed to be in some sort of radio shadow, unless the Iraqi authorities were actually jamming the broadcast. In the end, however, the whole affair turned out to be just hot air, and on the third day, the customs office reopened and we went on our way.

Even then, the trip was not without incident. I was booked back from Syria to Greece with a new company that had jumped on the bandwagon of offering ferries to avoid Turkey. The new ship was magnificent and could carry 120 trucks on three decks. Unfortunately, it appeared that the company had neglected to get insurance to carry more than the dozen passengers that every freight ship is licensed to load. The rest of us drivers had to fly, which meant we'd have to kill at least two days while the ship made its much slower progress across the eastern Mediterranean. I rather liked the arrangement. It was a change in routine, which is always welcome, and we did end up spending most of a day in Damascus, which gave me a chance to see the centre of the old city for the first time.

That was the good part; first, however, we had to get to Damascus. We loaded our trucks onto the ferry in Tartus, which then set sail, while we were driven to a dockside hotel for the first of two nights we'd spend apart from our mobile homes. Even to be away from my truck was unsettling, not least because it contained my entire life-support system, apart from the few clothes I was carrying in a small bag. Among the hundred-odd drivers was a handful of Brits and other Western Europeans, and a small army of Bulgarians. After breakfast the next morning, we were herded onto two buses, which would take us to Damascus, half a dozen hours away. I was just finding my seat when an Austrian driver shouted out, "Everyone off the bus." There was some argument, but he finally persuaded us and proceeded to show us why. He'd had the wit to inspect the bus – a Swedish Scania chassis with a colourful locally built body – and found that two of the six studs on one of the front wheels had sheared off. We could see this had happened recently, since the broken studs were still shiny where they'd snapped. We all knew the road to Damascus – we'd just arrived by it – and none of us fancied tackling the rough, often dirt, road up to the Syrian highlands in a bus that was likely to lose its front wheel, not to mention going down the fifty-kilometre Damascus Hill on the other side. The bus driver was highly offended, and demonstrated how safe his vehicle was by putting it in reverse and walking up and down the aisle, while we watched from the safety of the pavement. We remained adamant, however, led by our doughty Austrian spokesman, until replacement buses finally arrived and we proceeded to the capital without further incident.

In the afternoon I was able to be a tourist, freed from the responsibility of looking after my truck. I would never have left it in the outskirts of the city while I ventured into the centre; the risk of losing the whole truck, or part of it, would have been too great. While most of the drivers stayed in the hotel the ferry company had provided, I wandered through the centuries-old souk, which was even more picturesque than the famous covered market in Istanbul, and visited the magnificent Umayyad Mosque, dating from the early eighth century. I didn't venture any further in than the courtyard, however, because although the mosque didn't feel as unwelcoming as mosques in Saudi Arabia, there wasn't the same openness I'd found in Turkey in the past.

We were given dinner in the cheap Damascus hotel where we'd been boarded, but scarcely had time to sleep before we were roused at 3am for a flight to Athens in a somewhat down-at-heel Boeing 737 belonging to Olympic Airways. It was still well before dawn when we landed in Athens and were ushered into a bus for what turned out to be a seven-hour bus ride to Volos to meet the ferry. We were all exhausted, and many of us were suffering from food poisoning, for which we assumed our hotel was to blame. We politely asked the bus driver to switch off the raucous music blaring from the bus's radio, but he only turned it up, despite repeated requests. Thus rebuffed, we took matters into our own hands. A French driver in front of me simply reached up and yanked a speaker from its panel above his head. I happened to have a knife with me, with which I proceeded to stab the speaker above me until it was silenced. We proceeded grumpily to Volos and collected our trucks from the ferry. For twenty-four hours, I was unable to face driving and lay on my bunk wracked with stomach pains and attendant symptoms of food poisoning. It was the only time in seven years of driving that I ever fell ill, but given a choice, the dockside in Volos would not have been my ideal location for a sick day.

In any case, this turned out to be my last run to the Middle East, and I was lucky to get into Middle East driving before its golden age came to an end. Within a couple of years, first one country and then another started organising foreign trucks into escorted convoys, presumably for some kind of paranoid reasons of security on the part of their authoritarian governments. Apart from the inevitable delays this would cause, the convoys would also remove the feeling of freedom all of us drivers valued, and the desert emptiness that I had so enjoyed. In 1979, the year that Saddam Hussein was formally confirmed as president, there were already signs that the good times were drawing to a close, though this did have amusing consequences.

The economics of Middle East transport were greatly helped by the dirt-cheap diesel we could load into our belly tanks. Diesel was twice as expensive in Iraq as it was in Saudi Arabia, but that still amounted to a negligible £2 for a hundred litres, or twenty-two imperial gallons. Unfortunately for all international drivers, our Turkish colleagues had started buying fuel in bulk. Supplies of diesel were chaotic – and even non-existent – in Turkey at the time, so Turkish truck drivers were entering Iraq with tanks strapped to every available space on the underside of their trailers. I reckoned they could carry around 5000 litres, maybe more. Before running back empty from Iraq, the enterprising drivers would fill their underfloor tanks and presumably make a tidy profit back home.

The Iraqi authorities finally decided to clamp down on this lucrative trade and word came down that there'd be a limit of only 200 litres for foreigners at Iraqi fuel stations. To make sure the law was enforced, an armed solider was posted at every station. The new regulation was a potentially expensive disaster for us drivers. The limit was less than half the capacity of our standard road tanks and we'd have no chance of filling our belly tanks. Luckily, there was a solution. I don't recall how word got around among the drivers, but it didn't take long. The trick was to bribe the guard with a copy of *Playboy*, or some similar piece of illustrated literature. There remained the slight problem that such titles were illegal in Iraq – whose customs officers echoed the standard questions of their Saudi counterparts, "Whisky? Sex books? Pistol?" – and would have to be smuggled in. I solved that by making a cut deep into one of my mattresses, which would be hidden by the cover, and sliding a magazine inside. I had no idea how great the penalty would be if I were caught, but I made it through customs unscathed. When I came to fill up for the journey home, it couldn't have been simpler. The youthful soldier on duty at the filling station was more than happy with his *Playboy* bung and the attendant duly pumped a couple of thousand litres into my tanks. We parted the best of friends and I left Iraq with full tanks, as usual.

In the end, however, I didn't stay on Middle East work long enough to experience its decline, and my three Iraq runs marked the end of my desert-driving career, though the decision to quit was entirely a question of cash. Jack paid us 'trip money', a lump sum that could work out well enough when there were no delays, but became unacceptably thin as my trips continued to stretch out, largely because of the time I spent waiting for ferries between Greece and Syria. Jack paid only £700 for a 'local' run to Iraq, and on my last trip to Mosul, only £650, since it was in the north of the country and only next door to Turkey. In the days when trucks transited Turkey directly, a round trip could be completed in only three weeks. That, however, was before the disruption in that country began and we were diverted via the ferry from Greece to Syria. Now, instead of crossing south-eastwards through Turkey, we had to avoid that country altogether and lose time in waiting for a boat. The crossing itself took no longer than the drive across Anatolia, but the delays in each port often added up to a whole week lost.

On my last trip, the delays were compounded by Jack's apparent inability to find us a backload. I had to come back through East Germany (as it then was), all the way to Hamburg, where, with a number of other Harrison drivers, I waited for four days before reloading for England. If I'd been single, with no family to support, I would have stayed with Harrison, but my last trip took a total of five and a half weeks, amounting to barely £100 a week after my own expenses, so I threw in the towel.

CHAPTER 19
DO IT YOURSELF

I had been nervous about phoning Jack to give in my notice – so much so that I delayed until I returned to Dover – and he was far from gracious about it on the phone. By the time I returned with an empty truck to Brierley Hill, however, he'd calmed down and we parted amicably enough. I tried briefly to get a job with another Middle East operator, former owner-driver David Duxbury, from Lancashire, who had a number of trucks running for freight forwarder Davies Turner. I'd learned about Duxbury from one of his drivers, with whom I'd struck up a friendship as we waited for a couple of days on the dockside in Tartus. One night, as we sat up late into the night in my cab, our conversation somehow turned to esoteric matters, including the idea of exorcism. I discovered that my friend had spent several years studying to become a Catholic priest and had abandoned the idea only weeks before his ordination. At any rate, he claimed quite plausibly to have learned how to carry out the appropriate ritual. I can remember the slight feeling of disconnectedness as we sat in the dusty dockside parking area at about two in the morning, discussing matters that could hardly have been further removed from the reality of our surroundings, and the mundane fact of waiting for a ferry.

When Jane picked me up from Harrison's, she and I drove up to Lancashire together to meet David Duxbury, and I had a somewhat bizarre job interview, with Jane and a couple of other drivers, around a pool table in a local pub. It should have warned me that his organisation was somewhat loose, but he was offering more money than I'd been getting at Harrison's, so I agreed to work for him. I did a short job to Germany, driving an exotic American White Road Commander II – an impressive but crude vehicle that couldn't compare to the Daf or Volvos I'd been driving before, and was even outshone by my old Magirus. It did turn heads, however, which was amusing for a day or two, before I was swapped to a far superior Volvo F12. Nevertheless, after a week or so, it became clear that however amiable Duxbury might be, earnings might be more haphazard than they were at Harrison's, so I called Cadwallader to ask for my old job back.

Transport manager Phil Spittle answered the phone. "Are you going to stay this time?" I assured him I would. In truth, much as I'd loved Middle East work, I'd missed my colleagues at Cadwallader, and the company's resources and influence with the ferry companies, which was so much greater than Harrison's. I'd noticed this when booking my Harrison truck onto ferries to and from Zeebrugge. Cadwallader shipped so many vehicles each week that we drivers could nearly always be sure of getting any crossing we wanted. At Harrison, I'd had to be careful to book with plenty of advance notice, and even then I'd once been bumped off an overbooked ferry in preference for trucks from some larger operator.

When I arrived in Oswestry, having squeezed in a much-needed few days at home, both the Cadwallader brothers, and managers Phil and Mike, were very welcoming. After a week or two driving odds and ends, including one of the first Volvo F88s in Britain, which was later bought and restored by Volvo itself, I was very happy to be assigned to another big Daf 2800, with the same spec as my Harrison truck. I was also back in the fridge business, which meant I no longer had to strip down tilt trailers or worry about the correct loading of crates of machinery. And this time around, I was no longer a novice. I'd had unusual driving experience, which was shared by only one other driver at Cadwallader, Gordon Parry, whose two years on Middle East work had earned him the nickname 'Desert Wellies', a term usually applied to humble flip-flops. All the same, in my first few months back at Caddy's, I missed the distance and complexity of the Middle East runs, until we started running regularly to Romania, which posed an interesting challenge in what was still the Cold

War era. Meanwhile, my trips were mainly to France, Germany and Italy, with occasional short hops to Belgium and the Netherlands.

Pulling a fridge trailer again meant I once again had to get used to the noise of its engine behind me. On the move, the sound was almost inaudible, drowned by the noise of the truck itself, unless it was in the automatic defrost cycle, which revved up the fridge motor for several minutes every few hours. At night the fridge chattered away behind me, but never prevented me from sleeping. Fridges were less popular with other drivers, however, and I once nearly got into a fight with one of them, when we were up at the German border one Sunday afternoon, waiting for the truck ban to be lifted at 10pm. I was accompanied on this trip to Hamburg by my nine-year-old son, Ben, and after we'd made ourselves a late afternoon lunch, I lay down to sleep to prepare for the night drive to Hamburg. No sooner was I lying down than I heard the fridge motor stop, and Ben, who'd been reading in the passenger seat, said another driver had switched it off. I jumped down from the cab, turned the fridge on again and returned to my bunk, only for the same thing to happen again. This time I confronted the driver, who turned out to be a belligerent Dutchman, and explained that I had to leave the fridge running because I was carrying a valuable load of prime beef steak and couldn't afford to let it go off. He wasn't impressed and threatened to do some more significant damage to the fridge if I didn't stop it running. Not fancying a bout of fisticuffs, nor my chances against the heavyweight thug, I finally moved the truck away from him, which solved the problem. Years later, when Ben was an adult, he told me he was sure I was heading for a fight and I had to admit that I'd thought it was possible. Most drivers, however, were at least tolerant of what they knew to be unavoidable noise and that was the only time I faced a serious complaint.

The Daf I was now driving was a couple of years older than the almost new model I'd been driving for Harrison, but in every other respect it was identical. I continued to appreciate its height, imposing styling and the powerful, high-torque engine combined with the excellent 13-speed Eaton-Fuller gearbox. As a place to live, the cab was as good as it got in those days, which was just as well since I still spent, on average, four or five weeks at a time in it before making a quick run home. This was as long as a trip to Dubai and back, except that now I was running to and from the Continent, usually once a week, and returning anywhere across the UK from the West Country to Inverness. The cab may have been the most spacious on the market, but it was still only eight feet wide, and about six feet from the back wall to the windscreen, which was hardly generous considering it was both my workplace and my home. No manufacturer was yet building a high-roof cab, and at six feet three inches tall, I couldn't stand upright, even in the passenger-side footwell. In this confined space, I kept my clothes, food and cooking gear – no more Middle East trailer boxes – and a five-gallon water container. There also had to be room for a number of books and an ever-expanding collection of cassette tapes. It forced me into a tidy domesticity, which, I discovered, could be unexpected in a man.

I regularly loaded out of an abattoir run by T.N. Green in Oldham, a few miles to the north of Manchester, and one day I left the trailer at their site and drove my tractor unit to a nearby launderette, one of a row of small shops in a working-class neighbourhood. It was crowded, but I was the only man in the place. When my clothes had finished drying, I was folding them neatly as usual when I realised that several of the women were watching me curiously. Finally, one of them said, "You're making a nice job of that, love," as if it should be beyond the wit of a mere man to look after his own clothes. I made some joke about being away from home, but it made me realise that here was a male-female culture that was much more traditional than anything I knew. I'd felt a similar sentiment on an earlier occasion when I'd been in a supermarket in my hometown of Pwllheli, buying six weeks' worth of supplies for a trip to Dubai. At the checkout, the woman working the till clucked over the thirty single-serving cans of potatoes in my shopping trolley. Apparently assuming that I needed educating in the domestic arts, she said, gently, "You know, there are much cheaper ways of buying potatoes than that." I tried to explain why I needed spuds in small servings for a long solo road trip, but I could see that she didn't understand and probably thought I was beyond any sensible training.

My general self-sufficiency now stretched to the truck itself. I'd been used to the necessity of solving mechanical problems as far as possible myself, and I had gradually acquired a comprehensive toolkit, usually by adding one spanner at a time to my fuel bills across Western Europe. So, when the Daf's air compressor failed on the outskirts of Stuttgart one day, I didn't think of phoning the office until I'd tried to fix it unaided. I tilted the cab and discovered that the head of the compressor had come adrift from its 'cylinder block', in which the compressing piston was housed; all the nuts holding the head had vibrated off their studs. I had no spares, but as I pondered the problem, I noticed that the bolts holding the cab steps in place were the same size as those holding the compressor together, so I removed every third nut and bolt from the steps, leaving enough to keep the steps serviceable, and used their nuts to repair the compressor. It was enough to get me across the city to the meat market where I was delivering, before the temporary fix also failed. I now had to be towed into the local Daf dealer for a proper repair, but at least I had delivered the meat on time, which saved Cadwallader a penalty.

When Caddy's later began sending trucks regularly to Romania, we soon found that the modern, single-leaf trailer springs suffered and even snapped on the rough Eastern European roads. The company's response was to bolt a spare spring to the underside of every fridge trailer that was likely to be sent to the East. It was comforting to know it was there when we were far behind the Iron Curtain, but the only time I needed one was actually in France, at the Jacques Borel service area just north of Mâcon. I was walking around the truck on an inspection tour, as usual with a mug of tea in my hand, when I realised that one of the trailer springs had snapped. I had never changed a spring before, but it seemed obvious enough what to do. The only snag was that the trailer was loaded, so that at least five tonnes were being put through each spring, and the forces I would have to contend with would be considerable. Nevertheless, I managed it. I don't remember the details, though I have a vague memory of using the jack to take the weight off the axle and, later, to help locate each end of the spring. It was certainly very satisfying to be able to make the repair myself and next time I was back in the yard I had a new spare bolted to the chassis.

Sometimes, I got out of trouble by sheer luck. On one run to Bucharest, three of us were running back empty through central Romania. At one point, we stopped on the road for a quick consultation about lunch and then proceeded to the nearest parking space, a few miles further on. Once we'd parked, we noticed a pool of oil growing under the gearbox of the Scania 111 driven by my friend, Dave Matthews. A closer check showed that the drain plug had fallen out and the gearbox was likely to seize up at any moment for lack of lubrication. We had no idea where the nearest spare could be found, and since we knew that Romtrans, the Romanian national transport company, had no Scanias in its fleet, we didn't see much prospect of finding one, even if we were to backtrack to Bucharest. We debated whether we'd have to go on to Hungary or even Austria to find a replacement.

Finally, I made the absurd suggestion of driving one of the trucks slowly back the way we'd come to see if we could find the original plug on the road. It was a long shot, but we gave it a try. The other two joined me in my Volvo and we trundled back with dwindling hopes until we reached the place where we'd stopped briefly for our lunch planning. There, in a small patch of oil in the middle of the road, was the missing plug. If it had fallen out almost anywhere else, the speed of the truck would probably have bounced it across the road. Instead, the pool of oil had kept it in place, and we couldn't have felt better if we'd won the lottery. It didn't take long to replace the plug and fill the transmission with oil, and we managed to fit in lunch as well.

Eastern Europe may not have been as far away as the Middle East, but in some respects it was equally alien and inaccessible, and even locals had difficulty in finding quite ordinary spares. I was once parked up in a vast compound belonging to Romtrans, the government-owned company that covered everything from haulage to customs agency. The yard was in Arad, a town on the western side of the country near the Hungarian border. Ranged around the compound were at least fifty trailers, all equipped, as mine was, with American Thermo-King fridge units, showing that commerce trumped the American aversion to communism. As I was waiting, I was approached by a man who turned out to be the foreman fitter. He wanted to know if I had a spare belt for my own Thermo-King fridge. I can't remember how we communicated, probably in a combination of German and English, but I managed to understand that he needed the belt that transferred power from the fridge's diesel engine to the pump. Like all Cadwallader fridge drivers, I carried a spare – in fact, I had three – and I was amazed that an outfit with 50-odd refrigerated trailers didn't have a single belt on hand. The foreman explained that he'd have to order a new one from the capital, Bucharest, 550 kilometres away, and that it could take two weeks to get it. I was happy to give him the spare he needed – apart from anything else, it always helps to have a friend in faraway places – but the incident taught me more about the inefficiency of a communist command economy than any amount of western rhetoric could have done.

In any case, help went both ways. A year or so earlier, on a run back from the Middle East with my Harrison colleague 'Bubbles', I was cruising through Hungary when one of the injector pipes on my Daf cracked and started blowing fuel into the air. Not only did this reduce the engine to five cylinders, which made it sound rough and robbed it of power, but, worse than that, it meant I was driving in a cloud of malodorous diesel as it sprayed from the fractured pipe. We both knew what the trouble was before we tilted the cab, but neither of us carried a spare injector pipe, since this was a rare occurrence on what was then a modern truck. We were debating what to do when a Volvo F12 drew up. It belonged to Hungarocamion, a company that might have been owned by the Hungarian government, but which commanded much more respect among western drivers than Romtrans did.

Moreover, it was clear from the truck's equipment that it was also a Middle East motor, so there was an unstated bond between us. The Hungarian driver asked whether we needed help and, communicating with gestures and a few words of German, we described the problem and our lack of a replacement. Immediately, he returned to his own truck and brought us a spare injector pipe, which he insisted on giving us for nothing. It was for a Volvo and needed a little persuasion to fit the Daf engine, but we managed it between us and my Daf was ready to roll.

This wasn't the only time a Hungarian driver came to my rescue and the second time was considerably more spectacular. I was already a regular on the run to Romania, when, one evening, in the company of my friend and colleague, Peter Morris, and with my six-year-old daughter, Laura, sleeping on the bunk, I pulled into a parking area outside a roadside restaurant. It was late evening and there was hardly any room to park, so I ended up in the only available space, which I discovered too late was covered in soft sand. When we tried to leave again, my Volvo's driving wheels simply spun and dug themselves into the ground. We tried digging the sand away from the wheels, but it made no difference. As we struggled, we were approached by two Hungarian army drivers who were in charge of a huge eight-wheel-drive, Czech-built Tatra truck, and offered to tow me out. Yes, please. They reversed the Tatra to the front of my Volvo, hitched up a line to the towing pin in my front bumper and began to pull. Back in my cab, I tried to get some traction, but we were unsuccessful. Even with eight driving wheels, the Tatra couldn't cope with the dead weight of the F10 and its freighted fridge, and it too began to bog down. The soldiers held a hurried consultation and decided to pull me out with the powerful winch attached to the front of their truck.

Moving the Tatra away to firm ground, they paid out a long steel cable and attached it to the towing pin. I sat in the driving seat, ready to steer and give as much help as I could, as soon as my own wheels began to grip. As the army drivers wound in the winch, and the cable tightened to what might have been high C if we'd hit it, I tried not to imagine what would happen if it snapped, and having my small daughter in the cab made me more apprehensive. I imagined it damaging the cab at the very least, and possibly decapitating me in the process. Instead, however, the Volvo began to move, and within a couple of yards, I had enough traction to continue alone. Peter and I thanked the drivers profusely – I was almost weeping with relief – and urged them to accept some Deutsche Marks, a currency highly prized in the Eastern Bloc. However, they impressed us by refusing all payment and, with nothing more than enthusiastic handshakes, we were on our way.

CHAPTER 20
LIFE ON THE ROAD

The various breakdowns described in the previous chapter were a break in routine and interesting to solve, but some aspects of life on the road varied very little. For one thing, whether I was running to Dusseldorf or Dubai, much of my domestic routine was conducted in public. At night, my truck would be parked up in a motorway service area, a dockside, lay-by, or outside an abattoir or factory gate. So that, although my cabs were fully curtained once I began international work (apart from my month in the unlamented Magirus), I would usually have opened the curtains and be rubbing the sleep from my eyes in the view of any passing stranger. Having made a cup of tea, my first daily chores were to check the oil level, using a long dipstick behind the grille across the front of the cab; verify that all the lights were working around the tractor and trailer; and give the tyres a kick. Unlike the Magirus, Dafs and Volvos had wheel nuts that stayed tight, but I still checked them all every two or three days.

When it came to washing, I soon had to discard any idea of privacy or modesty. If a washroom were available, it would usually be communal and, in motorway service areas across Europe, I got used to doing my morning ablutions in a large public space, shaving, brushing my teeth and stripping to the waist (and further – briefly – if the coast was clear) to sponge myself down. The most reliable place to find a shower was on the ferries, though I usually only had time to use these on the longer crossings; Dover to Calais was too short for anything other than a meal. Some factories or abattoirs had showers we could use, often in the workers' changing rooms, and these were – incidentally – always for men. On one occasion, several of us were waiting as usual at the meat processing plant in Bucharest and in the group was Cadwallader's only female driver, a French woman who worked for the small subsidiary the company had set up in Cherbourg. The only way for her to have a shower – after three or four days' transit from Belgium – was for the rest of us to stand guard at the two doors to the communal showers and bar anyone else from entry. In those days, women drivers were still a rarity and the difficulties they faced as long-distance drivers were compounded by the lack of dedicated facilities. More often than not, drivers found themselves parked up far from a toilet, and the common practice – especially at night – was to piss against the wheel of the trailer. In high summer, the smell of truck parks in southern European service areas was a curious blend of hot tarmac and dried pee.

In the Middle East, there were few, if any, facilities. Even in the large parking areas in customs compounds, toilets were usually distant and dirty, so most drivers' choice was evidenced by the discreet piles of turds exposed when a truck moved off. The standard procedure throughout the Middle East was to crouch beneath your trailer to take a crap. Those who had widespread trailer axles often squatted between the tyres to gain a modicum of privacy, giving rise to the euphemism, 'having a spread axle'. The result was that any large parking area would be littered with little mementoes of each driver's delay, though at least the intense heat dried them out quickly, so the smell wasn't as overwhelming as it might have been.

The other problem was keeping one's clothes clean. It's not so easy to find a launderette with parking space for a fifty-five-foot truck, so I would often have to drop the trailer wherever I was waiting to load, as I did at Green's, and take the tractor unit in search of a laundry. In summer, being 'weekended' – stuck for a Sunday (and in Austria, a Saturday afternoon) by driving restrictions – would at least give me time for some domestic chores. I could wash my clothes in my plastic basin and dry them on a line hung from the trailer to some convenient tree or lamppost.

Even in Western Europe, I often cooked my own meals, to save both time and money. I had first begun cooking for myself when I was carrying straw across southern England back in my days at Abbey Hill, using a small single-burner 'Campingaz' stove, but more or less gave it up when I was doing relatively short-haul runs for Williams from Porthmadog. Once I started going 'over the water', however, self-catering became the norm. I quickly acquired a two-burner stove and two large, refillable Campingaz cannisters. All my cooking equipment was kept in a wooden box that had once been used to hold one of South Caernarfon Creameries forty-pound blocks of cheese while it was being cured. This fitted neatly under the bunk in my Dafs and my Volvo, and became part of the general life-support system I carried in my Middle East trailer box. Forty-five years on, I still have the unremarkable mug I bought in a Carrefour supermarket just off the A9 autoroute near Avignon.

I usually cooked in the cab, but on fine days, or when waiting for something gave me time to spare, I might set up my stove on the battery cover of the Volvo, or on a picnic table in a lay-by. In retrospect, I regret that so many of my cab-cooked meals came out of tins, but at the time it seemed sensible enough, and shopping for fresh food wasn't easy. Bread rolls and sometimes fruit were obtainable at motorway services and, if I had time, I could stop and shop in a French or German supermarket. In those days, very few long-distance trucks had in-cab fridges, as many of them do now, and the only un-canned food I carried in the cab were eggs and cheese. I gained a reputation for producing a passable curry from a couple of cans of stew and vegetables and a spoonful of Patak's curry paste, which disguised the processed taste of the meat.

It wasn't always cans, however, and in Romania we sometimes had the time and opportunity to cook an excellent meal, with high-grade ingredients. The meat processing plant to which we delivered in Bucharest was very slow in dealing with us, and we might wait two or three days before the hanging beef we were carrying was unloaded. The result was that I often found myself in the company of three or four other drivers, either from Cadwallader or from some Irish fridge firm, as we waited to be called forwards for unloading. And there were compensations. Not only did we have time to relax, but, since we had cleared customs, our trailers were no longer sealed. This meant we could climb into the back of the truck and cut the fillet from a beef hindquarter, which provided enough steak for several drivers. For some reason the packing plant either didn't notice, or didn't care, that we were removing prime cuts from our consignments, and by the time we'd taken a tractor unit out for a little vegetable shopping, we could assemble an excellent meal while our fridge trailers cooled the beer.

After a while, self-sufficiency becomes a state of mind for a long-distance driver, whether it's a question of fixing the truck or feeding the driver. Once I got used to making my own tea in Romania or Iraq, it made just as much sense to do the same in Britain. In the time it would have taken me to walk from the parking area of a British motorway service station and buy an overpriced cup of tea in the cafeteria, I would have the kettle boiled in the cab and be relaxing in my own surroundings, not to mention saving money in the process. When waiting anywhere – particularly in Eastern Europe or the Middle East – it was simply easier to cook in the cab, and it meant I would always be available if someone came looking for me to load or process some paperwork.

Not that all my meals were self-cooked. Ferry restaurants always served up a good steak, and in those days, there were still a large number of excellent transport cafes along all the major routes in Britain. If I had time, I would sometimes stop for lunch at a French *Routiers* restaurant – usually pronounced by British drivers as 'routears' – or park up outside one for the night. '*Routier*' is one of the French words for truck driver, and in those days, restaurants so named looked after us well. One of the favourites for Cadwallader drivers on the Italian run was in the Alps just before Chamonix, where the restaurant had a dining room for tourists and another room dedicated to truck drivers. Here, the menu tended to be fixed, but the price was much lower than what tourists were charged and the atmosphere in the drivers' room was usually more convivial. If we found ourselves running together, my tearaway friend, Dave Whitcombe, and I would make a point of stopping there, before continuing to the Mont Blanc Tunnel and Italy. *Routiers* menus could sometimes be quietly spectacular. Once a group of us, sent to Brittany to load the season's first new potatoes from Paimpol, went into a small *Routiers* in the evening to discover oysters on the menu as a starter, included in the usual fixed price of 25 francs (about £2.50).

When I was running alone, as was nearly always the case, *Routiers* restaurants gave me the chance to interact with other drivers, mostly French themselves, and enjoy a little company. A common dining-room layout consisted of one or more long tables, with places laid on each side. As each driver came in, he – or, rarely, she – would sit at the next available space, so that he'd have company for lunch. A bottle of cheap red table wine was placed between every pair of drivers and we had no hesitation in drinking it. A French lunch break takes one or two hours, so our drinks were spaced out and accompanied by water, so we were not incapable when we hit the road. In retrospect, it seems crazy that a long-haul driver would drink wine for lunch, but the practice was obviously so ingrained in French culture that nobody gave it a second thought.

The long table layout was considerably more convivial than the British practice of sitting at separate tables in transport cafes and it brought together people who were strangers, but still had their driving life in common. There was always something to talk about, whether it was the obstructive tactics of customs officers or the relative merits of a Mercedes over a Volvo, and my occasional *routiers* meals were a welcome break in my mainly solitary days. Once I was running regularly to France, I was soon able to converse quite freely with French drivers, and one evening near Nîmes in the south of France, I was chatting to a local driver who surmised that I must be from Belgium. I was flattered at first, but my smugness was tempered when I recalled how most French people viewed the Belgians, making them the butt of the kinds of jokes the English used to make, with no more justification, about the Irish.

Germany, too, was a good place to eat out, and irresistible once I began earning extra D-Marks on the East European fuel black market. When I first began running to the Continent, I went mostly to France, where my basic language skills helped make me feel at home. At first, I found Germany more daunting, but I soon discovered to my surprise that I could have a lot more fun in small-town German *gaststuben*, or bar-restaurants, than I ever did in France. I could also rely on them to be open reasonably late – unlike most provincial French restaurants – so that I would be able to order a schnitzel and beer well into the evening. Sometimes I found myself caught up in some communal merriment, such as the time in Waidhaus, before the Czech border, when someone put a lighted candle under the wooden stool occupied by a man enjoying a drunken nap. As the stool warmed up, and he began twitching from side to side in his sleep, the whole restaurant was howling with laughter, as was the victim himself when he woke up and saw the joke. As I became more familiar with Germany, I learned the custom of knocking the table twice when one left a small-town restaurant, as a short-hand for shaking everyone's hand. When I did the same, I would get a wave of acknowledgement from fellow customers, whether I'd been talking to them or not, showing a friendliness that was less common elsewhere.

Back in Britain, I often found myself spending one or two nights at an abattoir, waiting for all or part of a load to be ready, and whenever possible I would go to the movies. Since I often loaded for Romania at Green's in Oldham, north of Manchester, I tried to go to the local cinema and even drove into the heart of the city to find a good choice of films. Another common loading point was the abattoir in Lockerbie, in southern Scotland. Here the nearest cinemas were in Dumfries or Carlisle, twenty-five-odd miles away. That was no deterrent, however; I simply dropped the trailer and took off in the solo tractor unit. Technically I was breaking the hours rules, since a tractor unit, at over six tonnes unladen, still counted as a heavy goods vehicle. I never considered this much of an infraction, however, and nobody seemed to care. I was confident that my bosses wouldn't mind that I was using their truck as my private transport. They appreciated that we were away for long periods of time and would have been quite tolerant of my behaviour – if they'd ever found out about it, which, of course, they didn't. Nowadays, with satellite tracking and computers, such licence would have been out of the question, with both managers and 'the ministry' looking over every driver's shoulder.

One aspect of my trucking existence that I never tired of was the view from the wheel. Unless you have driven in a truck, you don't know what you're missing from the low vantage point of a car. In the days when all my work began and ended in North Wales, I was always able to see over the ubiquitous stone walls, which allowed me to view nearby detail and distant vistas. The moorland run between Bala and Trawsfynydd was one of my favourite pieces of road and rarely failed to stir me. When

I was returning home after dark, it ended with the dramatic lights of the Trawsfynydd nuclear power station glaring towards me, and on days when the cloud cover was low enough to feel like fog, I used to imagine Welsh soldiers vanishing into the medieval mists to evade the armies of the English. On fine days, the sky would be a deep, clear blue and I could see the mountains of Snowdonia to the north.

Contrast that with running down the Adriatic coast on a late summer afternoon in Italy, on the A14 *autostrada* between Pescara and Bari, and watching the sea change colour with the lessening light. The *autostrada* was often quite empty, and both the light and the view gave a wonderful feeling of freedom, boosted by the thought of spending a pleasant evening at the US Air Force base in Brindisi. Even the industrial north of Italy was interesting to look at from the cab, and the trans-Alpine route from Mâcon in central France to Aosta in Italy was a montage of arresting views and, in winter, sometimes scary roads. Another satisfying moment was the first sight of Lyon and the River Rhone, when my truck burst through the descending tunnels on the old A6 autoroute on the north side of the city. This marked, for me, the beginning of the south of France – my favourite region – and the long tunnels both defined and dramatised the change from north to south. Further east, the year I spent Christmas en route to Dubai provided a clear illustration of the variety of terrain and climate I might encounter. A week after driving through daytime temperatures of twenty-five to thirty degrees Celsius in Saudi Arabia, I was fastening snow chains to my Daf in sub-freezing Austria. And the long, open desert views in the vastness of Saudi Arabia were dramatically different from anything I could find in Europe. I soon counted myself as 'another of those Englishmen who love the desert', as Alec Guinness's Prince Faisal describes Lawrence of Arabia, in one of my top ten films.

Even when the view could lay no claim to beauty, there was always something to notice. My first sight of horse-drawn ploughs in Belgium, as late as 1977, was a surprise, while the view from the M1 motorway viaduct of empty factories in Sheffield – once a powerhouse of British steel-making – provided vivid proof of industrial decline. Watching people and businesses on their home ground was also fascinating, whether these were in roadside workshops on the outskirts of Damascus, in apple orchards and packing plants in the south of France, or in the streets of German and Italian cities. I remember seeing a shepherd in Yugoslavia, standing guard over a small flock of fifty-odd sheep, and realising that if he could devote his time to staying with his sheep, he must have been working in an economy where fifty sheep could support a man. Where I lived in North Wales, my friend, Harry Jones, needed 800 ewes and a herd of cows to make a living for himself and his two sons.

It would be gratifying to look back at my life as a long-distance driver as an opportunity to think deep thoughts, but much of the time I was in an almost meditative state, simply monitoring the road and the traffic, and driving on instinct and automatism. I literally took a long view. Back when I had first trained as a driver, I had been told to look further and further ahead, and I got into the habit of looking as far as the road ahead was visible. On a motorway that could easily mean a mile or more, so that I could see what the traffic ahead was doing, and was rarely surprised. I began automatically to anticipate when a driver ahead might move over to overtake, and to be ready when car drivers had not been looking far enough to see that they might have to pull out to pass a truck. The more you notice from the wheel, the less stressful it is to drive.

Years later, when I had become the editor of *Truck & Driver* magazine, I went on a two-day driver safety course run by British Road Services as a refresher for its experienced drivers. In a seminar session, our instructor asked whether a truck driver needs good reflexes; we all answered yes. On the contrary, he suggested. A good driver should be so aware of everything that is happening around and ahead of the truck that nothing should be a surprise. We wouldn't need to have quick reflexes because we should already be anticipating any event and any move made by other vehicles. It was a plausible theory.

As a driver, I often mentally calculated and recalculated my estimated time of arrival, particularly when I was on a familiar run. From time to time, I also set myself demanding driving schedules, which, though they did benefit my employers, were principally to amuse myself. One of these was to book ahead on a cross-Channel ferry that would give me just enough time to reach the port and catch the boat. Returning from Italy or the south of France, in common with most drivers I usually stopped at the autoroute services at Auxerre, about 150 kilometres south of Paris. Here, there was a phone operator who could put us through to any of the ferry operators and knew their numbers by heart. There were, of course, no mobile phones in those days and payphones required fistfuls of coins for an international call. Cadwallader had accounts with both Townsend Thoresen and the Anglo-French Sealink, and when we were homeward bound, the choice lay with us drivers. Though I generally preferred Townsend, I would sometimes book whichever ferry was leaving in eight hours' time, giving me exactly the seven hours I needed to reach Calais, and be in time to book in, as long as I didn't stop for anything except to pay the tolls. There was no pressure to do this from the company, but I enjoyed the challenge of driving to a self-imposed deadline.

I was once returning unladen from Saudi Arabia and stopped at a motel outside Belgrade in Yugoslavia, where western drivers congregated because it offered good phone service. It was mid-afternoon when I called Jack Harrison back in Brierley Hill. He told me to phone him again when I reached Munich in southern Germany, when he would have details of my backload to Britain. Munich was just over 1000 kilometres from Belgrade and I might reasonably have been expected to take a whole day, or even two, to reach it. Instead, since the weather was fine and I was in the mood, I simply kept on driving through the night in my fast, unladen Daf. I flew through Austria and reached Munich in time for breakfast. The surprise in Jack's voice, when I called him so soon, was my own private satisfaction. I wasn't the only driver who liked to beat the schedule, and I enjoyed those occasions when I found myself running with others who liked to drive under similarly self-imposed pressure.

The whole point of truck driving is to spend long hours at the wheel, and even with the variety of sights outside the cab, there was still need for entertainment within it. The days I spent struggling with the Magirus on my first Middle East adventure were not made any easier by the fact that it had no tape player (eight-track players already didn't count). In other trucks, however, I was able to play any of the several dozen audio cassettes I carried with me. The best cab in this respect was the Volvo F10's, in which some deft designer had supplied a shallow open compartment in the fascia that snugly stored exactly forty-eight cassettes. Some of these were recorded from LPs at home, but others I acquired in Italian motorway services, or near the docks in Tartus, in Syria, where the low-quality printing of the cassette sleeves, and the improbably low prices, suggested that the copies were pirated.

It was in Tartus that I acquired a copy of Bob Dylan's *Street Legal* album and its dynamic opening track – 'Changing of the Guards' – became one of my anthems. I used to set up the seven-minute song as I neared the end of a long run, playing it at full volume to coincide with my arrival at a delivery site in Jeddah or Bucharest, or in Zeebrugge after a hard charge to catch a ferry. I used to fantasise that 'Changing of the Guards' would be one of my choices for the radio programme *Desert Island Discs*, rather than the more obvious 'Like a Rolling Stone'. Other songs became associated with particular pieces of road and decades later they still remind me of them. For some inexplicable reason, Dolly Parton's 'Jolene' can still conjure up the sensation of my A Series ERF leaning into a sweeping left-hand bend on the A5 road before Corwen in North Wales, when I was heading off to England with a load of cheese. Another song that remains linked to a road in my memory is Dire Straits' 'Romeo and Juliet'. I first heard this on Radio Luxembourg as I was approaching the Turin ring road from Milan, at about 2am on a muggy summer night, before heading northwards to the Mont Blanc Tunnel with a load of Italian peaches. The taste and smell of a hot summer night in Italy, and the feeling of loneliness the track evoked in me then, still echo whenever I hear it today.

Although cassette tapes were the only reliable means of entertainment when I was far from Britain, long-wave BBC radio reached quite far south in both France and Germany, and it was the waveband itself that determined most drivers' choice of station. Until late 1978, BBC long wave carried Radio Two, so that I rather improbably found myself appreciating the Jimmy Young show, which appeared to be aimed squarely at middle-aged housewives with, among other things, a daily recipe. But it also included surprisingly acute political interviews, which I enjoyed. Another, even more unlikely, cult programme among long-haul drivers was the weekday Radio Two soap, *Waggoners' Walk*, set in middle-class Hampstead. This was so addictive that I can remember drivers cutting short a tea break in order to get back to their truck in time to listen to the latest episode. In November 1978, Radio Two was replaced on BBC long wave by Radio Four, so I was now able to listen to extended news and current affairs programmes, as well as becoming a fan of the comic *Just a Minute* panel game and *Woman's Hour*. Further afield, I often tuned into the BBC World Service, but this was often more elusive on my radio dial during daylight hours.

The Radio Luxembourg rock and pop music station was reliable night-time company and was available over much of Western Europe, even, when reception was favourable, as far east as Romania. The late shows had rock music more aligned to my taste and the station itself was – perhaps unwittingly – an important cultural export from the West. On one occasion, I picked up two East German teenagers on the outskirts of Dresden and took them over three days to Sofia, the capital of Bulgaria. They spoke excellent English and when I expressed surprise that they knew English rather than Russian, they told me that, yes, they did learn Russian at school, but had no interest in it. They were much more attracted by English and they spent long hours listening to Radio Luxembourg. This allowed them ample opportunity to practise the language, while also giving them an encyclopaedic knowledge of western rock and pop music. When the Berlin Wall came down less than a decade later, I imagined these two boys – by then, young men – helping to demolish it; Radio Luxembourg had long ago orientated them to the West.

Having been a regular hitchhiker in my student days – when I'd hitchhiked all over Britain and as far afield as Istanbul – I was happy to give other people lifts, but I wasn't indiscriminate. Hitchers had to look reasonably clean if I were going to share my mobile home with them and they had to be carrying a backpack, or some other baggage. This was a sign that they were going some distance; I wasn't interested in stopping and restarting my large truck for just a couple of miles. Even when I did pick someone up, I would offer them only a limited ride, perhaps to a service area a couple of hours down the road, and only after I had weighed them up I would extend the ride further.

Not only were hitchhikers company, but I sometimes learned from them, as I had with the Dresden teens. I once picked up a German student at Toddington Services, on the M1 motorway some forty miles north of central London. Having initially promised him a ride across London and onto the Dover road, I ended up taking him home to Nürnburg in Germany. In the process, I saved him the cost of a cross-Channel ferry ticket since I booked him onto the ferry as a second driver. If this had happened to me in my hitchhiking career, I'd have considered it a red-letter day. As we passed Würzburg, about a hundred kilometres short of Nürnburg, my hitchhiker gave a deep sigh and said, "Now I am home." I was surprised, because we had entered Germany at Aachen some six hours earlier. "Oh no," he said. "My home is *Bavaria*, not Germany." It was the first time I had realised how strong regional identities can be in Germany. Although I could by now recognise some differences in attitude and language between various German states – modes of greeting were a good example – I had never heard the distinction so clearly stated.

Even though I might have hitchhikers with me for a couple of days, I never went so far as to trust them when I crossed a border, particularly in Eastern Europe. Having no idea what was in their backpacks, I would make them get out of the truck with their luggage and cross the border independently, promising to pick them up on the other side, if they hadn't already found another ride by the time I got through. I had no intention of risking getting into trouble because a hitcher was smuggling something.

Nowadays, hitchhikers are a rare sight anywhere in Europe. Whether this is because young people are more affluent or more nervous, I have no idea, but in the days when I was a student, and later when I was the lift-giving driver, motorway service areas and slip roads across Europe often had a clutch of young people trying to hitch a ride. It was a system that worked for everyone; hitchers got a ride and we drivers had company to talk to and, sometimes, keep us awake. Even now, when I am driving a long distance alone, I miss the unexpectedness of giving a ride to a stranger.

Most of the time, of course, a truck driver is alone. I spent long hours every day with no company but my own, and I noticed that I became more chatty whenever I did meet someone, when stopping at a shop or a fuel station, or when loading or unloading the truck. My social life was concentrated on the dockside in the Channel ports, where I would often spend hours clearing customs when entering the UK, which gave me the chance to hang out with other drivers in the dockside canteen, or a convenient pub outside the dock gates. Wherever there was a customs delay, there was the positive benefit of having time to socialise and swap stories with drivers I knew or, much more often, new acquaintances. Our work as drivers was always something we had in common, whether or not we were fellow countrymen, and even if we spoke different languages. I found I could form close bonds with another driver – as I did with my Middle East mate, Joe Berrington – and then not see him again for months, perhaps ever again. Social life was precarious and we grabbed it when we could.

CHAPTER 21
HOME AND AWAY

Being back on European work didn't improve my family life. We had by now built on a large extension to our cottage, which gave us proper plumbing and a modern kitchen, so life at home was physically much easier, but I wasn't often home to share it. Nowadays drivers can easily stay in touch with home via their mobile phones, but back then it was hard to make affectionate conversation when standing in a draughty phone box, even if one were available. Moreover, even though I was in and out of Britain more often, I was still away from North Wales for several weeks at a time and my trips home became increasingly strained. Trying to make a normal family life squeeze into three days, after several weeks' absence, left nobody satisfied. Jane and her older son, Mark, now in his teens, managed perfectly well without me, and I had become a visitor who disrupted the routine of home, rather than enhancing it. It gradually became clear that we should leave North Wales and move to north London, where we both had friends.

Since I was away most of the time, Jane dealt with the business of finding us a large house in the north London borough of Tottenham, and in the days when the mortgage requirements were much tighter than they later became, she managed to find a loan through a broker who seemed – and later proved to be – decidedly dodgy. Nevertheless, we sold our now quite desirable house in Wales and moved. I rented a van that was just big enough to carry all our possessions and we drove away from the house that I had first seen as a young child, when my mother bought it as a cheap holiday cottage in 1958. Mark and I drove in the van, while Jane took the younger children in her car. Having installed them all in our new house – which I hadn't even seen before we bought it – I returned with the van to the hire company in Pwllheli and then drove my own car south to London.

Back in Tottenham, I was in for a shock. Without delay, and almost on the doorstep, Jane told me that she didn't want me to move in with her and the family, and that our relationship was over. In retrospect, I can see that she was justified in her decision, though her way of delivering it was shocking and its timing clearly planned. I should still have seen it coming, but at the time the news came as a complete surprise and left me shaken. I gathered the children together and explained the situation, assuring them that I would still be seeing them when I came through London. I retreated to my brother's house in nearby Holloway, where I spent a couple of nights before, unavoidably, having to return to work. There was some irony in the fact that from now onwards I would have been able to get home quite regularly, since I so often passed through London on my way to and from the ferries in Dover, but for Jane and me it was already too late.

The ending of our relationship was a serious blow to my often precarious self-esteem. With the hindsight of decades, I can see that for the seven years that we were together I usually deferred to Jane, probably because she was five years older than me, and I never considered myself her equal in experience. I may have acquired competence and confidence in my job, but domestically I felt neither – and regular absences had certainly not helped. It was doubly discomfiting that Jane rapidly acquired a new boyfriend, this time older than her, and I tried not to speculate whether he had been on the scene before I knew what was happening. At any rate, my driving life now made me feel isolated in a way that I hadn't experienced before.

It's a fine line between being a loner and being lonely, and a lot depended on my relationship with the world I'd left behind whenever I went back to work. Paradoxically, when Jane and I were getting on well, it was easier to leave, but when my return home had been rocky, there was too much time alone at the wheel afterwards for me to replay what had gone wrong. For a few weeks after I was given the elbow, I spent too much time in a useless self-pity. There were songs I no longer played in the truck because they were too closely linked in my mind with Jane, and there was no longer anyone to phone when I returned to England, let alone come home to. In some ways, I was lucky to have such a consuming job, because it took most of my attention, although there was still plenty of time for brooding at the wheel. It is only in retrospect that I can see the irony that my absorption and interest in my work, which kept me going in the aftermath of the split, was probably a significant contributor to it in the first place.

The only positive side to our separation, despite its abruptness, was that Jane and I managed to maintain a truce in deference to the needs of the children, which relaxed into a renewed friendship after a year or so. I don't know how this happened, and it wasn't a result of any discussion on our part. Instead, it just seemed natural to both of us to behave in a civilised and, ultimately, friendly manner towards each other, and the children were clearly the beneficiaries. Less creditably, however, it has made me rather judgmental since then towards separating couples who unfortunately have not been able to do the same. I think we were simply lucky.

Now I rented a room from my brother and his wife, so that I technically had a base in London, but I might as well have admitted that my home was effectively my truck, as it had been for some years. With little incentive to go back to my new address in London, I now spent more and more of my time on the road, and my work colleagues became almost the whole of my social life, both within the company and in the wider fraternity of international drivers.

Already my return to Cadwallader had allowed me to renew my friendship with Phil Spittle, one of the company's two skilled international transport managers. Phil, in particular, was an outstanding manager of vehicles and went on to run some major transport operations, including the nightly distribution of millions of newspapers for the then very influential Mirror Group. At Cadwallader, Phil and Mike Goffin managed to organise their seventy-odd trucks on international work so well that we never had to wait for instructions about where to go next, whether we were delivering an export load abroad or a return delivery in the UK. Phil treated the whole thing as a chess-like challenge and even if they had allocated all Caddy's trucks for a week ahead, he would pride himself on being able to take on further work at the last minute and juggle the trucks to accommodate it. Cadwallader's international fleet seemed to grow steadily as new work flowed in to the company.

As soon as I was tipped, anywhere in Europe, I'd phone, or sometimes telex, for reloading instructions, and it seemed as if both Mike and Phil were just waiting for my call. They always gave me my instructions quickly and efficiently, which was particularly useful in Italy where public phone boxes gobbled *gettones* at an alarming rate, and although Mike often allowed himself a few pleasantries, Phil was always brisk and to the point. Some drivers didn't like his brusque manner, but everyone recognised that he was good at his job. I discovered that it was satisfying to be well managed and that other drivers appreciated it, too. They didn't all like Phil, but they were happy to be deployed efficiently, and without wasted mileage between tipping and reloading. Nowadays, this is all handled by computers, which match loads to the nearest trucks, but in those days good transport managers, such as Mike and Phil, held the whole operation in their heads, with nothing more sophisticated than wall-mounted chalkboards displaying each truck's registration number and destination. Phil and I were of similar age and we enjoyed each other's company. In common with some of the other drivers, I occasionally brought duty-free spirits home from the ferries for both him and Mike, and on those occasions when I had a night in Oswestry, Phil and I would often spend the evening together, usually making inroads into the Gordon's export gin I'd brought back.

Unfortunately, within a year of my return to Cadwallader, he moved on to start his own business, and later went on to major transport management roles. If the Cadwallader brothers had had any sense, they would have done everything he asked to keep him on. Phil told me that he had been paid no better than an international driver, which, even as one of them, I could see made no sense, given the key role he played in the company. Nevertheless, he told me that when he had asked our employers for a substantial pay rise, they'd refused, not recognising that it would be worth paying double to keep him, given his skill in bringing in new work from the Continent and allowing the fleet to grow. Mike remained, but Phil was replaced by Colin, who may have had a more affable manner on the phone than Phil, but who was much less efficient. Whereas Phil had always had his reload instructions ready, Colin was quite likely to tell us to call back in an hour or two, saying there was a 'possibility of a load' at such-and-such. The drivers soon nicknamed him 'Possibilities', and although we all liked him as a bloke, we missed the way Phil kept us moving and the energy he brought to the job.

At the time, Gordon and Russell Cadwallader employed about 150 drivers, making them quite a sizeable transport firm in those days. There were also about fifteen fitters, who worked in a large workshop to which the office was attached. The workshop could accommodate several tractor units and at least a couple of trailers, and it was always busy. Every four or five weeks, I'd be called back to the yard and my truck would be given a service. The fridge fitters would look after the trailer and I'd drive my tractor unit onto one of the workshop's lifts, ready for an inspection and oil change.

One late afternoon, I put the truck on the lift and collected my outstanding paperwork to present it to the office. Finding that I'd left something behind, I climbed back onto the Volvo's steps and rummaged around for the missing papers. Having found them, I jumped backwards from the truck, but I'd failed to notice that it had been lifted up while I searched, so that I dropped twice as far as I'd anticipated. I landed squarely on my heels – I was wearing the international driver's standard wooden clogs – and it hurt like hell. Pursued by the laughter of the nearby workshop staff, I tottered into the office and presented my papers, but having sat down, I discovered that I couldn't stand up again and found myself in considerable pain. Luckily for me, Oswestry at that time boasted one of Britain's finest orthopaedic hospitals – a holdover from the war – and my feet were soon in good hands. X-rays showed that I'd cracked a bone in each heel and I was given a pair of crutches, and advised to take a couple of weeks off. However, I found that I could put weight on the balls of my feet and could still push down the pedals of my Volvo, so I went back to work.

It was by now quite late in the evening when I hauled myself into the cab, stowed my crutches and set off to load at Green's abattoir in Oldham. About an hour up the road, I noticed that my trailer lights had stopped working, so I pulled over to check them. Now I found that working with crutches wasn't so easy, because although I could do a fair impression of Long John Silver as I lurched around the trailer inspecting the lights, I was quite incapable of ducking under it to make any repairs. Instead, I drove on until I found a phone box and called Cadwallader's duty mechanic, since I was close enough to home for him to come out. He wasn't impressed to be called out at ten in the evening and sounded positively terse when I explained that I couldn't do much 'in my condition'. An hour later, he turned up in one of the company's vans and I climbed down laboriously from the cab, lugging my crutches behind me. As soon as he saw them, he laughed. "I'm sorry I sounded pissed off. When you said, 'in my condition', I thought you meant you were too drunk to get under the trailer!" Now in a quite different frame of mind, he found and fixed the electrical fault, and I was on my way.

I reached Green's in Oldham long after midnight, where I did manage to open the trailer doors to load, but hopping in and out of the cab wasn't so easy. Nonetheless, I managed it and set off for Dover, stopping for lunch at Birch Services on the M62. Here, I discovered something new about life on crutches; I was, of course, unable to carry my breakfast tray from the cafeteria counter to my table and had to ask for help. To make matters worse, the men's toilet was closed on the westbound side of the motorway and I had to negotiate two long flights of stairs to reach the facilities on the eastbound side. Within minutes, I became a vocal advocate for disabled rights and demanded to see the services manager. I explained how hard it was for a disabled person to deal with an out-of-order toilet and asked what would have happened if I'd been in a wheelchair. He may have been apologetic, but I had a sudden and very instructive snapshot of what it would be like to be permanently disabled. I also realised that even if I could drive, I wouldn't be able to climb down quickly from the cab to pay the tolls at French *péages* or do any work away from the wheel. Reluctantly, I threw in the towel, and after phoning the office, returned to Oswestry and hitched a lift down to London with a colleague to take a couple of weeks off. I didn't like it, because that meant surrendering my truck to somebody else. As soon as I could put weight on my heels, I went back to work.

CHAPTER 22
ROMANIA

Within weeks of returning to Cadwallader, I was sent on the company's first run to Romania, and for the next couple of years I was very happy that it became my main destination. The country itself, and the route we took through what was then communist Czechoslovakia and Hungary, was consistently interesting, and the mountainous parts of Romania itself were beautiful. The Romania run may not have matched the Middle East in complexity or strangeness, but it was far enough away to be challenging, with a thriving black market, and borders that made their own demands on patience and ingenuity. Since we were travelling outside the EEC, we had to use the TIR carnet system for customs with which I'd become familiar en route to the Middle East, but which was more convoluted than the T-forms used to cross borders in Western Europe. At the same time, being once again beyond the borders of the EEC meant I had the freedom to do as I pleased as far as hours were concerned. Moreover, I now had a new truck that could handle the work with ease.

Not long after rejoining Cadwallader, I was given a brand-new Volvo F10, which was at least as good as the Dutch-built Daf 2800, even if its cab wasn't quite as spacious. It had slightly less power to play with than the Daf, at about 275hp, but the relatively small 9.6-litre engine was coupled to an excellent 16-speed synchromesh gearbox, with a well-placed gearstick that had a short throw between ratios. If there was any difference in performance compared with the Daf, I didn't really notice it. As with my previous Volvo F88s, the basic eight-speed range-change gearbox was augmented with a splitter on each gear, but now controlled by a neat T-shaped switch mounted on the fascia just to the left of the steering wheel. The cab was mounted on four steel coil springs, which gave it a softer ride than the Daf's, and did a lot to mitigate the rigours of eastern roads. It was also much better insulated than the Dutch truck, which was very welcome in countries where the night-time temperature could drop well below minus twenty degrees Celsius in winter.

Where the Daf had been finished in soft-feel plastic across the engine tunnel, the F10 had a light orange carpet, which made the whole interior feel more luxurious, even if the colour made it hard to keep clean. Caddy's F10s had a single bunk, about two feet wide, and mounted above deep storage boxes across the width of the cab, with outside access at one end to a locker where I stored tools and snow chains. In the fascia, the wide shallow box that neatly held my cassette tapes meant I could keep my music in easily accessible order. The low, flat engine tunnel was finished off with a robust plastic storage box, which was an ideal place to put my two-burner camping stove, and I used to pride myself that I could have a kettle boiling within two minutes of engaging the handbrake.

Now that I had the new Volvo, I became something of a Romania specialist, though I still made long runs as far as Brindisi in the southern tip of Italy and occasional forays to the south of France. Cadwallader started hauling beef to the Eastern Bloc around the time when the EEC and the USA had imposed a trade embargo on the Soviet Union, in protest against that country's invasion of Afghanistan at the end of 1979, a considerable irony given what happened two decades later. All our Romania loads came from the T.N. Green abattoir in Oldham, and we drivers rapidly formed the impression that we were helping to break the embargo, at least in the early days. I took one of the first eastbound loads to the Hungarian capital, Budapest, and at the delivery point I had to reverse up to a line of refrigerated rail-freight wagons, into which my seventeen tonnes of frozen beef quarters were transhipped. I can't remember why I was so sure this train was bound for the Soviet Union, but I clearly recall my certainty that it was, a conviction shared by other drivers who made the same run. After all, if the load was destined to remain in Hungary, it made no sense not to deliver it directly to its final destination, rather than into a train. After a few months, however, most of our loads consisted of hanging fresh beef quarters, which we delivered to a variety of destinations in Romania, where they appeared to be processed for the domestic market and for re-export in cans.

The route to Romania took us through Belgium – and sometimes the Netherlands, if I felt like it – and on into Germany, which we entered near Aachen. From there, we ran south-east to Nürnburg, and then through Amberg and on to the German border with Czechoslovakia at Waidhaus. The German customs procedure was by now very familiar, and the first time I went through Waidhaus, the customs officers seemed particularly friendly. On the Czech side, however, their counterparts were unsmiling and unusually thorough, particularly when I returned through the same border to Germany. As we exited from Czechoslovakia, our cabs were carefully inspected. We were questioned about whether we were smuggling pornography, pistols or people, and the tops of our trailers were checked from a gantry, to make sure no one had cut a hole in them in order to hide in the trailer and be smuggled out of the country. However, as Rozvadov – the Czech side of the border – became more familiar, so did the officers who manned it.

One afternoon on the return journey, I was sitting in my cab being subjected to the usual litany of questions by a young Czech customs officer whom I'd come to recognise, and who spoke a little English. He asked me whether I would consider taking a person through the border. Something in his manner made me pause, but I answered that of course, I would never entertain the idea. He didn't pursue the matter and I gave it no more thought until a few days later when, back in England, I happened to see an item in *The Guardian* newspaper, reporting that a Czech customs officer had defected through the frontier at Waidhaus. Apparently, he had simply run between one border post and another. It didn't sound much of a feat, unless you knew, as I did, that the distance was several hundred metres along an exposed piece of road, and across a short bridge that offered a clear shot to any zealous border guard. I never saw the young officer again and I wondered whether he was the person in the report, and that his question had been a serious enquiry. Either way, my answer would have been no; some risks are just not worth taking, unless you're as desperate as he must have been.

Although we generally returned from Romania unladen, and reloaded from Germany, I once came back from Bucharest with a cargo of onion powder in large drums. When I reached Waidhaus, the customs officers were – like me – unable to read the Romanian paperwork and I couldn't explain what I was carrying. Finally, I remembered the German word for vegetables – *gemüse* – which I gave them, then mimed chopping a vegetable with tears streaming down my face. My growing audience of customs officers roared with laughter and said, '*Ah, zwiebeln,*' which solved the problem and, incidentally, taught me the German word for onions.

The village of Waidhaus, and its cosy restaurant, felt a little like the 'Last Homely House' in *The Hobbit*, much like the border at Spielfeld in Austria before I crossed into Yugoslavia on the Middle East runs. At both borders, I felt that I was leaving the modern world behind and going backwards in time to at least the 1950s. And in Czechoslovakia, the roads were considerably more primitive than they were in Yugoslavia. In those days, there was almost no dual carriageway in the country, except for one – a hundred-odd kilometre section of road south-east from Prague towards Bratislava, each now the capital of a separate country. Instead, the route from Rozvadov to Prague was a badly maintained two-lane road, black and dirty in winter and dusty in summer. It led through the city of Pilsen, past a huge Skoda truck factory and, more to the point, a brewery that seemed several blocks long. This, after all, was the city that had given 'pils' beer its name. Whenever I did return through Pilsen, I made a point of stocking up with beer bought very cheaply from the brewery's own store, filling up the passenger footwell with several cases, since we were then allowed to import up to fifty duty-free litres into Britain.

The capital, Prague, had no bypass around it and we had to find our way through the centre of the city. This did at least give me a chance to see how beautiful it was, despite its glum atmosphere and the smell of low-grade coal that pervaded the whole of the Eastern Bloc. Navigating, however, was fraught with difficulty, since the city was plagued with bridges of less than four metres' clearance and my fridge trailer wouldn't fit under them. Nevertheless, I soon learned my way through, and as one of Cadwallader's Eastern Bloc pioneers, I thought I knew the city quite well. After I'd done a few trips, I found myself heading to Romania with Peter Morris, the Cadwallader colleague I've mentioned before. I also had my seven-year-old daughter, Laura, with me, who was on her second trip to Romania. When we stopped for a break before tackling Prague, we met two more Brits, who didn't know the route through the city. I offered to lead the way and we set off in a convoy of four.

All went well, and we were already heading out from the centre again, when I found that the route I knew was closed for repairs. I followed what looked like a diversion sign and we suddenly found ourselves faced with a 3.8-metre tunnel, with tram tracks running through it. The four of us were effectively blocking the tram route with our four-metre trailers, and apart from the low clearance, we had no wish for a confrontation with a streetcar. Instead, we began to reverse, one by one, into a side-street to retrace our steps. Being originally the first in line, I would now be last, as we began to line up facing the opposite way. In the middle of this manoeuvre, a policeman turned up in a blue and white Lada – the ubiquitous Eastern Bloc car built in Russia – and we managed to explain that we were lost and needed directions out of the city and on to the road to Bratislava. To our surprise, the cop offered to show us the way, and even held back the traffic as we finished turning round. Off he went, with no regard to the fact that it takes time to get four large trucks through an intersection, and now I was bringing up the rear and was no longer the 'expert' leader. I also had no idea where we were, so I kept as close as I could to Peter's truck in front and hurtled through one red light after another, hoping that no bright spark would try to squeeze between us. After twenty minutes that seemed like forty, the cop had us back on a road I recognised and we parted with good will all round.

It took the best part of a day to cross Czechoslovakia, but entering Hungary wasn't as simple as it seemed because the main border crossing from what is now Slovakia required us to cross a weighbridge that weighed each axle. With hanging meat, our drive axles were often overloaded as the meat hooks slid forward on their rails under braking, and this meant a fine. Luckily, however, there was a longer alternative, which meant making a detour east of Bratislava and entering Hungary through Komárom, where there was still no weight check. All Eastern Bloc borders were slow and bureaucratic, and a queue of trucks might stretch one or two kilometres from the frontier itself. I often passed through Komárom at night and, quite naturally, there was usually a large number of drivers trying to avoid the weighbridge at the main-road crossing. There was no chance of sleeping. Instead, I had to stay in my seat, even if I didn't turn a wheel for half an hour at a time, for fear of being overtaken if I allowed a gap to appear in front of me. On the other hand, I had no compunction about taking advantage of any other driver who dozed off and allowed a space to appear into which I could overtake myself. The Czech and Hungarian border buildings were on either side of the Danube, and the line of trucks would creep across the legendary river before we could enter Hungary itself. East of Komárom, the Danube takes a big loop to the east and I crossed it again in Budapest, before continuing south-east to the Romanian border. The whole of this part of the route lay across the vast central European plains and it wasn't until well inside Romania that mountains appeared again.

We crossed into Romania at Nădlac, fifty kilometres before Arad, the first major town. Here, the Romtrans customs agent had a nice little scam. She was a plump, middle-aged woman, whose smile was only skin-deep. She had a quick look at my trailer and then explained with the aid of a chart that my axle configuration meant that, according to Romanian regulations, it was overweight on each axle. Smugly, she explained that I would have to pay a ludicrous fine of 1000 D-Marks before I could enter the country. On my first trip I was aghast until it became clear that the fine could easily be erased by a carton of Kent cigarettes, a brand much prized in Romania for reasons beyond understanding. Luckily, I knew about Kent from my experience with Harrison, when I had travelled down to Greece through the Eastern Bloc and I'd bought two cartons on the ferry from Dover. I handed one of them over, and the smiling bandit stamped my papers and let me pass.

This became a regular routine until the first time I brought Laura, then aged six. As soon as she saw this little blonde English girl, the

Romtrans lady forgot all about weight restrictions. Instead, she made a great fuss of Laura and invited her into her small office, where she showed her how to stamp the paperwork and let Laura amuse herself with other drivers' documents for ten minutes or so. My own paperwork was returned with no mention of the customary bribe and I congratulated Laura on saving me the price of the cigarettes. The following year, when she returned for a second trip during her school's Easter holiday, with the above-mentioned Prague adventure behind us, the woman greeted her like a long-lost relative. Once again, Laura was feted and this time she was even given a small bottle of perfume. For the second time she spared me from paying my bribe, but the next time I passed through, alone, it was business as usual.

This wasn't Laura's only exposure to petty graft. During our first trip to Romania, we were twice pulled over by traffic cops. The first time was in Czechoslovakia, on the short piece of dual carriageway south of Prague. The pretext was speeding, which was probably justified, given that the speed limit was a miserly 70kph. At any rate, faced with some fine whose value I can't recall, I offered the officer a pack of western cigarettes, which he happily accepted in lieu of official payment. In Romania, the same thing happened, though on this occasion my bribe was a can of Heinz baked beans. In both cases, I drew Laura's attention to what was happening – to show, whether she understood it or not, how differently life was conducted in the Eastern Bloc countries.

Our return trip took us through Austria, which I used as a shortcut to southern Germany, where I was due to pick up a load of cheese from Kempten, south of Ulm. Normally, I would have needed a permit to transit the country, but the Austrians allowed unladen trucks to pass without one, which saved some hundreds of kilometres, compared with continuing from Hungary to Czechoslovakia, and then heading south again through Germany. We crossed into Austria very late in the evening, and it was around two in the morning when I was caught in a radar trap as I speeded through what I had assumed was a sleeping village – only in Austria. Laura woke up when I stopped the truck and opened the door to talk to the cops. When I explained what was happening, she asked, in penetrating tones, whether I was going to give them a pack of cigarettes. I hastily hushed her; these were real cops, I muttered, and might be offended.

It might seem strange that a child would want to spend ten days travelling in a truck, but when I recently asked Laura (now in her mid-forties) about her memories of those trips, they were very positive, and she could remember a great many details after an interval of forty years. Some of her comments are worth repeating here, because they give a different slant from mine. They also show that, from a child's perspective, a long truck journey is very different from being strapped into a car:

"I can remember getting into your truck on Holloway Road, and pulling up to the red light and having the little car in front of the cab utterly disappear from view because we were so high up. I was so nervous about you crashing the truck into it. I remember being able to scramble right up to the windscreen to try and see the car in front of us, because there was no seatbelt!

"I was astounded by the bed in the back of your cab and how huge it was inside. If I could have had something to compare it with at the time, I would have said a Tardis for sure. I remember having to scramble to climb up the steps into the cab and how I was hardly as tall as your truck wheel.

"I also remember the special compartment in the cab where you had cans of food, your red metal stove-top kettle and your camp stove. Your huge collection of music tapes that you used to keep under a towel in the hope that customs officers wouldn't see them. Having the officers casually look through them, and you having to relinquish the odd tape or carton of cigarettes – the reasons for which only really made sense to me with the benefit of hindsight. I think at the time all you said about it was that it made it 'easier' to go through customs.

"I recall watching you take the tacho card out of the dashboard and thinking how incredibly high-tech that was, not to mention receiving telex messages from European offices so that you knew where to go next.

"I used to absolutely love driving at night and I vividly remember arriving at ferry terminals in the dark. Being able to drive down the special slip road for trucks and having an intense feeling of anticipation.

The strangeness of the sounds, the lights on high cranes, the lights from the ferry, seeing how big it was and being in a line of trucks waiting to board. And I loved feeling special because we were truck drivers; we had our own stairs and places to sit on the ferry.

"I clearly remember being in Prague where we were in a convoy of trucks and being immensely proud that you were the lead truck. Turning to bitter disappointment at being at the back because we'd gone the wrong way and needed a police escort when the convoy had to turn round.

"I remember collecting all the glasses that evening waiting to load on to the ferry in Zeebrugge and thinking it was lots of fun. I think you were outraged that I didn't get some recognition for that from the bar staff, but I just remember being up late and having a job to do. Those early experiences of long stretches on the road, with only your dad and the world outside your window for entertainment, have been an incredible gift."

Whenever I took Laura, or her elder brother, Jason, on a trip, I noticed that other drivers often made a fuss of them, and even gave them small presents or bought them snacks. It was as if my children reminded them of their own families back home and I certainly noticed the same feeling in myself when I met other drivers' children. On the occasion Laura remembered, when she collected glasses all evening as we waited for a ferry delayed by a gale, it was another driver, not me, who was outraged that she received not so much as a Coke for her trouble. From my point of view, taking the children away with me, and showing them this new and wider world, was very satisfying, and gave me an all too rare opportunity to spend significant time with them. Nowadays, it is much more difficult – if not impossible – for drivers to take family members with them, mainly for insurance reasons, but at Cadwallader our bosses were very supportive of the idea. We drivers always thought they encouraged us to take our children with us, so we wouldn't ask to go home so often. Whether it was pragmatism or compassion on their part, I was very glad to take advantage of it.

On my first trip into Romania, I was surprised to find a strong German influence, and I noticed graveyards where headstones were carved in old German, *Hochdeutsch* script. The following winter, just after I crossed into Romania, I came across a Dutch car stranded at the roadside. With a feeling of western solidarity, I stopped to help the driver and his wife, and it became clear that they would need a tow into Arad, some thirty kilometres away. Since I was pulling a fridge trailer, I had no need of ropes and had nothing with which to tow the car. As the Dutch couple and I searched the roadside for a piece of discarded rope – small chance in a country where anything might be scavenged – I noticed a small farm a few hundred yards away across the black-earth steppe. As I walked towards it in search of a rope, the farm looked more and more run-down, with tattered fences and lurching roofs. Finally, a tiny old woman appeared, dressed, as was typical, entirely in black.

"*Sprechen sie Deutsch?*" I asked her. She straightened herself to her full five feet and answered haughtily, "*Ich* bin *Deutsch*." I muttered something suitable and managed to procure enough rope to tow the Dutch car to Arad and the nearest garage. In the process I had learned something new about Romania, that its northern region had been settled in the inter-war years – and earlier – by German immigrants who still identified with their original homeland.

Respect for Germany also had its humorous side. I was once returning through Romania with two other drivers and we took the unusual decision to stop at a roadside restaurant, instead of cooking our own food. We knew the meal might be poor and we were right. Romanian food seemed to be a pale imitation of German cuisine, and the cook hadn't wasted any fuel in keeping our schnitzel and potatoes anything better than tepid. We were inclined to refuse dessert, but the owner was very insistent that we try his peaches, which, he was keen to tell us, came from Deutschland. To prove the point, he proudly produced the can they came in and pointed to the legend, 'Made in Germany'.

Sometimes Romania served up more serious adventures. On one mid-winter trip, I had loaded beef for the city of Suceava in the northern part of the country, near the Moldovan border. Near Amberg in south-eastern Germany, I fell in with a driver – I'll call him Mike – driving another Volvo F10, belonging to Swallow International, a small fridge transport firm in which the Cadwallader brothers apparently had some interest and which they eventually took over. Mike's load had been subcontracted from Caddy's and he was heading for the same destination. As we approached the Czech border, it began to snow and it was clear there would be bad weather ahead. I wasn't particularly alarmed since I had a set of snow chains and well-treaded tyres, but Mike did not. It was his first trip to Romania and given that his tyres weren't in great shape, I suggested that he phone his boss to ask permission to buy a set of chains at the large Shell service station near the border at Waidhaus. Permission was denied and we had to continue regardless. I was thankful that although Cadwallader wasn't the best payer in the business, we never lacked the right equipment for the job. Despite my misgivings, all went well until we entered Romania and headed off towards Suceava on a road neither of us knew.

It was already dusk when we met some sheep. There must have been a couple of hundred of them spread across the road. I was in the lead and saw them just in time to pull up short. Behind me, I heard a shuddering sound as Mike stood on the brakes of his Volvo. The Romanian shepherd was in no hurry to move his charges so I dropped down to third gear and edged my truck forwards. The sheep flowed to each side of my truck like the bow wave of a ship, leaving just enough room for us to creep through. The shepherd waved casually as we accelerated back to a steady cruise, this time with Mike in the lead. We'd thought we might even make it to Suceava that night, but I hadn't realised that our route would involve some fairly stiff mountain climbing and descents.

It was below freezing and there was now a thin dusting of snow across the road, so I let Mike pull ahead to leave some distance between us. Just as well; in the dark, there was little warning when the road suddenly began winding upwards. As I rounded an early, climbing corner, I had almost to swerve to avoid Mike's truck pulled untidily to the side of the road. He was standing next to his cab and waving. I slowed to a crawl, but he yelled, "Don't stop!" and jumped onto my bottom step, hanging onto the mirror arm. I lowered the window. "It's as slippery as hell," he shouted over the rumbling of the engine, "and I've got no grip. Whatever you do, don't stop." I didn't, and I didn't have to because my nearly new all-weather drive tyres were still gripping better than Mike's had. I kept the F10 in a low gear – fourth or fifth – and we snaked up the mountain, with Mike hanging on to the mirror. We dared not stop to let him into the cab in case I couldn't get going again. As the climb continued, we met new snow, which grew thicker with altitude. Finally, my own tyres started to slip and then to spin, and the Volvo slid to a halt at the side of the road. I set the handbrake and found the whole rig slipping sideways and backwards towards the ditch. I jammed the transmission into first, willing the truck to hold. To my immense relief, it did. Of course, having the Volvo in gear meant I had to turn off the engine, and with it went our source of heat. Mike stepped backwards to the ground and I climbed down from the cab.

Around us, the forest was dark and threatening; the air was harshly cold and already my hands were feeling it. I snapped open the Volvo's side locker and pulled out my snow chains; at least we had one set between us. We dragged them back to the drive axle and laid them out behind the wheels, at which point I realised they wouldn't fit under the mudguards. Most of Cadwallader's trucks had theirs cut away above the top of the wheels to accommodate chains, but my Volvo was then so new that it hadn't been altered. The heavy plastic mudguards were too thick to cut, even with the large butcher knife that had been left in my trailer at Hastings abattoir a couple of years earlier. Mike and I debated what to do, until I realised the cold was so intense that the plastic had become hard and brittle, and would break quite easily. I retrieved a large spanner from my toolbox and proceeded to smash the mudguards away from the top of the wheels. "Russell won't like that," Mike joked, referring to my boss, but I was long past worrying about that. The black plastic flew in all directions and in short order I'd made enough clearance for the chains, and now had the cut-down mudguards I needed; they could be tidied up later in the yard.

I climbed up behind the wheel, started the engine and gingerly rolled the Volvo back over the chains. This time leaving the engine running, with the security of the chains beneath the wheels, I jumped down again, and together Mike and I fastened the heavy links around the tyres. I always found it almost impossible to put chains on with gloved hands and the freezing steel was painful to touch. Every couple of minutes, I left the chains to warm my hands in the Volvo's exhaust. Once the chains were on and we were back in the cab, I revved up the engine to get the heater going. We took a couple of minutes to thaw our hands before I engaged first gear and let the clutch in as carefully as I could. The whole truck groaned slightly, the chains slipped a fraction and held. We were off.

After the drama of the past hour, the next few kilometres were plain sailing. We roared steadily up the mountain at about 25mph, with the chains gripping nicely in the thickening snow. Finally we reached the summit, and found a surprising and welcome sight. On the side of the road was a large, homely-looking restaurant. The couple of dozen trucks parked outside suggested it was a good one, but we resisted the temptation to go in until we'd done something about Mike's truck, ten kilometres back down the mountain. We couldn't leave it where it was; it was parked in a dangerous spot and anything of value might be taken if we left it unattended. Besides, Mike needed his cab to sleep in. We took the chains off my truck and debated how to get them back down the mountain. They weighed fifty pounds apiece and it was out of the question to walk.

The snow was coming more strongly as we looked about for a lift, but all the trucks were snug for the night. As we discussed what to do, a burly local emerged from the restaurant and headed towards a large agricultural tractor. Better than nothing. With gestures and pidgin German, we explained what had happened and that we needed a lift down the mountain. The Romanian farmer grinned and gestured for us to climb on to the step. We hauled the chains aboard and clung on as the tractor lurched forward and started trundling down the winding hill. It was the coldest ten kilometres I've ever covered. As the tractor lurched round each bend, I was praying Mike's truck would appear between the trees before my hands gave up the ghost. Finally, we reached it and, waving goodbye to our helpful friend, clambered into Mike's cab to warm up. He started the engine and floored the accelerator to get the heater working as soon as possible. Within ten minutes, we'd recovered enough to put the chains on his truck – and at least he had the right mudguards.

By the time we reached the top of the mountain again, we'd been battling with it for over four hours – an average of under two kilometres an hour. Mike swung his truck in next to mine outside the restaurant and in we went. Romanians know how to heat a building and the smoky, fuggy warmth was as welcome as the schnitzel and the beers that chased it down. We settled back for what remained of the evening and tackled the downhill side of the mountain in the light of a cold and sunny morning.

In all my time as a driver, I only used chains once in Britain, incongruously enough in the flat lands near Peterborough in eastern England. I had driven up from Italy with a load of apples bound for a supermarket distribution centre at Wisbech in the Cambridgeshire fens, and the trip had been quite difficult. I had hit heavy snow on the approach on the Italian side of the Mont Blanc Tunnel and black ice on the steep descent on the French side, with the result that I had been up all Friday night, crawling up and down the mountain. I can even pinpoint the occasion as the 13th December 1981, because I was trying to reach London by early Sunday evening, in order to attend a memorial service for my father on the date of his death. I did make it to the church on time and left London later in the evening in heavy rain, which turned into serious snow once I had left the microclimate of the city.

The radio was broadcasting regular messages from the police advising people to avoid travel if possible, and I pulled over at one point to brew a cup of tea and ponder the official advice. I had just decided to ignore it, when a sixteen-ton Leyland four-wheeler passed the lay-by where I was parked, unwittingly endorsing my decision. Besides, I had only just negotiated Mont Blanc in worse weather than this and in far trickier terrain. I set off and fell in behind the smaller truck, which was apparently unladen, judging by the imprudent speed with which he pulled ahead and eventually disappeared.

East of Peterborough, the road headed across flat open country, and the wind was creating surprisingly deep snow drifts across the road. At one point, I saw a collection of red tail lights and, between them and me, the Leyland, which had evidently slid out of control and was now stranded at right angles to the road. There was, nevertheless, enough room for me to pass, as long I was prepared to drive through virgin snow. I decided to put on my snow chains and, as I was doing so, the Leyland driver appeared and asked me if I could pull his truck straight again.

With the snow chains giving me extra traction, I hooked up to the rear bumper of his truck and reversed, pulling the sixteen-tonner back in line with the road. As the driver got back into his cab, I eased past his truck and continued a few hundred metres to the group of cars and one large van, which were trying to extricate themselves from a deep drift. In my mirrors I could see that the Leyland had once again slid sideways, but I was too far ahead to go back and help him further. I stopped to survey the half-dozen stranded cars, but quickly figured that there were enough people to look after themselves without any assistance from me.

As I was about to pass the whole crowd, once again venturing onto the new snow on the other side of the road, the driver of the van hailed me and asked if I could give him a tow. With the invincibility of the snow chains on my drive axle, I was happy to oblige. The van driver had a tow rope, which we fastened between the rear of my trailer and his front suspension, and I ended up pulling him through several miles of open country before we reached some woodland, where the road was relatively clear. I unhitched the van with its grateful driver and continued to the warehouse in Wisbech, where I parked up and had a few hours' much-needed sleep. The next morning, the staff were surprised that I had made it, given the conditions, but, although it's a cliché to say, 'it was all in a day's work' – it simply was.

The next time I needed chains in Romania was only a few days later. Less than a week before Christmas I was sent in to Green's abattoir in Oldham to load beef for Bucharest. When I protested to transport manager Mike that I'd be away for Christmas, he assured me that Green's had paid for a return flight from Bucharest to get me home for the holiday. The flight was on December 23rd and I'd fly back to Romania on January 2nd. That made the whole trip an adventure to savour and guaranteed me a week off for the holiday. Having loaded in Oldham, I detoured back to the yard in Oswestry for the truck to be serviced and to pick up my air ticket, an unusual addition to my normal paperwork. At the same time, I procured an extra set of snow chains to use on the trailer if the snow got bad. Whatever the weather, I had no intention of stopping and risking missing my plane, particularly since Mike told me it was the last flight before Christmas.

As I bowled down the A5 away from Oswestry, the Volvo ran as sweetly as it always did after a service and oil change. When you spend day after day driving the same truck, you are aware of the slightest alteration in its behaviour and I could always feel a difference for the first few miles after a service, before the sense of newness wore off. It was a good way to start any trip and particularly one in winter.

I was so determined to catch my plane home for Christmas that I hardly stopped – apart from at borders, of course – the whole way down through Germany, Czechoslovakia and Hungary, and by the time I entered Romania, I was a day ahead of schedule. It was just as well, because once again the snow started just as I entered the country. On the outskirts of Arad, about fifty kilometres inside the country, I parked at the side of the road and cooked myself some supper as I waited to see whether the snow would continue, and make it worth putting on chains. As I was eating and watching the snow get heavier, there was a knock on the door and I looked down to see a well-dressed man slightly older than me. He wanted a lift to a village some two hours down the road and, for some reason, I said yes. I was glad I did, because my passenger spoke quite good English and I learned that he was a professional icon painter. I was surprised to find that one could make a living by painting religious icons in a country that was supposed to combine atheism with its communism, though I later saw further evidence of how strong Orthodox Christianity was in Romania.

Meanwhile, my hitchhiker earned his lift by holding a torch as I put chains on the Volvo's drive axle and, unusually, a pair of chains on the trailer. Normally, I would only chain the drive axle, just to get up some mountain or other, but on this occasion I had no intention of stopping and aimed to drive more than 500 kilometres through the night, to reach Bucharest in the morning. I put a chain on the right-hand wheel of the front trailer axle and the left side of the rear axle, to prevent the trailer sliding sideways or attempting to jack-knife if I was travelling too fast downhill. It worked very well and I was able to maintain a steady 60–70kph, uphill and down, without drama. It helped that the snow continued falling the whole way, because chains work better when the snow is thick and suffer if they have to run on patches of bare tarmac. I didn't see any of that. The Volvo trundled through villages lit by occasional orange streetlights and with a couple of brief stops for tea, and to drop off my icon-painting friend, I reached Bucharest just as the city's customs office opened in the morning. With my plane not due to leave until the following day, I'd made very good time.

Our loads to Bucharest always went to the same large meat processing plant on the outskirts of the city, and for once I was the only western truck there. On other occasions, I'd waited up to three days to unload, but this time I was ready to leave by late afternoon. The plan was to park up the truck at the factory and take a cab to the airport. When I asked one of the office workers to find me a taxi, he immediately offered to drive me himself, for an appropriate fee, and even suggested I stay the night at his flat. However, I was determined not to miss my flight, having laboured so hard to be on time, so I asked to be dropped at the airport that evening and spent the night sleeping on a bench. I didn't miss the plane, though the sight of a Russian-built Tupolev tri-jet flown and, more ominously, maintained by Romanians didn't fill me with confidence. Now that I was based in London, it was a short hop home from Heathrow Airport and I was home early on Christmas Eve. No lonely porridge that year and, to cap it all, Jane invited me to join the family on Christmas Day.

I flew back to Bucharest on January 2nd, which was a holiday in Romania. Nevertheless, I managed to pick up my truck in the late afternoon and proceeded to head north. The temperature was just on freezing, ideal for snow, and I wanted to be well clear of the country while the sky was still cloudless. I now had a choice: to take the more direct route home through the centre of the country, past the oilfields at Pitești and through Sibiu, a town I knew quite well, or the longer but less mountainous route around the south-western corner of the country. Having an empty trailer, I opted for the shorter but hillier alternative. After a few miles, and when both routes were still available, I came across huge signs informing me with garish graphics that the road to Sibiu was closed. For some reason that I still don't understand, I ignored the warning and continued up the road that I now knew to be blocked. A second, and even a third, sign didn't deter me. It was crazy, because if I had to retrace my steps, I'd be adding at least six hours' extra driving and more if the obstacle proved to be far up the road.

Just after midnight, on what was now a beautiful clear night, I came to the road closure. The road, much diminished and with its asphalt ripped up, snaked ahead through a narrow gap between a high rocky cliff on the left and a fast-moving river on the right. I parked the Volvo and decided to reconnoitre on foot. It was only as I stepped down from the cab, by the brilliant light of an almost full moon, that I remembered I was in the heart of Transylvania and Dracula country. I told myself not to be a fool, but I felt distinctly uncomfortable as I walked forwards along what had now been turned into a rough dirt road and kept turning round to make sure I was alone. After a few minutes, I was startled to hear a vehicle coming up behind and a locally built 4x4 passed me, and continued boldly around the bend ahead. If he could do it, so could I, though this was a ludicrous assumption, given that his small jeep could get round a corner that would defeat my fifty-five-foot artic. Nevertheless, I decided to continue.

Glad to be back in the vampire-free security of my cab, I set off slowly up the road. The reddish dirt road surface was rough with the tyre tracks of construction vehicles and one bend was so narrow that I had to steer right to the edge of it. I found myself looking straight down into the river, some twenty feet below, while I had to let the nearside trailer tyres drag against a rock wall on the inside of the bend. If there really was an impassable barrier ahead, and no place to turn round, I'd never be able to reverse out again past this bend. I wondered darkly whether my truck would be stuck forever or how much it would cost to crane it out by helicopter. I now had no option but to go forward. I stopped to check the tyres but they were undamaged; the rock had been smooth and, with no load, the tyres had slid quite easily past it. I climbed back into the cab and tackled the next narrow turn. In all, I must have struggled through another ten kilometres, but finally I came to the end of the construction site and found myself back on a tarmac surface. My lunatic decision to go up the 'closed' road had paid off and I'd saved myself several hours. And I hadn't encountered Dracula. I parked up for the rest of the night, and continued on towards Hungary and Austria and the backload of cheese that awaited me in southern Germany.

CHAPTER 23
STRIKES

Running so often to Romania, and dealing with the Eastern Bloc's convoluted customs and laws, I developed a somewhat cavalier attitude to problems closer to home, which is perhaps why I got caught up in a strike that paralysed Dover docks for almost twenty-four hours.

It was the Dover customs officers themselves who started it. They were apparently in some salary dispute with the Customs and Excise Department that employed them, and to make their point, the front-line customs officers – the ones who processed our paperwork – had decided on a go-slow. No longer would they give twenty-four-hour coverage; instead, they would work only one shift a day. The result was chaos, and disastrous for international truck drivers. Tourists, of course, felt no pain, since their customs checks were minimal to non-existent, but in those days, trucks couldn't move in or out of the country without customs clearance and the appropriate paperwork – an impediment that was removed by the single market in 1992 and reinstated by the geniuses who pushed through Brexit nearly thirty years later. The result for us drivers was a wait of at least twenty-four hours. As we arrived in the port, we were given a raffle ticket whose number denoted our place in the queue waiting to board a ferry and then we parked, waiting for our number to come up. Kent-based drivers usually went home for a day, but the rest of us had to make the best of it. Every inch of the dockside was covered with trucks and the port's single drivers' canteen was crowded with their disgruntled drivers.

This went on for weeks. The Friday before what was then still called the Whitsun bank holiday, I arrived in Dover, en route for Romania with fellow Cadwallader driver, Peter Morris. I had my daughter, Laura, with me, having taken her out of school for a little geography education. We parked as usual and repaired to the drivers' canteen, where a row was brewing. A group of French and Italian drivers had had enough. Amid much yelling and gesticulating, they took themselves off to their trucks and, in short order, parked them across all six link-spans connecting the docks to the ferries, preventing any vehicle from disembarking or boarding. They flatly refused to move until customs went back to work.

Most of the Brits settled back for an even longer wait, but a few of us, including Peter and me and another Cadwallader driver, Gordon Parry, decided we couldn't leave the blockade to the French and added our trucks to theirs. I don't think the foreign drivers realised it was a bank holiday weekend, but they couldn't have picked a better Friday to make their point. Apart from the by-now usual backlog of trucks, the docks were crowded with cars and coaches off on a bank holiday break. None of them moved. The hours dragged by and tourist tempers frayed. At one point, a coach driver threatened to throw a jack through my windscreen, until I managed to calm him down by explaining that my six-year-old daughter was sleeping in the cab. Another coach driver asked me whether I thought he should take his passengers home, because they were only going for a three-day jaunt. I couldn't tell him; we British drivers were playing only a cameo role in the main drama orchestrated by the French and Italians, with a couple of Swiss supporters.

Together, they were implacable. By now, a number of senior customs officers had appeared and they came to talk to Peter and me. When they discovered that I had a workable knowledge of French, they asked me to act as translator. With me in the middle, the two sides began to talk to each other. Gradually, my role as a translator morphed into one of negotiator between the two camps. At first there was little common ground, but we eventually came to a compromise: the senior customs officers, normally too grand for paper pushing, agreed to work all night to get the backlog of trucks reduced if we would free up the link-spans.

Not so fast. The drivers wanted to know what guarantee there would be if everything were opened up immediately. Finally, after long discussions, the French and Italian drivers agreed to free one link-span for every fifty trucks cleared. By now we were into the early hours of the morning, but the senior officers went to work, and after an hour or so, enough trucks had been processed for the first link-span to be opened.

By early light, most of the loading ramps still remained blockaded. With the ringleaders, Peter and I had been up all night, and we were weary from hours of negotiation. All the same, I'd enjoyed the novelty of the whole situation and the fact that I had been propelled into the centre of the argument, mostly by chance. From time to time, I'd returned to my truck to check on Laura, but she was taking the whole thing in her stride. It wasn't until late morning that the French and Italian drivers declared victory; hundreds of trucks had been cleared through customs and the demonstrators opened the last of the link-spans. I didn't discover how the hundreds, probably thousands, of tourists had reacted, though many of them had shipped out as each ferry berth became available. Peter and I were much more interested in boarding our own ferry to Zeebrugge and catching up on our sleep during the five-hour crossing. Luckily, we were on a freight-only boat, so we didn't have to listen to any irate car drivers. With Laura in tow, we had breakfast in the drivers' restaurant on board and were asleep in our cabins before the ferry had cleared the harbour wall. I don't know how the customs officers' dispute was resolved, but by the time we returned from Romania a week or so later, the port was back to normal, so the drivers' direct action might have benefitted us all.

It wasn't the first time I had witnessed a French drivers' strike at first hand, and seen how resolute, and even ruthless, they could be. I'd been returning from central Italy, once again in late spring, when just south of the Mont Blanc Tunnel, near Courmayeur, I came up to the end of a long line of stationary trucks, extending down much further from the tunnel's entry platform than any normal hold-up. I pulled into the line and climbed down from the cab to join the huddle of drivers standing in the road. Here, I found out that French drivers had blocked their end of the tunnel, in protest against the slow pace of clearance by Italian customs in Aosta. Even though their cause was worth supporting, we were clearly in for a long wait.

I happened to be the only Brit in the line, at least as far back as I could see, and I found myself part of a group mainly consisting of Frenchmen, but including a solitary Luxembourger. We whiled away the morning exchanging trucking gossip and, as lunchtime approached, we set off for the nearest place to eat. Just up the mountain from Courmayeur, we discovered a small restaurant that catered for tourists with prices to match. When the *patronne* told us that lunch would be 20,000 lira – about £8 – we all turned to leave, at which point she appeared to realise how many potential customers she was turning away and dropped the price by half. We turned again and twenty-odd drivers quickly filled the place. The *patronne's* decision was a wise one, since we were still there for lunch and dinner the following day. Meanwhile, the Luxembourg driver had broken the seal on his trailer, which contained twenty-four tonnes of Italian red wine, and we were all very happy to help lighten his load.

By the afternoon of the second day, the French began to resent being trapped on the Italian side and a message went through the tunnel to their striking colleagues on the other side. The result was that the blockade was temporarily lifted so several dozen trucks could pass through the tunnel to the parking platform at the French end of the tunnel, 11.6 kilometres through the mountain. I was far enough up the queue to be included.

The French side was an eye-opener. Two tractor units were parked face to face across the road, preventing anyone from tackling the twisting road down from the tunnel mouth. I was waved into the parking area, where I left my Volvo and strolled over to the barricade to see what was happening. A cluster of drivers surrounded the blockading trucks, watched by a few policemen standing to one side and making no attempt to clear the road. As I chatted to the ringleaders, I discovered that some of them were in negotiations by phone with the ministry of transport in Paris, but that I shouldn't expect to be leaving any time soon. I had already phoned Mike Goffin back in Oswestry the day before and I found another payphone to give him an update. Now that matters were so clearly beyond my control, I began to enjoy the situation, until I saw that it could have serious consequences.

Late in the afternoon, a car came through the tunnel from Italy and tried to get past the barrier. In it were a couple and their daughter, about eight years old, whom they were taking from the little town of Courmayeur on the Italian side of the mountain to a hospital in Geneva, some ninety kilometres away. Despite the fact that the girl was due to undergo a serious operation, the French drivers remained implacable; no vehicle could pass. No amount of hand-wringing and tears on the part of the parents, or even appeals to common humanity by the police, made any impression. Finally, after protracted discussions, the blockaders agreed to allow the girl and her parents to pass through on foot and get into a car that was brought up from Chamonix on the other side of the barrier.

It was a chilling example of how single-minded the French can be when it comes to striking or demonstrating, but soon afterwards I had an equally telling illustration of their devotion to food. As dusk fell, and dinner time approached, these principled demonstrators had no compunction about opening the blockade to allow three tractor units to pass through in search of a restaurant for dinner. Each cab was packed with drivers, me among them, and the barrier was closed behind us as we descended to a Routiers restaurant down on the valley floor.

The following day, the phone negotiations had evidently reached a satisfactory conclusion, because the demonstrators lifted the blockade and allowed us all to descend from the tunnel, and normal traffic to resume. I had lost three days. Moreover, I never did discover what had been agreed and I can't say that I noticed any improvement in the Italian customs' leisurely way with paperwork, nor their propensity to lift a couple of lambs from my loads for 'testing'.

The only time that British truck drivers went on strike during my time behind the wheel was in January 1979, during the 'winter of discontent' that saw the demise of the Callaghan government and, in May of that year, helped usher in the era of Margaret Thatcher. The strike began as an official stoppage by fuel tanker drivers belonging to the Transport and General Workers' Union (TGWU). Other drivers joined the strike unofficially in early January and the whole affair became official a few days later.

This was the winter in which I celebrated 'Muslim Christmas' while driving for Harrison, and on the day that the strike was properly launched, I was struggling through snow in Austria on my way home from Dubai. I'd learned about the stoppage on the BBC World Service and I can't say I felt particular sympathy with my fellow drivers back home, though I would have applauded a pay rise. Any agreement would be irrelevant to me and, I suspected, to most small haulage businesses, including my former employers, Williams and Cadwallader. Moreover, I was no longer a member of the TGWU. I had joined the union when I worked for Williams, paying my dues at South Caernarfon Creameries, whose fifty-odd factory workers had their own small branch. I'd already concluded that the TGWU was out of touch with its truck driver members – who made up less than a quarter of its overall membership – since the union's official policy at the time was to oppose sleeper cabs, even though every long-distance driver wanted them. I'd let my membership lapse when I joined Cadwallader for the first time and, in any case, I'd become further disillusioned when I read in a news report that some four million members had taken part in the election of a new general secretary to the union, one Moss Evans. I knew that none of us at the creamery had seen a ballot and I later verified that the few TGWU members at Caddy's hadn't been balloted either. I concluded that either the election was, at least, somewhat fraudulent or that small union branches didn't merit inclusion.

Such considerations were quite academic as I put snow chains on my Daf, ready to climb towards a timber yard in the mountains of Austria. I had no strike pay to support me and if I had refused to pick up the load of timber that constituted my backload, Jack Harrison would have fired me on the spot. When I returned to Dover, the docks were much quieter than usual and, as I drove out of the docks, strikers were demonstrating at the gates, but not barring the way as their French counterparts would have done. They seemed resigned to the fact that international drivers weren't going to give up getting home and I encountered no trouble as I drove up the unnaturally quiet motorways to Stoke-on-Trent. The customer was surprised to see me and asked how I'd got past the picket lines in Dover. Without thinking, I told him there's been no trouble at all; it was only afterwards that I realised I should have talked up the difficulties and perhaps earned a tip for my efforts.

When the strike became official, most of Harrison's drivers were on their way eastwards and only a few of us were in the UK. This was just as well, since Spiers & Hartwell, the company for whom we were hauling to the Middle East was strike-bound, so we were unable to load for Jeddah and Dubai. Instead, Jack Harrison found work for his trucks pulling trailers to Holland for the giant international operator, Ferrymasters. Effectively, we Harrison drivers were black-legging, but the whole affair seemed so remote from the perspective of Middle East work that we didn't see it that way. At any rate, none of us could afford to do without wages for a month without the support of the union.

In the end, big-company TGWU members – fuel tanker drivers and the like – achieved a staggering twenty per cent pay rise, but that made no difference to what we were paid at Harrison and, I later discovered, what Cadwallader drivers received. The simple fact was that smaller independent hauliers couldn't afford such a wage settlement, and most of us drivers understood that, even if we would have welcomed such a boost to our earnings. As it was, wages at Caddy's stayed the same for the five years I was involved with the company.

CHAPTER 24
THE EASTERN BLOC

Visiting foreign countries as a working truck driver gives one an unusual perspective, and an understanding that a casual visitor might not pick up. I've already noted that truck drivers were the only category of traveller to be given multiple entry visas to Saudi Arabia, and in any country we came and went without drama, because we – and more particularly our loads – were needed. As a driver, I may not have visited the cultural landmarks of the countries I travelled to, but I gained an insight into the way ordinary people lived that would have been hard to replicate as a tourist. And the more time I spent behind the Iron Curtain, the more the contradictions of a communist command economy became apparent.

For a start, the Eastern Bloc countries seemed to be a breeding ground for small-scale capitalists. Almost any Romanian I came across was ready to change my D-Marks on the black market and, if I agreed to do business, the money-changer would produce a fat roll of Romanian *lei* from his pocket. I often wondered how such a large sum could be accumulated in a country where wages were pitiful. At the meat-packing plant in Bucharest, one worker had a sideline in bootlegged rock music cassettes and regularly tried to acquire my tapes to copy them. I didn't play ball, not least because he showed no inclination to pay me, and I doubted whether they would be returned. When I worked for Harrison, I'd learned about the black market for fuel in Czechoslovakia and Hungary, and now that I'd become an Iron Curtain regular, I made good use of it. In Western Europe, we used a Shell credit card to fill up, but, before I left for the first trip to Romania, I impressed on Gordon Cadwallader that even if we could find a Shell station, we'd save money by buying diesel with cash. In Hungary, the regulations stipulated that we should buy our fuel with tokens acquired at the border, for about 1.2 Deutsche Marks a litre, and I did indeed buy some tokens, but only enough for fifty litres. I never used them.

Instead, I would go to one of several fuel stations I came to know where they preferred D-Marks in cash, and where we could get four and sometimes even five litres for one mark. It was potentially risky, but the transactions seemed so routine that it seemed absurd to pass up the opportunity, particularly since we Cadwallader drivers agreed among ourselves that we would charge the company one mark per litre and pocket the difference. The company saved about twenty pfennigs a litre and we drivers made sixty to eighty. I justified this to myself on the grounds that it was I who was risking ten years in jail if I were caught. I always kept the fifty litres' worth of tokens in case the police should appear while I was filling up, in which case I planned to zero the pump and then appear to buy fifty litres legally. I never needed to. Instead, I found a few filling stations where I became recognised by sight and became quite relaxed about the whole black-market routine.

The system often worked slightly differently in Romania. Here again we were supposed to buy overpriced coupons at the border and exchange them for fuel at the state-owned filling stations. However, the fuel station attendants were happy to be paid cash in Romanian *lei*, and black marketeers were keen to give us a rate for D-Marks that meant I was effectively getting the same four or five litres per mark as I could in Hungary. The only snag was that the black-market money-changers were in the big cities and I usually needed fuel before I got to them. My solution was to buy *lei* in readiness for the next trip and hide it in the cab when I passed through the border. The centre of the steering wheel consisted of a Volvo emblem on a plug of plastic that covered the nut holding the wheel in place. If I levered the plug out carefully, it revealed a space just big enough to hide a roll of cash, and thus I illegally exported *lei* and reimported them to buy fuel on my next trip.

The local cops were apparently in on it, too. One evening I pulled into a filling station on the outskirts of Arad, just over the border from Hungary, where I had become a reasonably familiar face. As I pulled up next to the diesel pump, the attendant came over and asked, "Lei?" I was about to say yes when I noticed a police motorbike parked outside the gas station office and its owner leaning against the doorframe. I gestured towards him, but the attendant shrugged and made a gesture that clearly meant 'no problem'. And there wasn't; I filled up, handed over a fistful of lei instead of the compulsory coupons and went on my way. The cop even waved to me as I left. I didn't relax completely until I'd put a few kilometres between us, but I assumed that the officer simply took some kind of cut.

It was too good to last, of course. Gradually, as more and more western trucks passed through the Eastern Bloc, the black-market rate went down. We Brits blamed the Greeks most of all; they bought fuel in bulk – in extra tanks along the chassis of their trailers – and flooded the market with marks. By the time I left Cadwallader, the rate had fallen to three or even two litres per mark; still worth doing, but not a patch on the price I was used to getting.

There were several other ways in which the Eastern Bloc countries defied the communist stereotype. In Romania, one of these was religion. Communist ideology may have been atheist, but evidently this had made no impression on ordinary Romanians. The icon painter I'd met on my Christmas run to Bucharest was no aberration, as I discovered over Easter the following year. I was travelling with my daughter Laura, who was then seven years old. I'd picked her up in London and taken her north to Oldham to load for Romania, before calling in at the yard in Oswestry for a service. We then drove south to spend the Easter weekend with my mother near Westbury in Wiltshire. The fact that Westbury isn't in a straight line from Oswestry to Dover was a measure of how much freedom drivers had in those days – you'd never get away with such a detour in the era of satellite tracking. Laura and I set off again on Easter Monday morning and made up for any lost time with a rapid transit to Romania. By the time we'd unloaded and were ready to return, it was Eastern Orthodox Easter, a week later than the western calendar.

As we drove back through Romania on the Saturday evening, we passed through a succession of villages where the Easter liturgy was unfolding, so that in each one we had a different snapshot of the event. In the first village, I pointed out a throng of worshippers surrounding the traditional fire outside the church as prelude to the service, with which I was familiar from my Catholic upbringing. A little later, we came across a small town that seemed totally deserted, apart from the light pouring from the church windows. Around midnight, with Laura sound asleep in the bunk behind me, I drove into another village where the congregation was just emerging from the church and people were walking down the main street carrying lighted candles. Not wanting to blow them out with the backdraft from my truck, I slowed down to a trundle and quickly woke up Laura. She scrambled into the passenger seat and we watched the people returning home, clearly in a very good mood. Some of them raised their candles to us in greeting and we waved in return. It was one of those moments that stood out in my whole experience of the country and filled me with affection towards it.

Another seemingly incongruous incident happened in Hungary in the summer of 1981, when I stopped at a fuel station to fill up with cheap diesel before crossing into Austria on my way home. The attendant was so absorbed in some TV programme that he left me to my own devices and only appeared when I'd finished to check the pump. Then he beckoned me into his small hut where he was watching the wedding of the British Prince Charles and Diana Spencer on a small TV. He invited me to watch with him and seemed slightly surprised when I left a few minutes later, having stayed just long enough to be polite. Evidently, this Hungarian 'communist' was a better royalist than I was.

A few months later, my personal life finally took a turn for the better, although not the way I had been hoping. Returning from Romania early in 1982, I had picked up a load of cheese, as I often did, from a creamery in Kempten, in the Allgäu region about 130 kilometres south-west of Munich. I had loaded there so often that I had come to recognise, and chat to, a very attractive girl in the Kempten customs office who prepared our paperwork. A couple of visits earlier, I had finally decided to ask her out, only to find that I'd left it much too late; by then she had acquired an engagement ring and my long-shot invitation bit the dust.

On this trip I was due to deliver the cheese to Coleraine, in Northern Ireland, and the week worked out so that I had time to stop for the weekend in the flat I was now renting in my brother's house in London. I arrived in time for dinner with my brother and his family, and there I encountered Amy, a friend of my sister-in-law who was visiting from the USA. We had met once or twice before, but this time we hit it off immediately, and at short notice she agreed to travel north with me for a romantic trip in my truck. So instead of spending the whole weekend at home, we set for a leisurely run north to Stranraer, 420 miles away in south-west Scotland, where I was due on Sunday to take an evening ferry across the Irish Sea to Larne.

This was the first and only time I visited Northern Ireland as a driver and I wasn't prepared for the level of security when we entered the docks at Stranraer. The police officers at the gate were highly suspicious of Amy, once they learned that she was American. One of them spent several minutes questioning me about her, while one of his colleagues observed me impassively as I explained that she was my girlfriend, and that she had no Irish connections. The two cops then went to the passenger side and asked Amy almost the same questions. This was at the height of the 'Troubles' and the IRA was known to have considerable support in the United States. The police, probably quite rightly, were taking no chances, but we were finally allowed through and were able to board the ferry.

In the drivers' restaurant on board, I asked a couple of drivers who regularly crossed to Northern Ireland for advice about the road to Coleraine. I had been slightly spooked by the cops' almost hostile questioning and the other drivers were not reassuring. Hearing I drove for Cadwallader, whose fridge trailers were decorated with two large crossed Union Jack flags, they insisted that I park for the night in the docks at Larne with my truck between theirs, so the flags wouldn't be visible and couldn't provoke any response from Irish nationalists. Nor, they said, should I stop in Belfast, but head north to Coleraine without delay. For Amy, this wasn't turning out to be quite the relaxed trip she had anticipated, though the rest of it passed without incident. Returning from Northern Ireland, I was sent to reload at Lockerbie, and as a vegetarian she found it less than ideal to be parked for two days at the abattoir as I collected a load of lambs for Germany. I dropped Amy back in London, and despite this somewhat unconventional beginning to our relationship, it continued to flourish, albeit at a long distance. Eventually it played a major part in my decision, a few months later, to give up driving indefinitely.

Amy was inconveniently living in northern Florida, where she was completing her training as a doctor at the medical school in Gainesville. When she was hired for an internship in Seattle, at the opposite corner of the country in the Pacific North-West, she suggested that I join her for a three-week overland camping trip across the USA, with the possibility of staying for longer. The idea was very attractive, but it would mean quitting my job, and despite the attraction of a new girlfriend, and an American adventure, it wasn't a straightforward decision. I was well established at Cadwallader, with good friends among the drivers; I was travelling to interesting countries in an excellent truck, and earning a reasonable living. Not only did I love the work, but it had made me a very different person from the somewhat callow ex-student who had begun his truck-driving career seven years earlier. I had travelled over every part of my homeland, and after five years of international driving I'd visited more than twenty different countries. I had driven all kinds of trucks, solved all manner of technical and procedural problems, and had learned to relate to a wide variety of people and nationalities. I had also developed a worm's-eye view of international commerce that still colours my attitudes. Four decades later, for example, I understood far better than apparently anyone in the British government just what would be needed on the ground to go back to border controls in post-Brexit Dover. I gnashed my teeth at the government's unpreparedness and insouciance, and how much it would affect the people who now did the work that I had once done.

Such crises lay in an unforeseen future, but meanwhile I did decide to give up my satisfying job. Although I wasn't yet ready to consider living with Amy in America as my long-term future, or how it would affect my children, from the employment point of view the move wasn't as rash is it might seem. I was confident that the Cadwallader brothers would take me back if I returned, and when I did finally give in my notice, in May of 1982, both Russell and Gordon assured me of a welcome any time. Thus fortified with a safety net, I left the trucking world behind. Or so I thought.

LIFE AFTER TRUCKING

I spent several months in the USA, first travelling across the continent from one corner to the other, and then helping Amy organise her new home in Seattle. In the process, I learned my way around the city and some of its surroundings. It was an idyllic few weeks, until Amy began her internship in a large Seattle teaching hospital. The arrangements for junior doctors required them to work hours that were so brutal they seemed more like a weird initiation rite than a serious training. Amy was frequently gone for forty-eight hours at a stretch, and was sometimes so exhausted that she dozed on her feet in the operating theatre. Not surprisingly, she didn't have much time for me when she got home, and in an ironic reversal of my long absences from home as a driver, it became clear that her job had become all-consuming. I decided I might as well go back to England, particularly since I had no way of working legally in the United States. Amy and I did have a couple of reunions in the ensuing months, but our relationship didn't survive the twin pressures of distance and Amy's total immersion in her life as a junior doctor. I was in the same movie as before, but playing a different role.

On my return, having taken my children on holiday, I spent three months slimming down my bank balance while I wrote a film script based on a story of smuggling a whole truckload of whisky into Saudi Arabia. The plot evolved from the plan my old Middle East mate, Joe Berrington, and I had cooked up, while waiting for two days at the Saudi border. This was, of course, purely theoretical; nothing – not even the half a million dollars we figured the smuggled load would be worth – would have induced us to try it in practice. Still, I thought it made a good story, and a year or two later I was even paid a modest amount of money for the rights to the script, and to develop it with a more experienced writer. Needless to say, the movie didn't get made. Meanwhile, I found myself back in London living, as before, in the same flat above my brother in Holloway. And by the end of the three months, I was broke.

I called Cadwallader and was promised a job in a week or two, as soon as they had found me a suitable truck. Then, something life-changing happened. My brother, Ben, was working as a photographer and regularly scanned *The Guardian* newspaper's Monday 'creative and media' pages. One morning, he came across a small advertisement posted by *Truck* magazine, which was looking for a journalist who could test trucks and write about them. With no experience as a journalist, and with my last major pieces of writing a dry, 25,000-word MA dissertation on the politics of US President Kennedy's tax cut, and the speculative film script, I dismissed the possibility that I might be qualified, but Ben persuaded me to apply.

Truck was the market leader among the fifteen or more road transport magazines then published in Britain, and I had read it on and off since its first edition back in 1974. It was known for its uncompromising style, its refusal to kowtow to truck manufacturers, and the high quality of its road tests and reports on every new truck that came onto the market. It was published by F.F. Publishing, a tiny and creative company that also produced *Car* magazine, then the outstanding motoring magazine in Britain and, indeed, the world. Both magazines had the same independence of mind and always put the interests of readers ahead of the demands of advertisers. I made an appointment to see Paul Barden, the editor of *Truck*, and found him in a cramped set of offices above a bank in West Smithfield, in the City of London. In the street outside, fridge trucks I recognised were delivering to the Smithfield meat market, as I sometimes had. Paul – who turned out to be slightly younger than me – was unimpressed by my academic writing and the script, but after a friendly conversation, he told me to bring him a couple of sample articles.

Since I knew the magazine liked stories about unusual trucks, I thought of Athol Addison, who owned a left-hand-drive Swedish Scania with a drawbar trailer – the only combination of its kind in Britain. Athol operated from his base in Aberdeen down to the Persian Gulf, so the chances of finding him were slim. Nevertheless, I called Davies Turner, the Middle East freight forwarder I knew from my time with Jack Harrison. To my surprise, I found that Athol was due to load in Davies Turner's yard in Battersea the following morning. I had met him once or twice on Middle East trips, and we had got on well enough that I felt able to bang on his door at eight in the morning and wake him up for an interview. With the addition of a couple of calls to Scania to gather a few technical details about Athol's truck, and my best attempt at mimicking *Truck's* writing style, I had my first article.

But I still didn't have the job. I discovered later that Paul had had fifty-odd applicants, several of whom were established journalists, and he was taking his time to make a decision. I called Cadwallader, who were sympathetic and prepared to wait for me until I knew about the job at *Truck*. Meanwhile, I had to unearth another story. I decided to find out why a French transport company would run British-built Leylands, when they had access to perfectly good French Renaults. Using an old tacho card to attract attention from truck drivers, I hitched a ride from Holloway Road in north London, where I lived, down to Dover docks. There, I found a few French-registered Leylands and picked one owned by L. Giraud, whose new Roadtrain was one of Leyland's latest models. The driver gave me the name of his transport manager and I learned that the company was based in the small village of Sonnay, some sixty kilometres south of Lyon, where Renault had a large truck factory. Back home, I marshalled my fading French and called Giraud's transport manager, who told me the firm employed several English drivers, running regularly between France and Britain. We arranged that one of these would call me the following week and give me a ride down to visit Giraud's headquarters. I didn't tell the manager that without a lift I couldn't afford to travel down to see him.

On Tuesday, I picked up the phone and heard, "Is that George Bennett?"

"Yes," I said.

"You arsehole!"

What? Who was this?

"That *is* George Bennett?"

"Yes."

"You bastard. It's Frank; Frank Ward."

I was surprised, but happy to hear from him. I had worked with Frank at Cadwallader and we had similar driving styles, which sometimes found us tramping south together to pick up peaches from Italy. He picked me up in his Roadtrain the following day and, after one of *Truck's* photographers had taken numerous pictures, Frank and I set off. We had a merry time driving the 800-odd kilometres from Calais to Sonnay, making very good progress since we shared the driving. On the way, Frank talked up Giraud as an employer; the company paid better than Cadwallader, he said, and ran all over Europe and the Middle East. It sounded a good job prospect if the opportunity at *Truck* fell through. As a result, during my interview with the transport manager, I was trying to research a story while at the same time leaving a good impression in case I later needed to ask him for driving work.

After a day at the company's yard, Frank and I headed home, and he dropped me off in London to write my second probationary article. I was gratified to discover that Paul intended to publish both of my pieces immediately and, since I had nothing pressing to do, I began to spend my days in *Truck's* offices, beginning to learn the rudiments of sub-editing and journalism in general. After a few more weeks, Paul made up his mind and took me on full-time. In short order I was being sent all over the place in search of stories, including a three-day trip to Mercedes in Germany to drive and report on two of their latest truck models. I acquitted myself well enough, but I still had one major hurdle to clear before I could be accepted as a competent truck tester.

In those days, *Truck's* number one tester was one Pat Kennett, the magazine's founding editor, and a legend among readers and rival magazines alike. Although the magazine itself was based in London, Pat worked from his own office in Derbyshire, and the first time I met him was when I was sent north to accompany him on a road test of a new truck, and learn the test route and procedure. Pat was known to have a poor opinion of any road transport journalist he deemed incompetent behind the wheel – which was most of them, it transpired – so despite my varied experience as a UK and international driver, I was somewhat nervous when we met at the yard of haulage company F.B. Atkins, on the A38 near Derby, to begin the two-day test. The main aim of the road test was to maximise fuel economy and minimise journey times, and this was our first test at the new 38-tonne maximum truck weight that Britain had just adopted. Our subject was a new German MAN 321 and, as always (as I later discovered), the test truck was accompanied by a knowledgeable and fiercely attentive development driver from the manufacturer. So, while he occupied the passenger seat, I perched on the bunk and watched Pat's every move.

At the end of the second day, having looped around the north of England and across the Pennines, the test ended at a fuel station off the M1 south of Derby, where we filled the tank for the last time, recorded the diesel used for the last stage of the test and checked the final fuel figures. Abruptly, Pat told me to take the wheel for the half-hour run back to Atkins' yard, skirting Derby via the old ring road. He didn't say that this was my personal audition, but I knew I was going to be watched, even as Pat busied himself with a calculator to work out the test results. I was pleased that the MAN had a 13-speed Eaton gearbox, the non-synchromesh transmission I'd so much appreciated in the Dafs I'd driven in Europe and the Middle East. In a couple of minutes, I had stopped worrying about Pat and simply enjoyed the truck.

At one point in Derby the road climbed a fairly steep hill, with a set of traffic lights halfway up. The lights were red as we approached and I let the MAN slow down, in what was still quite a high gear. Just before we drifted to a halt, the lights switched to green, so I double declutched, flipped the range selector switch to low, and skipped down from tenth to third. The MAN surged on up the hill without stopping. "Good recovery," was Pat's only comment. Later, I discovered that most truck journalists would probably not have been able to make a double declutch 'skip' shift so quickly, if at all, and would have ground to a halt before having to do a hill start from scratch. I'd taken the gear-change for granted, but in a test, stopping would have cost precious fuel. That single gearshift put Pat permanently on my side, and his endorsement made a difference both at *Truck* magazine itself and, more significantly, among the manufacturers' meticulous development drivers.

I began to travel all over Britain and the Continent, reporting on the launches of new trucks anywhere from Sweden to Italy – which always involved driving them – and then testing them around *Truck*'s test route. At the same time, I learned to research all manner of articles, ranging from transport café reviews to interviews with heavy hitters in the truck manufacturing and road transport industries. Within a few months of joining *Truck*, I was promoted to the magazine's deputy editorship. This was not as grand as it sounds, since there were only two full-time journalists on the magazine's staff, but I felt it was a satisfying landmark, considering that six months previously I had been an unemployed ex-driver. Within another year, I was appointed as editor of *Truck & Driver*, a new magazine which Paul and I developed specifically for drivers. Truck drivers were an audience whose interests I understood very well and the magazine was a success. When Paul left the company to work as a freelance journalist, I was given the editorship of *Truck* itself.

Two years later, my career again developed along unexpected lines when my boss, Ian Fraser, invited me to take charge of the production of *Car*, F.F. Publishing's flagship. I enjoyed the challenge of working on a larger and more prestigious magazine, not to mention the chance to drive all kinds of new cars, but I missed the personal and business stories I had covered at *Truck*. However, my career at *Car* lasted less than two years because Ian and his business partner, Andrew Frankl, sold their company to a subsidiary in Rupert Murdoch's sprawling media empire. Murdoch Magazines was building a stable of high-circulation consumer titles and had little interest in F.F.'s two trucking monthlies. As this became clear, Paul Barden and I – with *Truck*'s former advertising director, Nick Payne – bought them back from Murdoch and set up our own small publishing business, which we called 'Village Publishing'.

I once again took on the role of editing *Truck*, which Murdoch Magazines had combined with *Truck & Driver*, a move we reversed as soon as we could. I also found myself in a new position; managing people.

As editor of *Truck* when I'd worked for F.F. Publishing, I'd had to run the small team that put the magazine together and the freelance journalists we hired. Now, Paul, Nick and I were responsible for a wider range of employees and when we hired new writers who knew about trucks, but little about journalism, I became their mentor. Although we had set up shop in the unfavourable circumstances of a recession, we learned fast and Village Publishing grew successfully over the next seven years. We eventually employed a dozen people before we too sold out, this time to our main rival, another huge publisher, just before the magazine world in general began its long downwards slide. Timing is everything.

For twenty years from my vantage point as a journalist covering both the road transport and truck manufacturing industries, I was able to observe the long series of developments described in the Introduction that transformed the business in which I had once played an active part. Trucks became more sophisticated and more automated, following every manufacturer's explicit aim of making them 'driver-proof', a description which, as a former professional driver, I found almost insulting. Drivers – even those on long-distance work – had less need for self-reliance, while communications were revolutionised as mobile phones and satellite tracking became widespread. As borders opened and permits disappeared, following the establishment of the EU's single market in 1992, international trucking became less of a niche business. Between 1980 and its pre-Brexit peak in 2017, the number of trucks entering the UK through Dover, and later the Channel Tunnel, grew from fewer than 1400 trucks a day to 11,500 – an eightfold increase. The chance of running into a driver you knew was greatly diminished, and even allowing for nostalgia, the comradely world of international road transport that I knew had largely disappeared.

Nevertheless, many drivers still simply enjoy the act of driving and the challenges it presents, just as I did. The vehicles piloted by modern truckers are quiet, sophisticated and, for the long-hauler, have well-appointed and spacious cabs that we couldn't even dream of back in the 1970s. For all that, however, the dearth of drivers that grew in 2021 and, at the time of writing, showed no signs of being solved, suggests that the significant changes in all other aspects of the work remain a continuing disincentive to recruitment. Pay is low considering the responsibility and pressure of being a modern truck driver, and although major pay rises might go some way to solving the driver crisis over time, working conditions have deteriorated, particularly in the UK. British motorway service areas – unlike their continental counterparts – make a hefty charge for overnight parking and for long-distance drivers, there are few other parking areas, apart from narrow and squalid lay-bys at the side of major roads. All truck drivers, whatever the distance they drive, now suffer from the combination of 'just-in-time' deliveries, heavy traffic and having the boss constantly looking over their shoulder, which effectively nullify the sources of job satisfaction that we enjoyed forty years ago. In describing a driving life of variety, self-reliance and independence, I have tried to show how much of that world has been lost, and perhaps to explain why potential drivers are no longer attracted to a job that was once challenging, satisfying and, often, simply fun.

ACKNOWLEDGEMENTS

Though time has erased the names of many of the drivers I worked with, I am grateful to all those who gave me advice and help, particularly in the early days. I am especially grateful to Bert Navey at Abbey Hill, who made me a better general haulage driver; to Joe Berrington, who showed me how to thrive in the Middle East; and to Dave Whitcombe and Peter Morris at Cadwallader, with whom I shared various adventures in Italy and the Eastern Bloc.

I am very grateful to Buzz Cousins, Ben Young and Bob Tuck, who read early drafts of this memoir and made useful suggestions about how it might be improved. For many reasons I am thankful for my daughter, Laura Jacobsen, who features in this tale as a child and whose early enthusiasm for the book kept me going.

To say I feel gratitude to my wife, Ana, is a woeful understatement. She has been my true partner for nearly forty years, and has listened more than once to many of the stories in this memoir, with only an occasional rolling of eyes.

I very much appreciate the work of Joshua Howey de Rijk and Jonathan White at Troubador Publishing, who have patiently guided me through the process of making my raw 'manuscript' ready for publication.

Finally, I am indebted to my friend and former colleague at *Truck*, Andy Salter, who has gone far further in the publishing business than I ever dared to and who has now taken on the publication of this book.

 Matador

For exclusive discounts on Matador titles,
sign up to our occasional newsletter at
troubador.co.uk/bookshop

Printed in the USA
CPSIA information can be obtained
at www.ICGtesting.com
LVHW061539061123
762867LV00028B/145/J

9 781803 137155